Fantastic!

The Life and Vision of James V. Goure

TULLY MOSS

Outskirts Press, Inc.
Denver, Colorado

Outskirts Press
http://www.outskirtspress.com

ISBN-10: 1-43270-014-6
ISBN-13: 978-1-4327-0014-0

Outskirts Press and the "OP" logo are trademarks belonging to
Outskirts Press, Inc.

Printed in the United States of America

Grateful acknowledgement is made for permission by the United Research board to include excerpts from Jim Goure's lectures. All quotes from these lectures as well as The Effective Prayer are copyrighted material of United Research, Inc.

THIS BOOK IS DEDICATED TO YOU –
AND THE MAGNIFICENT, DIVINE BEING THAT YOU ARE

Table of Contents

PART I: LIFE

Prelude

This is the story of a man who lived as every great religion has taught us to live – with a heart full of love, a life dedicated to serving others, and a spirit absorbed in the Divine. It is the story of a man who changed thousands of lives. It is the story of a man who offered a vision for transforming the planet into an enlightened world.

On the surface, he did not appear to be extraordinary. He had had the simplest of upbringings. He was the father of eight children and had been a Naval officer and a government employee. His attributes appeared to be relatively straightforward. Those who knew him well described him as "a real gentleman" and one might have noticed that he had a simple dignity and honor about him. One also might have noticed that he was honest. Zealously honest.

Perhaps it was his normalcy that allowed so many people to feel comfortable around him. Despite his absorption in things of the Spirit, he did not have otherworldly airs about him. He is remembered as being "such an unlikely combination of people. He seemed remarkably human and un-preacher-like. He could talk sensibly. He had none of the preacherly aura. He didn't rely on his status and what he knew." People also remember "the amazing humor," that "it was serious but not serious. You could laugh at things."

But beyond the surface, he was a man on a simple – but ever so challenging – mission. He was going to live as Jesus had asked us to live.

It was the fullness of his dedication that made him extraordinary. At his home in North Carolina, he welcomed all comers. His exceptional generosity and the depth of his commitment to serving others was captured in his belief that, "We cannot own anything on planet Earth. Everything that is belongs to God. My home, that I call my home, isn't mine. It's God's. I am a tenant. And people from all over the planet, if they want to come, it's their home, too."

And come they did - by the thousands. He turned away no one. For things had come to him that "required proving Jesus' words for man to see and know. The first thing to prove was 'Love thy neighbor as thyself.' Loving thy neighbor as thyself means one hundred percent love. Nothing less. That meant that we must, as a family, open our door to everyone." They did just that.

"Love thy neighbor as thyself" wasn't the only admonition of Jesus' that he sought to prove. There was also the one that people "ought always to pray." And he took to heart the statement in the Sermon on the Mount, "Ye are the Light of the world." He interpreted these statements as meaning that each one of us has the Light of the Divine within us, that each one of us has a mission to use that Light for the betterment of the world, and that the way to use this Light is to put it into action through continuous prayer.

Sensing something extraordinary, people flocked to him. Many came wanting to deepen their spirituality – and they found God in refreshingly direct ways, in ways they had been seeking all their lives. Many came wanting to be healed – and most were. Drug addicts came wanting to break their habit – and they did. The suicidal came – and found a new life.

He had an infectious confidence and optimism that with God anything is possible and that the power of prayer has no limits. His buoyant nature lifted people and made them feel that life was a thing of infinite possibilities and beauties and that the future was only going to get better. In his presence, it was as if one's problems and worries and inner knots had dissolved.

For hundreds who met and knew him, the time they spent with him remains the high water mark of their lives. He created a space in which people felt free to be, to experiment with letting the Divine direct their lives. Those who did so almost invariably found themselves and their worlds changing for the better. Burdens were lifted. Relationships became smoother. Those with dormant artistic abilities began creating a new type of music, a new type of poetry, a new type of painting.

His presence radiated love and joy. People felt he loved them unconditionally - no matter what they did or who they had been. Around him, they felt "that great river of love, that flood of love for us, so that we would become what we are meant to be." With a few words, with a look, with his beaming smile, he could make a person feel they were the most special being in the universe.

But there was nothing mushy about this love. He could push people's buttons – and push them hard. He did this so people would move out of their personalities and move into a consciousness of the Divine.

There was a strength about him. And it took a strong person to do what he did – to be so generous, to be so uncompromising in living his truth, to be so welcoming to all comers. It took a strong person to remain open and generous when so many used him or were charlatans or were emotionally unbalanced. It took a strong person to continue giving – housing and feeding scores of people at any given time - even though he never had much money. Many took advantage of this generosity without giving back. Some even wanted to hurt him. At least one or two wanted to kill him. And yet, he pressed on.

Despite condemnation and threats, he was uncompromising in speaking the truth as he knew it. In the face of condemnation from those of a more conservative religious persuasion, he never flinched or backed down. He was unshakeable. The truth he knew, he spoke. No matter what others said or did to him, he spoke that truth.

He lectured extensively. What he had to say was fresh, distinctive, unlike what anyone else was saying. It was never based on dogma. When he spoke of God, people sensed that it was from a place of knowing. Not theory. *Knowing*. People felt they were hearing the truth they had sought all of their lives. They felt, "This is *truly* a man of God. From the depths of his being, he loves God with all of his heart, mind, and soul. He *really* knows God."

His teachings were simple. Deceptively simple. His basic message was this: Know your Divinity. Do something with it. Do as Jesus admonished us to do: pray without ceasing. You can do that. Saying, "I am Light" is a prayer that you can have going on inside of you at all times. But don't stop there. Pray for the planet. Help Earth give birth to its new life. And in doing so, you will give birth to the new life within you.

He made it clear that spiritual development was not just for self. It was so that you would get on with your mission of helping others and helping all of creation. And this help was not to be given in a place isolated from the rest of humanity. He himself had lived in the world and wanted everyone to bring an enlightened spirituality into their daily lives.

He had a worldview that cried out for us to "be about our Father's business," to get on with knowing the Divinity within and engaging that Divinity to create Good. The world was a troubled place and we had to get beyond our personal problems and get on with our collective mission of healing planet Earth and everyone and everything on it.

He had felt the urgency of this mission himself when he took early retirement so that he could dedicate his life and that of his family to prayer for planet Earth. He had felt that the planet was in a precarious state, particularly given international political tensions. He believed that everything that mankind could think of had been tried – aid, diplomacy, war – and that none of these had worked. But there was one thing that had not been tried and that was prayer without ceasing. Prayer for people. Prayer for nations. Prayer for peace. Prayer for the planet.

If we would get on with the Divine's business, if we would get on with knowing and expanding the Divine within, if we would get on with our mission of praying for the planet, then the world would become a paradise. It would become a place of peace and harmony. It would become a place of great beauty and splendor.

It was not his global vision that left the deepest impression on most people. What touched them more was a sense that he knew them at a very deep level, at a level deeper than anyone else. And they felt that even though he knew them so intimately, he still loved them, still accepted them as they were. He was remembered as having "this uncanny ability to go inside and see what was cooking. It was amazing. What he could sense about my history and psychology was so on the money it was spooky. He would say things and I immediately knew what it was about. He could say things – not much – and get right at you. He would say things about my past that rang seven hundred bells and got me thinking about acceptance, forgiveness, understanding, and not carrying around baggage. Amazing that this was communicated in relatively few words. I really felt he was a Divine being who had the ability to get people right where they lived."

His legacy is in the lives he touched and in his teachings and in the love of which he gave so abundantly. After he passed away, it was remarkable how many people said, "He was my truest friend" and "I owe him my life" and "Whenever I think about it, I'm still blown away. He gave me everything. I know I can handle anything."

Like all spiritually advanced people, almost everything he said and did was memorable. But he never wanted the story to be about him, and he could be brusque with those he sensed were putting him on a pedestal. He wanted the primary focus to be on you and your Divinity and your engaging this Divinity to help others and help the planet.

He was an example of what is within each of us, an example of the essence of who we are – generous, loving, attuned to the Divine. He showed that when we get on with being the Divinity within us, great things happen. In his case, the proof is in the thousands of lives he touched.

He favored the word "Fantastic!" to express his feelings about God and about the magnificent Divinity in each one of us. "You are fantastic!" he would say, speaking not to your ego, but to that spectacular Divinity he saw within you.

Fantastic! is the story of this man, James V. Goure, who believed in you. You may not have ever met him, but he would have believed in you and would have known that your essential nature is Divine and would have loved you no matter who you were or what you said or did. This book was written to help you tune into that spirit – and thereby tune into your own Divinity.

BEGINNINGS

James V. Goure was born on June 2, 1921, in Nebraska City, Nebraska. He was the middle of five children – four boys (Hudson, James, Richard, and George) and one girl (Helen). His parents, Raymond Riley Goure and Lenora Hudson Goure, ran a dairy farm.

Lenora had a fondness for horses, and she delivered the dairy's milk with a team of horses that she said were the prettiest and fastest in town. They must have been fast because people in town got after her for the speed with which she drove them. Those who, decades later, were white-knuckled passengers in her son Jim's car, as he sped up and down mountain roads in North Carolina, swerving around corners and cutting across median lines, may wonder if some of his driving habits weren't inherited.

Speedy delivery would not be enough to save the Goure dairy farm. It was one of the casualties of the Great Depression. The Goures simply couldn't make a go of it, and like a number of other families affected by the Depression, they decided to migrate to California. In 1929, when Jim was eight years old, they packed the car and started driving west.

They got as far as Denver – and then they ran out of money. While they were in Denver, Raymond heard that a steel mill in Pueblo, Colorado, about 100 miles south of Denver, was hiring part-time labor. That mill proved to be the financial salvation of the family – and the catalyst for Jim's spiritual quest.

The Colorado Fuel & Iron (CF&I) mill, where Raymond found work, was the largest steel mill west of the Mississippi River. It was also the large private employer, the largest private landowner, and the largest mining operation in Colorado. In the early part of the twentieth century, the CF&I employed one tenth of the state's workforce. Its rails, nails, and girders helped build the western United States.

The CF&I could be somewhat benevolent. It encouraged employees to have their own land and provided them with irrigation. The Goures had ten acres of land, where they grew beans, raspberries and grapes as well as alfalfa hay, field corn, sweet corn, and popping corn. They also had a small cherry and apple orchard and raised cows, horses, pigs, rabbits, and chickens. George, the youngest of the Goure children, grew the popping corn and sold it to the movie theaters in town. Each summer the Goure family canned enough vegetables to last through the winter. Jim worked in a neighbor's fields for fifty cents a day, picking green beans or other vegetables.

The Goure cornfield became the scene of a little family drama. One day Jimmie (as Jim was called until early adulthood) had a heated argument with his mother, who had become quite provoked with him. She chased him into the cornfield with a broomstick - and then returned to the house. The other children must have been startled and upset at the intense row and the subsequent disappearance of their brother. No doubt to relieve their worries, Lenora calmly announced, "Don't worry, kids. He's got to come home to eat." And he did.

Jim came to appreciate Lenora's having disciplined him. Reflecting on her nearly fifty years after the cornfield incident, he said, "She was a wonderful person. I got spanked by her. This was before Dr. Spock, and it was totally acceptable to be spanked. She had the right and I warranted it. There's no question about that."

A little farm and a father with a steady job: things appeared to have settled down for the Goure family after the trauma of having lost the Nebraska dairy farm. But it was not to be so. Every few years, a significant part of their lives would be taken away from them. This time it would be their house. It burned down.

While Lenora and Raymond built a new adobe frame house, the family lived in a tent and in the chicken coop. As primitive as living in a tent might have been, it was a relatively insignificant experience compared with what would follow.

Back at the steel mill, Raymond Goure, who had been working for the CF&I seven years, was a mill ride. This was dangerous work. Pig iron floated in the open hearth while workers threw in ore. Protective clothing was worn, but it was still a dangerous job. There could be flashbacks.

In 1936 an oxygen manifold exploded at the mill, injuring Raymond. He did not have much external damage and was expected to live. But Jimmie, then 15 years old, had a premonition that his dad wouldn't make it. Within a few days of the accident, Raymond Goure, forty-six years old, father of five children, was dead of internal bleeding.

This death would trigger Jimmie's spiritual search. He began to ask, "Why life? Why death?" He began to study religious texts. The first – and throughout his life the core one – would be the Bible.

As with most Americans of his generation, Jim learned about the Bible in church. The Goure family attended Grace Community Church, a non-denominational, one-room church that at most could seat fifty people. The preacher, Reverend Edwards, was a farmer who donated his time. Mr. Edwards is remembered by George Goure as being "tall, very quiet. He was a very good man. His hands were farmer's hands – wrinkled. He was not eloquent, but he had the faith. He preached from the Bible. He had no airs. He was a down-to-earth man." And in the little Grace Community Church, "That Bible was it."

Lenora Goure (as remembered by her son George)

It wasn't just the Bible that had an early influence on Jim's spiritual outlook. His mother also shaped his perspective. George recalls that, "When Jim and I were young and he talked about religion, he sounded like my mother." Lenora was "very spiritual," although "She did not believe in denominations. She lived a life more than she preached it. She believed more in practice than preaching. She was a strong-willed woman. She believed you could heal yourself if you had faith. But, if you were really sick, you prayed for a doctor. She believed God gave us doctors to help us be healed."

Lenora must have been a strong-willed woman. At age forty-four she had become widowed and was suddenly a single parent with responsibility for five children. In taking on those responsibilities, she proved to be a woman of faith, strength, frugality, goodness, and pride. "She was a good Christian woman. She took care of us." In doing so, "She wasn't demonstrative. I can't ever remember her hugging me. No doubt she loved me and her other children with all her soul."

One of the ways Lenora expressed her love was by having faith in the strength and capabilities of her children. George remembers, "I was in a 4H pig catching contest at the county fair and won a pig. I told Mom, 'I've got to pick up the pig.' She said, 'Where are you going to put it?' I hadn't thought of where to put it, but she said, 'Well, you can build a pig pen.' She hadn't even shown me how to hammer, but said, 'You can do it. I've got faith. Don't tell me you can't. You've got a brain.' That was her way: she had faith you could do it even if she hadn't showed you."

She also had physical endurance. "She taught me how to irrigate, how to clean ditches. We came in – I was dead tired - and she cooked the meal" and didn't seem to be tired despite having worked hard.

In addition to her faith and strength, Lenora had pride. For people in her generation, pride in self extended to a concern about how others perceived your behavior. "She was a very proud lady. She never went to town without a hat." When Lenora was eighty-five years old, "She called one day. 'Hey, Kathy [George's wife], can you come over? I fell.' She had been on a step ladder painting the gutters [and had fallen]. She didn't break any bones. Her biggest concern was that a neighbor might have seen her fall and have thought she was drunk. She was a teetotaler."

She was also frugal. When he was young boy, George was a janitor at the church. "I'm sure they gave me the job [recognizing that my mother and I were probably scraping to get by]." George earned fifty cents a month. "When I brought home the fifty cents, Mom said a certain percent went to savings, another percent went to the church, and I got a nickel for spending money. The next day, she took me to the bank and opened a savings account in my name. She was always saving a little, even when we didn't have much." (This frugality was one character trait that her son Jim did not inherit. He was always one to spend money freely. Later in life, Jim gave a lecture in Colorado Springs and afterwards took a number of people out to dinner at a Hilton Hotel. Lenora was among those at the dinner, and she remarked, with some exasperation, "That's Jim – always spending money.")

Lenora's frugality wasn't rigid or selfish. "She always thought of others. She was a treat to be around." While it was her habit to turn off the lights to save pennies, when there was a storm she turned on the outside light, saying, "What if there is someone out there? It's a chance to save themselves."

Frugality may have been a wonderful virtue during the Depression, but one still needed a source of income with which to be frugal. The CF&I did not provide Raymond Goure's family with any death benefits, but his co-workers, at the height of the Depression, collected $300 for the family. (That $300, adjusted for inflation, would be the equivalent of over $4,000 today.)

The sons also helped with the family finances. After Raymond's death, Hudson, the oldest son, went to work in the mill, in the same dangerous, mill ride position his father had had. Jimmie worked as a Western Union boy, delivering telegrams on his bicycle, and then, as soon as he graduated from high school, followed his father and older brother to the steel mill, also working as a mill ride. Richard and George, too, worked in the mill after graduating from high school.

Despite circumstances that might have crushed a lesser soul, Lenora would maintain throughout her life that "We were never poor. We never had to worry about money." In a family photograph taken shortly after Raymond's death, Lenora and her children appear well dressed, well groomed, and smiling. You would never guess, from the photograph what the family had been through.

Lenora's attitude, that "We were never poor," was absorbed by her children. Reflecting on his early years, George Goure said, "I never thought I was poor. She never asked for money. She had the faith."

Lenora's fundamental conviction was, "You're never alone in this world. No problem is insurmountable. You can talk to Him and those problems will be resolved." This resounding faith in God and in the power of prayer would be a signature characteristic of her son Jim.

Jimmie Goure Learns about the Ways of the World

He would need that kind of resounding faith when, as a young boy, he confronted a big prayer challenge. "The Great Cataclysm has been forecast by almost every prophet since the beginning of time. I can remember when I was a child, we had a man that came to our house and he said that within two years, and he gave the date, that according to the Bible, this was in the early thirties or late thirties, the world is coming to an end and the only thing that will save it is you've got to read the Bible every day and pray and pray. And it won't be saved and it's coming to an end on such and such a day. I never prayed harder in my whole life. I was a young boy and I didn't want the world to come to an end because I was just beginning to enjoy it and I still had a whole bunch of time yet to go. So the day came and went and I knew my prayers were successful – no one else prayed as hard as I did. Then it wasn't very long – about another year and a half – another person came, 'The world is coming to an end in about two more years.'"

Jimmie would have other experiences in Pueblo that would teach him about the ways of people, not all of them uplifting. Before he worked in the mill, Jimmie worked for Western Union, delivering telegrams. For this job, he rode his bicycle six miles into town to the Western Union office, then rode the bicycle to deliver telegrams, and finally rode the six miles back home. Decades later, Jim recalled, "I remember when I was fourteen I worked for Western Union. The manager came to me one day, and he had noticed that I was getting more tips than the others – we had to record all of our tips – and he came up to me and said, 'Isn't money wonderful! It's the greatest thing in the world!' And I said, 'Well, there are other things that are a little greater.' And he said, rather sharply, 'Like what?' And I said, 'Health.' He turned and walked away and didn't talk to me anymore. That was one of my greatest educations.

"I remember one time I had to go to the red light district of our town. So, I walked in to deliver a telegram to one of the women in there. They weren't wearing very much. And me, a church-going young man, I forgot what I was doing there for awhile. And that was an education.

"And one of the other times I delivered it to a private home and the woman opened the door and she had no clothes on. That's when I stopped being a Western Union boy.

"I thought, 'How strange we people are. What are we doing?'"

High School

Not all of his experiences in Pueblo were strange, by any means. Jim attended Pleasant View High School, which was a small, country high school. In some ways, it appeared to be a typical high school experience. He had friends, he had a role in the school play, and he was a forward on the school basketball team.

More than sixty-five years after Jim left Pueblo, Colorado, his friends from high school still remembered him as an exceptional person. He was remembered for his leadership, for being a gentleman, for being trustworthy, for his sense of humor, for his courage, for his quickness in sports, and for being an athlete with heart.

It was in high school that Jimmie Goure clearly began to show early signs of leadership and strength of character. The school's principal, James L. Bongirno, would rely on Jimmie. If Jimmie was told to do something, he would get it done. Jimmie's exceptional strength of character made such an impression on Jim Bongirno that, nearly fifty years after Jimmie graduated from high school, Bongirno, upon learning that Jim had passed away, had a mass said for him.

Jim's leadership was not just a show for the school principal. A friend from high school, Frank Bartolo, remembers Jim as a standout from the beginning of his time at Pleasant View High School. "Here's a guy who appeared out of the blue. Jim appeared out of nowhere. He had gone to another school [until his junior year]. He made an impression on me. [I never forgot him.] If it were a new girl, you looked to see if she were pretty. If it were a guy, you looked to see how tough he was. What impressed me more than anything was his leadership qualities. He would sit back, kind of quiet, Jim would always speak up and say something positive. What he said was always very, very sensible. You could tell immediately that Jim had something special. He was very respectful."

Frank remembers another incident that showed Jimmie Goure's willingness to stand up and face unpleasant circumstances, if he felt it were the right thing to do. "We had fun hitting a ball across the highway. There weren't too many cars going down that highway, but finally we hit one. The rest of us ran. Jim was the only one who stayed behind. He talked us out of trouble."

Frank also remembers Jim as one who stood up for those who were younger and prone to being ignored or bullied by older boys: "I was younger. Jim was the only one who looked out for me [and allowed me to play sports with the group of older boys]. Jim always stuck up for the little guys. The others thought us little guys were in the way."

Another of Jim's high school friends remembered that on Jim's way home from school one day, Jim saw two or three boys bullying another boy. When others might have frozen or fled, Jim, against the odds, stepped in and broke up the bullying. He would be stepping in to rescue someone in need to the last day of his life.

Frank also remembers Jim as simply being a fine individual. "I never saw a finer gentleman. He was a gentleman through and through." Franks's sister, Helen Bartolo Mosco, also remembers Jim as a gentleman and says of him, "He was as fine a gentleman as you could expect." She also remembers Jim as "a good student. Punctual. Honest. If he said he would do you a favor, he would. He had a wonderful sense of humor."

Regarding Jim's athletic abilities, Frank's impression was, "Others had greater natural athletic ability, but Jim had a bigger heart. He tried harder. Jim would never quit. He was the last one to quit." Jim's bigger heart was on display not just on the basketball court. Frank recalls that "Jimmie was one of the better boxers. We had no choice: [if you got in a scuffle, you had to defend yourself.] Nobody got hurt."

Since they did not have much in the way of material things, the people of Pueblo had to improvise for entertainment. In an era before cinema multiplexes, one thing they did was to take an evening drive to a hill overlooking the CF&I steel mill and watch the slag burn red against the black of night. Frank Bartolo's memories of how the boys of Pueblo improvised were that, "We had no toys. We played kick-the-can. We would stuff pants with something to play football. If any of the boys had a ball, we thought it was the greatest thing. Jim was one of the fastest."

Jimmie Goure's legs always seemed to move him quickly. Frank remembers that, "In the afternoon after school, the kids would dilly-dally so they wouldn't have to go home and work. I would be walking down the highway and somebody would pass me with long legs." It was Jimmie.

It was not all sports and playing with other boys for Jimmie Goure. In the high school play, *Girl-Shy*, Jimmie played the role of Anthony Arsdale, a father trying to prevent his girl-shy son from marrying what Anthony considered to be the wrong woman. In this play, there were several moments of art foreshadowing life. Jimmie is remembered by Helen Bartolo Mosco as having played his role in an "authoritative" manner, and the good Mr. Goure, later in life on the stage of many a conference, would speak authoritatively about matters of the spirit. The play's notes on characters describe Anthony Arsdale as "a nice-looking gentleman of forty-five or fifty, rather dictatorial and peppery. He likes to have his own way. He wears a business suit of good quality throughout." After he had retired from government and established a spiritual center in North Carolina, at close to the age of fifty, Jim would still wear a jacket and tie and, especially to some of the younger people who came to him, would appear to be not only "authoritative" but, on occasion, "rather dictatorial and peppery" at times. The play even has one scene where Anthony slams a door, something the occasionally provoked Mr. Goure was known to have done.

Jimmie Goure himself was not girl-shy. He was courting Winifred Dall. They were high school sweethearts. Jimmie and Winifred lived in a time and a place where fun could be had from small things, among them, nicknames. Classmates of Jimmie Goure had nicknames such as Corky, Pee Wee, Pluto, Steamer, and Toots. Jimmie acquired the nickname of Zeto and his girlfriend Winifred Dall's was Pupa.

Pueblo, Colorado was a town of European immigrants, as was the nation as a whole in the early part of the twentieth century. Over half Jim's graduating class of twenty-six had Italian surnames. Some of their parents had come from Italy and, prior to attending school, some of their children spoke not a word of English. (The Goures have traced their ancestry to France. Raymond Goure's family had been in North America for generations.)

The relationships between boys and girls at the time Jim was growing up were monitored closely by parents and kept somewhat formal. For the girls, there was no dating alone with boyfriends. At the graduation party for Pleasant View High School, held at the Mineral Palace Boathouse, the parents took their children to the party and waited outside while the children danced.

The material world of Jimmie Goure and his classmates may been very basic, but some of the values on display at Pleasant View High School were of the highest caliber. Helen Bartolo Mosco remembers that "The teachers we had could never be replaced. They were interested in our welfare." She also remembers that for the students, "It was one for all and all for one." Reflecting that oneness, everyone in Jim's high school class stayed in Pueblo but Jim and one woman who went to California. The surviving class members, after all these decades, are still close to one another.

Jim himself must have felt close to them because he returned for his twentieth high school reunion. With humor, he announced to his classmates how many children he had (six at that time) and that he had done "the uppermost to propagate the human race. Can anybody do better than that?"

Despite the fondness many in Pueblo evidently had for him, Jim would leave the city, as would his sister Helen and his brother Richard. Two brothers, Hudson and George, would remain in Pueblo.

Another Loss

Two years after Jim left Pueblo, the Goure family would experience another sudden loss. Hudson was on vacation from his work at the Colorado Fuel & Iron mill, driving his motorcycle at night, on his way to see his grandmother, whom he was close to, when he ran into a farmer's buggy that had no lights. He was dead at age twenty-four.

For all of Lenora's inner strength, with Hudson's death, the family's traumas finally caught up with her. With Jim, Richard, and Helen away from Pueblo and her husband Raymond and son Hudson dead, only George, the youngest of the Goure children, remained. And as George put it, "It was just Mom and me hanging on by our finger nails."

Lenora and George would dress up for church every Sunday and get as far as the church door when Lenora would tell George, "I'll start crying if I go into church. You've got to represent the family." George remembers, "She used to tell me the worst thing that could happen to a man or woman was to bury one of your children." Lenora would eventually emerge from her grief, but it took her five years before she could return to church.

Before she died in 1981 at the age of eighty-nine, Lenora would lose a second son, Richard, to a heart attack, in 1968.

The Family and the Times

George was only six years old when his father died. He was nine years younger than Jim and thirteen years younger than the eldest Goure child, Hudson. Having been so much younger than the others, he remains curious to this day about the family's early years. George said that, "I used to beg my sister to talk about the family." But her response was, "Nah, it was just an average family."

Average? Maybe it was "just an average family." But then all the more extraordinary that from such simple origins, from a family of such modest means, from a family that experienced so much loss, came the greatness that was James V. Goure.

And maybe the "average" nature of Jim's upbringing is what would make it so easy for others to relate to him later in life when he embarked on a most atypical venture into the world of Spirit. Even those not comfortable with religion of any sort would still be comfortable around Jim Goure.

Some of Jim's childhood experiences were typical of early twentieth century America. He grew up in a one company town of modest size (Pueblo had a population of 66,038 in 1930). His father worked in manufacturing. The family scraped by during the Depression. Children weren't given toys, because there wasn't money for non-essentials, so they relied on their innovative spirit to create their own toys. The values on display, particularly in the Goure family but also in society at large were not materialistic ones; they were ones of pride, dignity, resiliency, optimism, discipline, hard work, and faith in God. First generation immigrants didn't speak English, but they made sure their children did, and they valued and honored education.

Experiences and Values

By the time he had left Pueblo, at age eighteen, Jim had lost his father, would soon lose a brother, had been a member of a family living on a financial precipice during the Great Depression, had experienced the family house burning down and the family having to live in a tent, and had seen something of the realities of life - as a Western Union delivery boy and as a steel worker.

The Depression left many of Jim's generation scarred for life, obsessing about money and survival and attached to whatever material things they could acquire. Not Jimmie Goure. In his case, having had a simple existence as a youth may have left him unattached to material goods. And having survived what for many others would have been traumatic events may have given him the confidence that he could make it through anything. And it would be remarkable how, despite the poverty and hardship and traumas of his youth, Jim would develop such a loving heart. Despite the disruptions of his youth, he had not been broken, but strengthened, and he would become firmly anchored in a knowing that the Good ultimately prevails. This knowing would be so deep that others would feel completely secure in his presence.

What would also remain with Jimmie Goure the remainder of his life would be the values he learned from his mother: pride, dignity, physical endurance, a gentlemanly nature, and an unshakeable faith in God. He would use these values to good effect when he had his own family and, later in life, when he was surrounded by an extended family of spiritual seekers. To every situation, he brought optimism, courage, and the confidence that through God's presence he and his family – whether it be the immediate or the extended family - would see themselves through difficult circumstances.

In the Pueblo, Colorado, phase of life, there already were intimations of Jim being someone exceptional. There was the intuition about the fatal nature of his father's injuries, the courage and confidence that enabled him to step in and stop the bullying by others when he was out-manned, and his exceptionally fine character, so exceptional that it would lead his high school principal to hold a mass in his honor nearly 50 years after his graduation.

And then there was his spiritual education that had been simple and experiential. He heard about the Bible and about Jesus from a simple farmer who preached on Sundays. And his early experiences were of searching hard for answers – answers to questions about life and death – and of praying hard for the salvation of Earth, so that the Apocalypse would not occur. From his material existence to his spiritual education, everything for James V. Goure had been from the ground up.

Leaving Pueblo

For all that he had gained from his Pueblo experience, remaining in town as a steel worker for the rest of his life was not what Jimmie

Goure had in mind. We don't know exactly why Jim made his next move. It could have been that he had a desire to see the world. The first transatlantic flight by a commercial airliner was in June of 1939 and in today's dollars a roundtrip fare cost $8,000. If you were a boy of modest means from Pueblo, Colorado, you were going to see the world by ship or not at all. His decision also could have been prompted by the fact that he did not have the money to go to college. Whether it came from a desire for adventure or for an opportunity to see the world or a desire to serve his country or perhaps some inner, intuitive prompting, Jim was ready to try the United States Navy.

Raymond Goure with Helen (on his knee) and Hudson

Raymond and Lenora Goure

The Goure family, shortly after Raymond's death. Back row, left to right:
Richard, James, and Hudson. Front row: Helen, George, and Lenora

Jimmie Goure's high school graduation picture

Certainly not *Girl-Shy*

With Lenora

Jim shortly after he enlisted in the Navy in 1939

NAVY

Jim enlisted in the United States Navy in September of 1939, the month German troops invaded Poland. Britain and France quickly declared war against Germany. World War II had begun. Jim was eighteen years old.

In October 1941 - two years after joining the Navy and two months before the U.S. entered the war - Jim was sent to officer training school. He was trained as a radioman and was assigned to a ship stationed at Pearl Harbor. In what could be seen as an act of Divine intervention, he was transferred out of Pearl Harbor just prior to the Japanese attack.

All radiomen have access to commanding officers, and Jim's commanding officers must have been impressed with his leadership capabilities, because the following year, in July of 1942, Jim was appointed as a midshipman at the U.S. Naval Academy. A relatively small portion of Naval Academy enrollees – currently only about five percent - enter as enlisted men or women. Appointments of enlisted personnel are made by the Secretary of the Navy after recommendations have come through the Navy chain of command. So Jim would have been recommended for an appointment to the Naval Academy by his superiors, and the leadership qualities that began to display themselves while he was growing up in Pueblo must have caught their attention.

The Naval Academy is considered by many outside of the Academy as a place that trains people for war. But the Academy does far more than that. It prides itself on developing leaders - people who have courage and who have the ability to make the right decisions under extreme pressure. An example of such a leader from Jim's class is Walter Shirra, who became one of the Mercury 7 astronauts. Another prominent example, from the class immediately following, is Jimmy Carter, who became the thirty-ninth president of the United States.

In creating leaders, the Academy emphasizes values and ethics. The core values taught at the Naval Academy are honor, courage, and commitment. The *Bluejacket's Manual*, a training manual for Navy recruits, states that, "Before you make a decision or do something, you must consider whether your action will reflect a loss of honor, a failure of courage, or a lack of commitment. If it does, then you should not do it. You should keep in mind that…maintaining honor will often require courage and commitment. You should remember that…sometimes you have to make a decision that is not easy and may not result in you getting what you want, but because it is the right thing to do, you must find the courage to do it. And you must be committed to doing what you know is right, what is honorable, what is courageous."[1]

It can be difficult to live up to these values, so difficult that midshipmen for decades have invoked God's assistance in remaining true and honorable. The Prayer of a Midshipman asks God's help in "…guarding me against dishonesty in purpose and in deed, and helping me so to live that I can stand unashamed and unafraid before my shipmates, my loved ones, and Thee."

Whether he learned it at the Academy or from his years in the Navy or simply always had the qualities, Jim, later in life, when he was leading people spiritually, would exhibit discipline, leadership, and ethics. And there were numerous times during his years of leading people spiritually when Jim would demonstrate - under strenuous circumstances - the Naval Academy's core values of honor, courage, and commitment.

---

[1] *The Bluejacket's Manual*, Thomas J. Cutler, Naval Institute Press, Annapolis, Maryland, copyright 2002 by U.S. Naval Institute, p. 9-10

The Naval Academy was a demanding institution. Out of the one thousand two hundred eight men originally admitted in Jim's class, one hundred sixty-two or thirteen percent did not make it to graduation. At their sixtieth reunion in 2005, men in Jim's class, even ones who had attained relatively high rank in the Navy, still talked about how demanding an experience the Academy had been.

It was difficult for Jim, also, particularly because of his impaired eyesight. His roommate, Ken Lampton, remembers that Jimmie Goure had to work extra hard because of his eyesight. The exact nature of the problem Jim had with his vision is not known. He was farsighted - Jim could see ships at sea long before others could. (And, as the story develops, we shall see that he had an ability to see into people's pasts and futures.) But, it is not known why this farsightedness couldn't have been corrected with glasses so that it would have been easier for him to read or if there were other problems with his vision that kept Jim from being able to read without effort.

It was not all pressure and challenges at the Academy. The Naval Academy divides classes into companies, and Jim was in 8th Company, which had about fifty men. With a sense of humor and self-deprecation, they nicknamed it the "Eight Ball Company" (as in, "always behind the eight ball").

If there was one thing Jimmie Goure was known for at the Naval Academy it was speed. He was a member of his 8th Company intramural track team, which came in first out of the twenty company teams in the Class of 1946, and a friend of Jimmie's, Scotty Parish, remembers Jimmie as frequently being the fastest on the team. All that high school basketball and bike riding as a Western Union boy at high altitude in Colorado must have given Jimmie the extra lung capacity that allowed him to outdistance the others in track.

Jim continued his pursuit of the Divine at the Naval Academy – quietly. At the sixtieth reunion of his Naval Academy class, Jimmie was remembered enthusiastically as a "great guy" - but no one mentioned his spirituality. Those who were in the 8th Company seemed unaware that he had started a Christian Science group while at the Academy.

Jim also had another interest while at the Academy that stayed with him for life, and that was music, the most inspiring of which he heard in the Naval Academy Chapel. Because of its enormous size (it seats two thousand five hundred people), the Chapel has been called the "Cathedral of the Navy." It also has been called "the jewel of the Academy." It is located on the highest ground in the Yard of the Naval Academy and its copper dome can be seen throughout much of Annapolis, Maryland, where the Academy is located. The Chapel's classically-inspired architecture follows principles of proportion and symmetry and its simple interior features stained glass windows designed by Tiffany Studios.

No music would move Jim more than when he heard the great Chapel swell with the voices of the Naval Academy Glee Club singing *Eternal Father, Strong to Save*:

Eternal Father! Strong to save,
Whose arm doth bind the restless wave,
Who bids the mighty ocean deep
Its own appointed limits keep;
Oh, hear us when we cry to Thee,
For those in peril on the sea!.

O Savior, whose almighty word,
The winds and waves submissive heard,
Who walkedst on the foaming deep,
And calm amid its rage did sleep;
Oh, hear us when we cry to Thee
For those in peril on the sea!

O sacred Spirit, who didst brood
Upon the chaos dark and rude,
Who bad'st its angry tumult cease,
And gavest light, and life, and peace;
Oh, hear us when we cry to Thee
For those in peril on the sea!

O Trinity of love and power!
Our brethren shield in danger's hour;

From rock and tempest, fire and foe,
Protect them wheresoe 'er they go,
Thus ever let there rise to Thee
Glad hymns of praise from land and sea.

Jim was not a saver. He did not hold onto things of the past. But, in evidence of his fondness for inspiring music, one of the very few things he kept from his Naval Academy days was the brochure for the March 27, 1943 concert performed by the Trapp Family Singers of *Sound of Music* fame, which was held in the Naval Academy's Mahan Hall.

Because of the war and the need for large numbers of officers, Jim's Class of 1946 was rushed through the Academy in three years, graduating in 1945. Jim received a degree in Marine Engineering and Electrical Engineering from the Academy, and in June of 1945 he reported for active duty. The war against Germany was over by then and the fight against Japan would end in another two months. He would never be in combat.

Jim would stay in the Navy for another thirteen years. Including his three years as an enlisted man and his three years at the Naval Academy, Jim would be associated with the Navy and its Academy for a total of nineteen years. Early in his Naval career, he was assigned to a destroyer, the USS Weiss, and later to an aircraft carrier, the USS Ticonderoga. Toward the end of his time in the Navy, he was a commander on an amphibious ship. During his years with the Navy, he would serve three years with the Chief, Armed Services Special Weapons project at the Pentagon, and draft classified documents with the Joint Chiefs of Staff, the Chief of Naval Operations, and the Assistant Secretary of Defense. He would also spend two years as an instructor in electrical engineering at the Naval Academy, two years training personnel in nuclear physics, and another two years training men in navigation and seamanship.

But before he did all of that, he fell in love and got married.

Lieutenant Goure (note the ring on his left hand,
which is believed to be his Naval Academy ring)

DIANA

Lenora Goure came to Washington, D.C., in the fall of 1946 to visit Jim, who at the time was attending a course at the Army War College. While in Washington, being the good Christian woman that she was, Lenora wanted to attend church services. Jim usually went to the Christian Science church and suggested that the two of them attend a service there. But Lenora had a different idea. In Pueblo, Colorado, where she still lived, she had started attending the Divine Science Church, and she had seen an ad in *The Washington Post* for the very first services being held at a new church, The Church of the Healing Christ: Divine Science.

Jim wasn't convinced, but Lenora persisted and got him to agree to attend the service. Lucky for Jim that she did. It was at that church that he met his future wife, Diana Lightfoot Patch, who was the daughter and only child of the minister, Grace Faus.

Diana was not at the first service Jim attended, but the next Sunday Jim was ushering people up the church steps when Diana arrived and he came part way down the spiral marble staircase and ushered her the rest of the way up the stairs.

Diana's first impression of Jim was that he was "joyous, outgoing." He must have been taken with her, too, because he started attending The Church of the Healing Christ every Sunday. Both of them then were twenty-five years old.

After three or four Sundays, Jim went home with Diana and Grace. That particular Sunday, Diana and Jim decided to try something Diana had seen with another couple: the woman would go into a very deep, meditative state and the man would ask questions. Answers would then flow through the woman. When Diana and Jim tried it themselves, it worked. They got answers. "So, we did that for the rest of our married lives," said Diana. "He would ask or I would ask." What they received from their Higher Selves would guide them in some of the most critical decisions they would make.

Later on, Jim started teaching Sunday school at Grace's church, and in preparation for his classes, he would ask questions from within regarding the meaning of things in the Bible. The answers he received to those questions became the basis of what he would teach not only at Sunday school but also at the spiritual center he would found more than two decades later.

Jim and Diana courted for eight months and then, on a day late in May, Jim asked Diana to marry him. Twelve days later, on June 5th, 1947, they were married. This was exactly two years after Jim had graduated from the Naval Academy (although it was no longer required, Jim was honoring a requirement the Naval Academy had had that graduating midshipmen had to wait two years before they could marry.)

Grace Faus married Jim and Diana. In a scene not uncommon today, but a rarity in 1947, the bride's father was the divorced husband of the minister, who was the bride's mother, and the groom's best man was the bride's stepfather. (Jim had wanted the executive on his ship, Pete Fissler, to be his best man, but Pete was shipped out before the wedding occurred.)

Charlie Patch, Diana's biological father, gave Diana away. With his keen eye for humor and coincidence, he noted that Diana, who had been born next to Gore Creek in the Gore Range of the Colorado Rockies had married a Coloradoan whose name was Goure.

Diana and Jim wrote their marriage ceremony, excerpts of which include:

We are assembled here to establish a new union in LOVE.

This is a covenant between this man and this woman in which they each maintain toward the other an expression of LOVE beyond the love of self. Only such supreme expression of LOVE can fulfill the universal obligation to "Love the Lord thy God with all thy heart, with all thy soul, and with all thy mind." This is possible through the Divinity, which is the essence of your life. God is LOVE and LOVE is all there is.

In this LOVE, you are each an equal cooperator with Almighty God. In this union, God radiates LOVE through you to all.

LOVE is the only LIGHT on LIFE's path. It is the morning and evening star. It is the builder of every home, the kindler of every fire on every hearth.

LOVE is God. God is LOVE. LOVE unites all in one Spirit of Truth.

Inasmuch as Jim and Diana have consented together in Holy wedlock, and have witnessed the same before God and those present and thereto have given and pledged their troth each to the other by giving and receiving these rings and by joining hands, I pronounce them united in LOVE, husband and wife. In the name of the Father and of the Son and of the Holy Spirit. Whom God hath joined together, no man can put asunder. Amen.

And now I charge you, united ones, that you be mindful of the vow you have taken. Remember that happiness comes not from the outer, but is spiritual, born of Truth and LOVE and comes from within.

Know that the love between man and woman will be perpetual only as it is pure and true. Therefore, be ye watchful of your thoughts. See that you remain steadfast in love toward the one whom you have chosen out of all the world. Let your love for each other, faithful and true, be the means of leading you to broader and fuller living. In this joy that has come to you, there will be ever greater and still greater blessedness as together your hearts live in radiant LOVE and service to your fellow man.

Therefore,
Be perfect
Be of good comfort
Be of one mind, living in peace
And the God of LOVE and peace shall be with you forever.

And now may the grace of the Father, the power of the Son, and the consciousness of the Holy Spirit be and abide with you in your Union in LOVE now and forever. Amen.

If there were one line from this marriage ceremony that expressed how they would end up living their lives, it would be, "...together your hearts live in radiant LOVE and service to your fellow man." Love and the service, love and service, and yet more love and service would be the themes of Jim and Diana's life together.

Given where he went in life, it is hard to imagine a better match for Jim than Diana. She was behind the scenes much of the time while Jim was front and center with his spiritual ventures. But, it was Diana who oftentimes kept order in the family – both the Goure family and what came to be their extended family of spiritual seekers. It was Diana who saw to much of the practical side of things. And it was Diana who held up Jim and got him refocused at times when it was getting to be too much for him.

Diana was able to do this because she was born to a life of Spirit, married into a life of Spirit, and lives a life of Spirit. And she got her start from one extraordinary woman, her mother, Grace.

The wedding party, left to right: Floy Harding,
Dr. Charles Patch, Jim, Grace Faus, and Ray Faus

Jim and Diana
at their reception

Off to the honeymoon

Jim and Diana
in South Carolina

Lenora Goure

Lenora with Diana in Pueblo, Colorado

GRACE

Diana's preparation for a life with Jim came about because her mother, Grace, was a pioneer of the spirit, in what was then called the New Thought movement. Grace wrote in her book *The Eternal Truth in a Changing World,* "You and I living today are not among the early pioneers who went across the country in a covered wagon…We are moving on: We are literally pioneers in relation to our own human minds." The pioneer in Grace would do things that were unheard of in the early 1900s.

As with many people who achieve great things, Grace's life started with a big challenge, which she eventually overcame. Her challenge was a physical one. From youth through early adulthood, she frequently got severe migraine headaches. They would become so debilitating that Grace routinely would miss two to three days of school a month. The migraines would continue through college and into the first part of her married life. It was only after Grace had been introduced to Divine Science by her first husband, Charles Patch, that Grace would engage Spirit to heal herself.

Her own health problem led to an interest in the healing arts. While in college at the University of Colorado in Boulder, against her parents' advice, she switched majors from home economics to nursing. Her parents didn't think she was strong enough to be a nurse, but in an early example of her determination and independence of mind, Grace embraced the nursing courses with energy and enthusiasm.

Grace would never complete her nursing degree. What intervened was an extraordinary experience. As Grace tells the story, "One night I was going up a stairway [of University Hospital in Boulder, Colorado] when I was stopped and I heard, 'You are working with effects, not the cause. The cause is in the mind.' It was such a strong experience that it took all the medical desire out of me. It was that strong! So I went to my sister's home in Denver to nurse her husband back to health and I never went back to nurses' training. I had three months left to finish the course."[2]

Out of school and living in Denver, Grace answered her first ad for a job, to be a dental assistant to Dr. Charles Patch. Charlie Patch was a graduate of Harvard Medical School, where he also had been a crown and bridge instructor.

When Grace first saw Charlie, she was taken aback. There was the man she had seen in a vision when she was in Miss Clark's eighth grade class in Manhattan, Kansas. Grace had been at an open window looking at the flat stretch of the horizon when the image of a man appeared out of nowhere. From her vision, Grace had a feeling that this man was an outdoorsman involved in medicine. She felt that she would meet this man and someday marry him.

Dr. Charles Patch himself was taken aback when he saw Grace. He, too, had had a vision. There before him was the face he had seen on a New Hampshire horizon at sunset nine years previously.

With Charlie and Grace having had visions of each other long before they met, both were strongly motivated to know each other and in relatively short order they were engaged.

Thus began another challenge for Grace. Her father, William Lightfoot, forbade her to marry Charlie Patch, saying that a man twenty-three years her senior would be an old man, or perhaps dead,

---

[2] Nearly all quotes of Grace Faus are from *Proof of Truth* and are reprinted with permission of the author, Dorothy Elder. Grace's statement about Jim, towards the end of this chapter, is from a taped lecture of Jim's, and is part of material copyrighted by United Research, Inc. *Grace and Truth* by Lula Zevgolis was also a source of biographical information about Grace.

when she reached the prime of her life – leaving Grace and her children alone.

With her trademark determination, Grace did not let this deter her. She married Charlie.

Soon after their marriage, Charlie introduced Grace to the First Divine Science Church and College of Denver, where he at one time had been superintendent of the Sunday school.

The Divine Science Federation International, as it was called, had its origins in Pueblo, Colorado (what *was* it about those people from Pueblo, Colorado that they became so deeply spiritual?), when three Brooks sisters, in the spring of 1887, began their study of metaphysics. As Nona Brooks told the story, "We were, as a family, in sad condition physically and financially....I myself was in very poor physical condition, being able to eat only very soft, especially prepared food. For more than a year, I had been praying almost constantly, 'God, give me light.'....It was during [a class on metaphysics] that my whole being was completely flooded with a great light – a light brighter than sunlight, brighter than any other light I had ever seen. It filled me! It surrounded me! I was conscious of nothing but that intense white light! I thought that...all in the room had seen the light, too, but they had not. I alone had experienced this wonderful light which flooded my entire being and which I discovered had healed me instantly and completely."

Grace began attending the Divine Science church in Denver and started to have lots of questions. Grace said of that period that "Charlie Patch...taught me a great deal....We used to sit up until 2 a.m. arguing certain points [about the teaching]. I was hard to convince. I said, 'You can't tell me there isn't any disease. I've seen it. I've experienced them.' He patiently taught me."

Charlie's patience finally paid off. Grace reached a tipping point. The Divine Science church had a service during the middle of the week when people would testify to the healing that they had through the Omnipresence. After Grace had heard many of these testimonials of healing, she decided, "If they can do that, so can I. And so I went home and healed myself, or rather the Omnipresence healed me. I just had to let go and believe. I never had another headache after that. I accepted the idea of spiritual healing and became a spiritual healer myself. And that was proof of the truth!"

When Grace became pregnant, Charlie's reaction was, "We've got to get out of town." Grace asked why, to which Charlie responded, "To get away from old wives' tales. I don't want anyone to tell you a negative thing about birth, about conditions that happen to lots of women. We are Divine Science now. We are LIVING it. We are going to the top of the world with our Consciousness. We're not going to have any trouble of any kind."

Grace was all for Charlie's plan and off they went. Charlie closed his dental practice. They bought a mule and hiked into the mountains. When winter set in they found a homesteader's cabin and set up housekeeping. The cabin was in the Gore range of the Rocky Mountains near Mintern, with the Gore Creek running through the property. Charlie got work as a ranch hand.

Grace loved it. "It was lots of fun. Such freedom! You cannot imagine. No clock. No office. No calendar. No anything. No business calling. It was terrific freedom."

During the day, while Charlie was working as a ranch hand, Grace cut wood, kept the fire going, and cooked. She also talked with the fetus "about how healthy and happy I was" and she danced, by herself: "The Spirit was just bubbling in me. I tried to impress the fetus about dancing." Decades later, after Jim had passed away, Diana, whose fetus had been in the womb while Grace danced, became an award-winning ballroom dancer.

Charlie and Grace prayed a great deal, and the birth was an easy one. Grace said, "I never remembered any birth pains. I will tell you what my husband did. He had saved his best stories and jokes for the best psychological and physical moment. Then, when the pain would start, he would tell a joke. So, Diana was born on laughter. In enjoying his joke, I forgot the pain. He told his funniest story, and out she came." Diana was born January 14, 1921.

It was during the birth that Grace came to know the Omnipresence. "It was so apparent to me that I couldn't have that baby without the help of the Omnipresence, and as the baby was born, I knew what It was. I experienced It. It was like a conversion. And I never lost that awareness, that Presence, in all the days and years to come. I gave physical birth to a child and at the same time the awareness of the Omnipresence was born in me!"

Grace, Charlie, and Diana spent two years in the mountains, then returned to Denver. Grace started attending Divine Science classes and took Diana with her. In Grace's words, "She really had grown up in Truth."

Meanwhile, Charlie reopened his dental practice. When he had left his practice previously, his patients had returned. But this time the response was slow. By the third year, Grace and Charlie had to give up their house and rent an apartment. The decline of his practice and his inability to provide for his family was so upsetting to Charlie that he became mentally ill and had to close his practice.

Then the Patches ran out of money. Grace wrote her parents asking for assistance. Grace's father, who had opposed the marriage of Charlie and Grace from the beginning, refused to help the struggling couple. This was quite a shock for Grace, but she did not allow it to defeat her.

She got to work on putting Charlie back together again. In talking with him, she found that Charlie had not wanted to be a dentist. He was a man more comfortable in the mountains than in a dentist's office. With Grace's help, Charlie began to heal.

When Diana was about five or six years old, Grace and Charlie and Diana would again head for the mountains – this time for an ashram in Mooredale, Colorado founded by Vitvan, from whom Grace had her first exposure to Eastern philosophy.

Vitvan had been born Ralph Moriarty DeBit. He had grown up on a farm in Kansas and had been raised as a Methodist. He migrated to Oregon, where one day he went to hear a lecture by an East Indian man named A. K. Mozumdar, founder of the Christian Yoga Society. Down the aisle of the lecture hall came Mozumdar, who stopped where Ralph DeBit was sitting and said, "I've been waiting for you." Mozumdar said that he had been sent to find an American to work with and that Ralph was that person.

Mozumdar instructed Ralph in ancient Oriental teachings and renamed him Vitvan, which means "one who knows." Vitvan himself evolved into a teacher whose ideas reflected a confluence of Gnosticism, philosophy, semantics, and science. To propagate those teachings, he founded the School of the Natural Order. Grace and Charlie had heard Vitvan lecture in Denver, and when he started his ashram in the Colorado mountains, they wanted to join him and be a part of his work.

At Vitvan's ashram in Mooredale, Grace, Charlie, and Diana would live for a year and a half. They rented a small house in Mooredale, and Charlie commuted every day to his dental practice in Denver. They couldn't afford the ashram's tuition, so they earned their way by cooking for the people who were staying at the ashram. Grace also tutored Vitvan's older son, who was then in high school.

Grace and Charlie were so taken with Vitvan that they almost left Divine Science to follow him. But, Vitvan eventually closed his ashram and moved to California, at which point Grace and Charlie returned to Divine Science.

They would soon need all the wisdom and strength that Divine Science could offer. While Charlie had pulled himself together during the mid-1920s and reopened his dental practice, when the Great Depression came, many people felt they could no longer afford dental care and Charlie's practice began to decline precipitously. As that occurred, his anxiety and tension resurfaced. As with the Goure family dairy farm in Nebraska, the Great Depression would destroy Charlie's business.

But Grace would receive a message that would change their lives. One morning after she had taken Charlie to work and before she returned to their apartment, she went to Cheesman Park to look at Mt.

Evans and talk to and love the mountains. This particular day, she heard a message that she experienced as coming from Mt. Evans, and the message was, "All that you love and adore is not out here; is not up here. It is in you." Within two weeks she was in Washington, D.C. attending her father's funeral. She was to live in Washington for the next thirty-seven years.

The Patches had struggled to stay afloat for nearly eight or nine years, but Grace, buoyant and full of faith, said of this period, "…some of my greatest spiritual growth occurred during that time. That is proof of the truth. For if I had not had the Truth, the Omnipresence faith, I could not have survived."

Grace came to believe that "Charlie Patch could not make a living for Diana and me, so I decided to move in with my mother. Remember, this was during the time of the Great Depression. A whole new life opened up for me." Diana was then about ten years old.

Charlie Patch returned to the Boston area where he had contacts. At one point, Grace and Diana went to Boston to see him. Grace and Charlie had a talk and decided that it made sense for them to seek a divorce. Divorces were not common at that time and it bothered Grace, who said, "I was troubled by it, but I knew that the Omnipresence had opened doors for me to teach and to be on my own. It was a Divine plan."

During one of the early years that she was in Washington, Grace met another teacher of Eastern philosophy, Sri Deva Ram Sukul, who was the president of the Yoga Institute of America. There had been an advertisement in *The Washington Post* for a class that Sukul was giving. Grace said, "At that point, I was in such a dither about my life that I thought I would go and see if I could get some help. I didn't know what I was going to do with my life. I had left Denver, was living with my mother, and knew my marriage was not working. So, I decided to go see him and be in his class.

"At the end of the class, he invited any of the students who wanted to have a private interview with him. When I saw him, I presented him with my major problem. I said, 'I am supposed to become a minister.

My great question is how can I write all of those sermons? How can I prepare a sermon for every Sunday? I don't feel I know that much.' He replied, 'You only do them one at a time.'"

And that's all it took – a respected teacher telling Grace that it would be one sermon at a time – for Grace to have the confidence to begin her ministry.

But Grace faced skepticism. She was told that people already had tried to establish a Divine Science church in Washington, D.C., but that it had failed – and so would she – because the population was transient. But Grace thought, "If I teach a few of them from Washington, D.C., they will take it all over the world. The people in Denver said, 'You know, that's a Catholic area. There's not much chance for us.' But I didn't believe I couldn't at least start a class. I was so hungry to share."

Once again, Grace would not let others deflect her from what she felt was the right thing to do. She had gone into nursing school despite the fact that her parents thought she was too weak to be a nurse. She had married Charlie Patch, despite her the fact that her father forbade her to do so. And now, she was going to set up a church in Washington, despite the fact that a number of people told her she would fail.

Some time after establishing the church, Grace remarried. Ray Faus had been a client of Grace's when she was in Denver, and when he had come East looking for a job, he had called Grace. After more than a year of courting her, she agreed to marry him.

Ray evidently was a decent man, but he developed a problem with alcohol after he lost his job. While Diana was spending a summer in Florida with friends, she had been taking flying lessons. Her flight instructor told her about an Alcoholics Anonymous book. She bought it for Ray, who was an avid reader. That one act did much to change not only Ray's life but also Grace's. Ray joined Alcoholics Anonymous (A.A.) meetings and, at least for a time, became sober.

Grace, typically, saw the greater good in the whole experience. "I feel that Ray did more good for me than anyone else because I was able to help more people through my speaking at A.A. meetings than I could have through my little church."

Reflecting on her life, Grace at one point said, "…as I look back I can see how the Omnipresence brought me through many experiences that could have defeated me." One of those experiences, which occurred after Jim and Diana were married, was of being relieved of her position as minister of the Divine Science Church. The congregants, in a more puritanical era than the current one, felt that, by making donations on Sunday and by paying Grace a salary, they were supporting Ray's alcoholism. So, they asked Grace to leave.

Another shock. And after the shock, a realization that this was another opportunity to see the Omnipresence in action. Grace decided to start a new church, The Church of the Healing Christ, Divine Science, which she headed for the next two decades.

By the late 1960s, Grace was ready to retire from being the minister of The Church of the Healing Christ. She had blessed hundreds with her laughter, her positive attitude, her joyful presence, her healing counsel, and her dedication to spreading the Word. But, she felt it was time to go. The one thing that remained to do was to find her replacement.

She had hosted many New Thought ministers at her church, hoping to get one of them to take over her pulpit so she could go live in the mountains of Colorado, where she had been building a house – The House of Grace. But, all of them wanted to remain at their own churches.

Finally, after Grace and her son-in-law, Jim, had talked it over, Jim contacted Max Ballard of the Pueblo Divine Science Church. He was thrilled to hear of the proposition and eventually became the minister of The Church of the Healing Christ in Washington, D.C. Grace then returned to her beloved mountains in Colorado.

Grace and Jim had a great deal of admiration for each other. Grace said of Jim, "I'm so proud to know I have a son-in-law who knows the truth." Jim, for his part, introduced Grace at one of his lectures with some gentle kidding along with genuine admiration: "There's a lady here close to two hundred years old – a lot closer than I am. She's been a minister longer than most people have been alive. She's saved a lot of people. She's healed a lot of people. She changed Washington by herself. Her name is Grace Faus."

Grace gave much to Jim and Diana. Her greatest gift to Jim was, of course, Diana. But it also was in preparation for teaching Sunday school at Grace's church that Jim received many of his revelations about the Bible. And Grace gave much to Diana. Grace's adventurous spirit, her willingness to take gambles against long odds for what she believed in, her dedication to helping others bring the Divine into their lives, and her optimism in the face of challenges were all qualities that would serve Diana as well. Grace also gave Diana a pioneering spirit. Similar to what Grace and Charlie Patch had done twice – first when Grace became pregnant with Diana and then, six or seven years later when they went to Vitvan's ashram for two years – Diana and Jim, twenty-three years after they were married, would take off for the mountains of North Carolina to found a spiritual center.

But, before that came to pass, Jim and Diana would establish a family and meet many interesting people, one of whom was Walter Russell, a sculptor, portraitist to American presidents, and spiritual leader who Grace introduced them to, and who Jim said was the most spiritual person he had ever met.

FAMILY

The moving and changes that Diana experienced with Grace prepared her for the life of moving and changes that she would experience with Jim. Their early years together were ones of moving and babies and babies and moving. By Jim's count, they moved twenty-one times. Neither of them seemed to mind it. Diana's life was made easier by the fact that the Navy took care of the moving. Jim's viewpoint was that all the moving prevented them from getting too attached to any one spot.

Early in their married life, Jim was assigned to a destroyer based in Norfolk, Virginia. They lived with a family in Norfolk for several months. Then, they moved to an apartment. Navy assignments kept Jim away much of the time.

In October of 1948, Diana gave birth to twins, James, Jr. (Jay) and Jonathan. Not even the doctor was expecting twins. When Jim called Grace to tell her the good news about the birth of twins, she at first thought he was playing a joke on her.

<u>Jim and Diana's Personal Bible</u>

A month after the twins were born, Jim was at sea for six weeks. Before he left, Jim and Diana wrote, on one page, their personal bible. Jim held that, "If you really analyze the Bible, you can narrow it to one page." What he and Diana wrote was a document they would refer to time and again throughout the years. Here is what they created:

Listen always.
Think Love and Light always – let them do the work.
Pray regularly.
Let Love and Light make relations smooth.
Let Love and Light put peace and goodwill in all hearts.
Let Love and Light awaken all to God and His goodness.
Be faithful about keeping time for your Father to speak to you.
Be constant about thinking Love…every moment of the day and night.
Be peaceful and calm in your constant flow of Love and Light.
Be thankful to God.
Let nothing disturb you or ruffle the feathers of your inner peace.
Let nothing keep you from your communion with God…for there is nothing that can direct your thoughts away from God, if you desire to keep them centered in God.
Let God's perfect work be done through you always.
Be patient, for Love does all things at the right time.
Be kind, for all are the children of God and all are your well beloved brothers.
Be helpful, for that was Jesus' way.
Be Love and Light…for you are Love, and it is up to you to express Love always in all ways.
Love is all there is!

This personal bible was not just words. It was something that Jim and Diana lived. This personal bible used the word "love" eleven times, and this love would be the enduring impression that many people would have of Jim, years after he had left the physical. This personal bible also called upon them to "Be helpful, for that was Jesus' way." We saw early signs of this attribute during Jim's youth, when he would step in to break up a scene of bullying, when he would help younger boys participate in the activities of older boys, and when he would be helpful to his high school principal. But the generosity and helpfulness that Jim and Diana would extend to total strangers, thousands of them, would prove a wonderful testament of how they lived their personal bible.

As the story unfolds, we shall also see how the Goure family – first the immediate family and then an extended family of friends – would "pray regularly." We shall see how they "Let love and light awaken all to God and His goodness." We shall see how Jim continually praised and was "thankful to God."

Although Jim based a lecture on his personal bible (excerpts of which are in the *Code of Life* chapter in *Part III: Teachings*), he encouraged everyone to write their own bible. His view was that, "The whole of the Bible is basically a story of man, of you, of your growth. From being primitive and caught up with the world to the evolution of yourself into a Christed being."

In March of 1949, Jim was transferred to Yorktown, Virginia, for a month or so, then to Charleston, South Carolina, and they lived in Isle of Palms, South Carolina, for a couple of months.

Liana, Jim and Diana's third child, was born in January of 1950.

In September of 1950, Jim was assigned to the Naval Academy, where he taught electrical engineering for two years, and the family moved to Maryland.

In March of 1952, Jim and Diana's fourth child, Christine, was born. In June of that year, Jim would perform one of his last duties at the Naval Academy by accompanying Naval Academy plebes on their first sea voyage.

New Mexico

In August of 1952, there was another move, this time to New Mexico. Jim was assigned to Sandia National Laboratories in Albuquerque, New Mexico, where he worked in nuclear physics and propulsion systems. Sandia was engaged in ordnance engineering – turning the nuclear physics packages created by Los Alamos and Lawrence Livermore National Laboratories into deployable weapons. Over time, it expanded into new areas as national security requirements changed: in addition to ensuring the safety and reliability of the nation's nuclear stockpile, Sandia applied the expertise it acquired in weapons work to a variety of related areas such as energy research, supercomputing, treaty verification, and non-proliferation.
The move to New Mexico brought new adventures where Jim would

display his exceptional intuition and caring for others – and how he was living his personal bible. As Diana tells the story, "For the first month, we were able to stay in a classmate's quarters on base while he and his family were on leave. We had thirty days to look for a place to live.

"We had looked at several places in town, but this one day we drove up a hill above and to the east of the city. Jim got out of the car, paying no attention to the huge, furiously barking dog. He went right up to the door and knocked. The young man who answered (as we were told later) was so amazed that anyone would knock while the dog was still barking. This man had been holding a gun to his head ready to commit suicide. Jim must have known the urgency to get to that door before the trigger was pulled. But the fact that Jim wanted to rent the house and was not afraid of the dog was enough to save the man's life. We even adopted the dog to go with the house and the man became a good friend.

"[The house] was off by itself on the side of the hill with no close neighbors. Perhaps many people would be afraid to live so far away from everything, but it never entered our minds. Since we were both from Colorado, we were thrilled to be back in the West with sunny skies, large mountains, and a drier atmosphere.

"And that furious dog turned out to be a life saver for the three older children. While the baby was asleep and I was finishing up dishes or beds, the three older ones [the twins, who were four-and-a-half, and Liana, who was three], were playing right near the house with their tricycles. First thing I know they are off down the road getting closer and closer to the highway.

I quickly got in the car (thank goodness I had it at home [that day]) and went down there. Just as I got to the highway, there was Amigo (the dog) standing in front of them, not letting them go out in the busy Interstate 40 traffic. The trip back up was a three block, uphill climb – such a hard climb that they never went down there again."

<u>Continuing To Live the Personal Bible</u>

In the mid-1950's, it was back to the East Coast. Jim was again assigned to a ship based in Norfolk, Virginia. While in Norfolk, Jim and Diana connected with the Quakers and with the Association for Research and Enlightenment (A.R.E.), the organization founded in 1931 by Edgar Cayce to explore intuition, personal spirituality, ancient mysteries, holistic health, and dreams and dream interpretation. Many of those who came to Jim soon after he established his own spiritual center also had been associated with A.R.E. in Virginia.

Paula, Jim and Diana's fifth child was born in August of 1954.

About the move back to Norfolk, Diana remembers a story that "shows Jim's extraordinary generosity and his knowledge that nothing is impossible. Part I begins in Virginia Beach about September, 1955. We moved from Albuquerque, New Mexico to Virginia Beach, Virginia and got there just after a huge storm. The streets were flooded with two inches or more of water. Temporarily we moved into a small furnished cottage with two rooms, kitchen, and bath. The baby, Chris, slept in a dresser drawer with pillow mattress. The children loved playing in the sand box in the yard.

"Then we moved to a furnished two story, four bedroom house east of Atlantic Avenue at 55th Street. It was just a walk past three to four houses, over the sand dunes to the beach and the Atlantic Ocean. Jim was assigned to a ship out of Norfolk and [it was] worth the drive [from Virginia Beach to Norfolk] each day his ship was in port just to be near the beach.

"While there, I met a neighbor, Jane Waller, and her two children, Janie, who was four, Liana's age, and Johnny, two, who was Chris' age. Eventually, she and I began to trade off looking after the children so one of us could shop and do errands without the kids along. Janie, Liana, Chris and the boys would read or play quietly, but Johnny was always moving: he was a great knob-turner and always into everything. (He may been undiagnosed ADHD). So, I had him in the kitchen with me making cookies or jello or something so I could keep a eye on him and involve him in simple tasks (stirring, cookie cutting, etc.) to keep him constantly busy. Or he and I would get into the huge rocking chair and rock uproariously back and forth. This fast rocking motion seemed to satisfy his longing for speed and it soothed him.

"Years later, after we'd moved a couple of more times and were in Bethesda, Maryland and he [Johnny] was in a private Quaker school in Ohio, we get a phone call from Jane. She was in tears, not knowing what to do with Johnny. He'd been fighting with others, difficult to discipline, called 'incorrigible,' and kicked out of school.

"Right away, Jim said, 'Send him here to live with us.' (Here's his generosity and [belief that] nothing's impossible.) It was about March. Johnny was in eighth grade, middle school. He slept on a cot placed between Jay and Jon, who were in tenth grade. Johnny was way too big for middle school. Jim went to the high school and got permission for him to be in the [high school's] after-school track and field activities with Jay and Jon.

"So, Johnny began to apply himself at school and found a great outlet in being with other guys his size and beginning to learn and soon excel in events, discus and shot put. He also began wrestling. When he went back to Virginia Beach, he became a champion wrestler and won first place in discus and shot put."

"I Am a Family Man"

While he was away on Navy assignments, Jim stayed in touch with his own children through prayers and letters. In a letter he wrote on U.S.S. Ticonderoga stationery, dated February 7th,1955, Jim talked about how warm it was in Guantanamo Bay, Cuba (both the air and water temperature were 82 degrees Fahrenheit). "God be with you, Diana, in all you do. Be of good cheer, for I am with you alway. All the children's stars and moon are all together in the heavens. They brighten the sky with Light."

Regarding family, Jim said of himself, "I am a family man. I believe in the family as the right way for this planet. Because there we *are* 'two or three gathered together in My name.' In our family we prayed together every day. We held hands. And prayed out loud. And some of the children's prayers were *far* exceeding anything I'd ever heard before. They were fantastic."

Witnessing Nuclear Detonations

In September of 1955, Jim was assigned to the Atomic Energy Commission, splitting his time between the Pentagon and offices in Germantown, Maryland.

From its inception in 1947 until its abolition in 1975, the Atomic Energy Commission (AEC) maintained programs for nuclear weapons research. It conducted biomedical research into the effects of radiation and nuclear weapons; promoted a civilian nuclear power industry; and conducted international Atoms-for-Peace activities.

While working for the Atomic Energy Commission, Jim observed the detonation of nuclear explosions in Nevada. Seeing firsthand the devastation that nuclear weapons could unleash probably contributed to his decision years later to dedicate his life to prayer for peace.

Jim's basic belief about weapons was that, "If all of the countries of the world laid down their arms, then obviously within a few months there would still be a power struggle. So, we need to look into this concept of war and peace and things of this nature in a different way."

Probably reflecting his own experiences in witnessing nuclear explosions, Jim said that, "Anyone who has ever seen a nuclear weapon go off would obviously never use it. This is true of Russia and China and it is true of our country. We would not use it now because we know the devastation that would exist and *they* know no one can win in those conditions. There is a proposal to the United Nations by our country that every five years we put on a demonstration of nuclear weapons – actually exploding them and showing what they do, so, at the end, all of the leaders will say, "We can never do this." As leaders who are aware of what nuclear weapons can do die off, the new leaders don't know. No matter what they say, they really don't know. If there were a demonstration of the destructive power of nuclear weapons every five years, eventually then, nuclear weapons would be done away with."

More Children…and a Career Change

On a more life-filled note, in September of 1957, another star came into the Goure galaxy: Gloria was born.

When Jonathan was nine or ten (around 1957 or 1958), he developed asthma and, as Diana put it, "gave us a full opportunity to increase our prayer power. He got into such violent midnight wheezing bouts that his life was in jeopardy. Fortunately, it was revealed to me to give him tiny sips of salt water in the wee hours of the night. In action this was similar to having a blood transfusion, and he lived! He pulled through with the help of Dr. Maiesmond Panos, a homeopathic physician and Dr. Florence Everhart, an osteopath. Having had asthma prior to twelve years of age kept him out of Vietnam. The first year [we were in Bethesda] the children were on the Bethesda Country Club swim team. Jonathan progressed from a frail, weak boy to a strong, winning swimmer."

Towards the end of the 1950s, Jim decided to shift his career, and he resigned from the Navy in April of 1958. His resignation was accepted under honorable conditions. He was a lieutenant when he resigned and had spent nearly nineteen years being associated with the Navy and its Academy, about sixteen years in active duty and three years as a midshipman at the U.S. Naval Academy. Jim then went on the staff of the Atomic Energy Commission.

In 1959 Jim and Diana took classes with Sri Sukul, the teacher of Eastern philosophy who had given Grace the confidence to face writing sermons by telling her, "You only do them one at a time." At the final ceremony for Sri Sukul's class, he gave each student a rose. Diana's rose also had a bud attached to it. Diana took it as a sign. At the time, she was two month's pregnant with Will. "Nobody else knew of it. But Sri Sukul knew!"

Jim would eventually be the father of eight children. But he would become far more than that. Over the years, the man who had lost his own father at a young age would become the father to many who sought his guidance and counsel.

His ability to do so came from his deepening spirituality. This spirituality was advanced by contact with other like-minded people. Of those, he said the most spiritual person he had ever met was someone his mother-in-law, Grace Faus, had introduced him to: Walter Russell.

The twins (Jay and Jonathan) with Diana,
Ray Faus, Grace Faus, and Jim

WALTER RUSSELL [3]

As one person who spent several years with Jim put it, "Jim pretty much thought he was it." But there was one man, one of the great, self-made renaissance men of the last century, Walter Russell, who Jim thought was very special.

The Artist

Walter Russell was born in Boston on May 19, 1871, and lived until his ninety-second birthday, in 1963. He attended a local school until he was nearly ten years old, when, because of a reversal of family fortune, he was told to get paying work. He got a job as a clerk in a dry goods store, for which he had to walk six miles each way.

He later considered it fortunate that he was taken out of school and put to work because, in the words of his biographer, Glenn Clark, he "thus escaped the encyclopedic educational systems of information-cramming and memory-testing which filled other children's lives."

Walter did eventually attend an art school, which he financed, at least in part, by playing music, even though he could not read music. At the age of thirteen, he became a church organist, for which he was paid

---

[3] Quotations are from *The Man Who Tapped The Secrets of the Universe* and pictures of Walter and Lao Russell and of Swannanoa are from the University of Science and Philosophy's web site. All are copyrighted by and reprinted with the permission of the University of Science and Philosophy.

$7.50 per week. He was also paid $2.00 a week to play the piano at Friday evening prayer meetings.

Walter married in his early twenties and spent several years in Europe studying art. He returned to the United States in 1897, when he was in his mid-twenties, to join *Collier's Weekly*, where he was art editor for two years. He then became war artist and correspondent for *Colliers* and *Century* in the Spanish-American War of 1898. Between 1901 and 1904 he wrote a series of children's books.

Having been a musician and an illustrator, Walter developed proficiency in a third artistic field, portrait painting. At first he specialized in children and painted the offspring of notables, including the children of President Theodore Roosevelt. At the zenith of his fame as a child specialist, he was commissioned by the *Ladies Home Journal* to tour America and select and paint the twelve most beautiful children in the country.

In 1914 Walter stopped painting children and became a portraitist of prominent people, including the likes of Mrs. Theodore Roosevelt, wife of the president.

The Roosevelt family must have liked Walter. In addition to painting portraits of Teddy Roosevelt's children and wife, he would sculpt a large bust of TR's cousin, Franklin Delano Roosevelt, who would also request that Walter create a sculpture of the Four Freedoms.

Artistry was not the only talent Walter Russell developed. He also worked on his athletic abilities. It was said that Walter was "an ardent and skilled horseman." He kept twenty-seven Arabian horses at his property in Oyster Bay on Long Island and he rode horses with Teddy Roosevelt. Horse riding was not the only sport in which he became proficient. When he was in his mid-forties, he formed the New York Skating Club. At age sixty-nine, he won three prizes in figure skating against competitors, all of whom were under thirty.

Lecturer on Values

Being the Renaissance man he was, Walter's interests extended to areas beyond the arts and athletics. He was also interested in uplifting society at large and engaged in several activities whose purpose was to do just that. He was the first president of the Society of Arts and Sciences, which he and Thomas J. Watson, chief executive officer of IBM, founded in 1921, when Walter was in his late forties.

Executives of IBM had been intrigued by the way Walter Russell had multiplied his capabilities. As Walter's biographer, Glenn Clark recounts it, "For many years, he lectured upon the philosophy of life, self-multiplication of the individual, and ethical principles in business to the officers and salesmen of International Business Machines Corporation, in the effort to build a finer race of manhood through greater comprehension of the Light of omniscience which is in all men awaiting their awareness of it....He began to infiltrate the Sermon on the Mount principles into big business. In his first lecture to this great organization, he told its directors that he was utterly shocked at the two slogans that were then the very fundamentals of business. They were: 'Let the buyer beware,' and 'The sale is the only thing that counts.' I say that equal interchange of goods and services between buyer and seller is the keynote of tomorrow's business world....'"

Sculptor

At the age of fifty-six, Walter added yet another artistic skill, that of sculpting. It was not a change he had planned. The Society of Arts and Sciences, of which Walter was president, was to give a medal to Thomas Edison. The artist who had been commissioned to create the portrait-sculpture for the medal had failed. So Walter wired Mrs. Edison that he would do it himself.

He later said, "It was very unwise for me to do, perhaps, because with such a great man as Edison as my subject, I might not have survived a failure. But I never let the thought of failure enter my mind. My knowledge of my unity with the Universal One and the fact that I *must* do this thing, and the inspired belief that I *should* do it as a demonstration of my belief in man's unlimited power, made me ignore the difficulties that lay in the way. So, I went to Florida with a mass of clay, but on my way down, I spent the entire time absorbed in inspirational meditation with the Universal Source of all inspiration, in order to fully realize the omnipotence of the Self within me as a preparation for doing in a masterly way what I would otherwise be unable to do. If I had followed the usual procedure of the superficially minded man and played bridge all the way down to Florida or otherwise enslaved my mind by sidetracking it from its creative purpose in order to entertain that great aggregation of sensed corpuscles which I call my body…I know I would have failed. In fact, I knew in advance, from long experience in trying to achieve the unachievable, that meditation and communion between my Self and the Universal Self was the only way to achieve that impossibility."

Other portrait busts followed, including those of Thomas J. Watson, George Gershwin, and Charles Goodyear. He became known for executing large, complex sculptures and for being a sculptor who could make the eyes of his subjects exceptionally expressive.

He also liked things on a grand scale. He made a head of President Roosevelt nine feet high, and his large statue of the Four Freedoms appeared as winged angels seventeen feet tall. The bust of President Roosevelt was exhibited at the World's Fair in 1939.

Most of Walter's work was created in New York City, where he lived and worked for over fifty years, and where he maintained a studio in Carnegie Hall.

Cosmic Consciousness

When he was fifty years old, Walter Russell had an extended, thirty-nine day experience of cosmic consciousness. During this period, he wrote thousands of words and drew many diagrams about the nature of the universe which he was experiencing.

In his own words, "In May of 1921 God took me up into a high mountain of inspiration and intense ecstasy. A brilliant flash like lightning severed my bodily sensation from my consciousness, and I found myself freed from my body and wholly in the Mind Universe of

Light, which is God.

"And then, God said to me, 'Behold thou the unity of all things in Light of Me, and the seeming separateness of all things in the two lights of my divided thinking. See thou that I, the Undivided, Unchanging One, am within all divided things, centering them, and I am without all changing things, controlling them.

"And the secrets of the universe were unfolded to me in their great simplicity…the universal kaleidoscope was but moving mirror waves of dual light extending from their equilibrium in God from Whom all creating things spring in octave electric waves….

"For many days and nights I was made to write down all these things…in *The Divine Illiad,* which is my record of my teachings while in the Light.

"Thus I was made to see the universe as a whole and its simple principle of creation as one unit, repeated over and over, endlessly and without variation, as evidenced in the universal heartbeat to which every pulsing thing in the light-wave universe is geared to act as ONE UNIT OF THE WHOLE.

"…all knowledge exists in the Mind universe of Light – which is God…all Mind is One Mind…men do not have separate minds…all knowledge can be obtained from the Universal Source of All-Knowledge by becoming One with that Source."

Philosophy and Science

Walter Russell's experiences in life and his thirty-nine-day experience of cosmic illumination led him to a perspective on life and on science, in which he said, "I believe sincerely that every man has consummate genius within him. Some appear to have it more than others only because they are aware of it more than others. I believe that mediocrity is self-inflicted and that genius is self-bestowed. Every successful man I…have known…carries with him the key which unlocks that awareness. That key is *desire* when it is *released* into the great eternal Energy of the universe."

Walter's biographer, Glenn Clark, further articulated Walter's perspective as, "He...believes that every man should be master of anything he does and should do it in a masterly manner, with *love*, no matter what it is, whether hard physical work, menial or boring work, or inspirational work. This is fundamental with him. He believes it to be the reason for his perfect health and great physical strength throughout his entire life. With an overwhelming desire for intensive expression, a love of all tasks of every nature, and a deep love of life and of all people and things in life, he believes that every person can remain vital and effervescent throughout one's entire life."

In Walter's own words, "There should be no distasteful tasks in one's life. If you just hate to do a thing, that hatred for it develops body-destructive toxins, and you become fatigued very soon. You must love everything you...do. Do it not only cheerfully, but also lovingly and the very best way you know how. That love of the work which you must do anyhow will vitalize your body and keep you from fatigue."

In response to questions from his biographer, Walter gave these answers: *The greatest passion of your life?* "Beauty. Beauty and worthiness to live life as a masterful interpreter of the Light." *What do you mean by beauty?* "Perfection of rhythm, *balanced* perfection of rhythm. Everything in Nature is expressed by rhythmic waves of light. Every thought and action is a light-wave of thought and action. If one interprets the God within one, one's thoughts and actions must be balanced rhythmic waves."

Walter went on to say, "The Life Triumphant is that which places what a man gives to the world in creative expression far ahead of that which he takes from it of the creations of others. And it should be every man's greatest ambition to be that kind of man. With that desire in the heart of every man, there could be no greed or selfish unbalance, nor could there be exploitation of other men or hatreds or wars or fear of wars. The impregnation of that desire into New Age thinking will be the makings of a new race of men which will mark the next stage of his journey from the jungle of his beginnings to a full awareness of the Light of God which awaits all mankind on the mountain top of its journey's end."

According to Walter Russell, the five laws of success are humility, reverence, inspiration, deep purpose, and joy.   He said, "I have absolute faith that anything can come to one who trusts to the unlimited help of the Universal Intelligence that is within, so long as one works within the law, always gives more to others than they expect, and does it cheerfully and courteously."

The University of Science and Philosophy, which Walter Russell founded, summarizes the Russell philosophy as being this: "There is a gold thread of fundamental Universal Truth woven throughout all the ancient teachings of the world, and through their modern counterparts and enlightened interpretations.   The Russell Philosophy expounds Universal Fundamental Truth and the Law of Rhythmic Balanced Interchange in terms of philosophy in ACTION.   Ethics is the science of conduct, and to know the nature of the Law of Balance is to understand the unity of all things and the cause and effect nature of existence.   A living philosophy demands that we look within to centering cause rather than outwardly to the sensed world of effect. Through understanding cause and through becoming consciously aware of working with centering Cause, the joy of co-creatively ordering and living one's life cosmically from the mind turns life into an experience of meaning and beauty."

In addition to his artistic pursuits and his development of a philosophy of life, Walter Russell had an interest in science.   He was keenly interested in hydrogen as an alternative fuel source, as are many people today.   He conducted experiments at a Westinghouse Electric laboratory in 1927.   And of his overall view of nature, he states in page after page of his writings that this is an electric thought-wave universe.

Lao Russell and Swannanoa

In his mid-seventies, Walter Russell was still active as an artist and a lecturer, but he felt he was not making optimal use of his capabilities. So he started to make changes.

He allowed Daisy Stebbing, a divorced Englishwoman, to bring greater organization to his life.   He became impressed with her spirituality and renamed her "Lao" after Lao Tzu, the Oriental philosopher whose works became the foundation for Taoism. Walter believed that Daisy's spirituality was so advanced that she was the reincarnation of Lao Tzu.

Walter and Lao fell in love. Walter divorced his wife of over fifty years and shortly thereafter, in Reno, Nevada, he married Lao.

He was finding it "impossible to work in New York" any more because of the many business and personal calls upon him. In 1948, Walter and Lao leased a marble Italian Renaissance palace, sculpture garden, and 500-acre estate on a Virginia mountaintop so they could devote the rest of their lives to the arts, to philosophy, and to science – with the intent of fostering better human relations and helping to unfold the inherent genius they believed lies within every person. The Russell Foundation, established at the same time, was to be a "force for unifying mankind."

The name "Swannanoa" had been given to the mansion by its original owners, the Dooleys, to recognize Mrs. Dooley's fondness for swans. Lao herself liked the name because in West Indian it meant "land of beauty" and in East Indian it meant "the absolute, or mother of heaven."

Walter and Lao's intention was to move into part of the mansion and turn the rest of it into a public museum of Walter's work. It was to be maintained as a memorial to him after his death.

On May 2nd, 1949, Swannanoa was dedicated as a "shrine of beauty." The ceremonies were led by Colgate W. Darden, president of the University of Virginia and former Governor of Virginia. Between 1,000 to 2,000 had been invited to attend.

Over the succeeding years, the Russells continued to enhance Swannanoa as "a shrine of beauty." They also developed a home study course for spreading their message of the Light within man and taught courses on that subject at Swannanoa.

Several well-known people in government, business, and the arts were attracted to the Russells' teachings. Among them were the actor Eddie

Albert, the singer John Denver, the actress Gloria Swanson, and Senator Stuart Symington

Grace Faus, Jim's mother-in-law, also found Walter Russell's teachings appealing. She had learned about Walter Russell from a friend, and she had traveled from Washington to New York to visit Walter at his studio in Carnegie Hall. The two recognized quickly that they shared common perceptions of life and God. Walter subsequently spoke at Grace's Divine Science church in Washington, and Grace and Ray Faus were among Walter and Lao Russell's first students after the Russells began teaching classes at Swannanoa.

Among those who had been in attendance at the dedication of Swannanoa was one James V. Goure. He had been introduced to Walter Russell by Grace and was accompanying Grace and her husband Ray to the dedication (Diana stayed behind with the two very young twins, who were less than seven months old at the time). In succeeding visits, Jim and his wife Diana were among the most warmly received guests of the Russells. The Russells would have Jim and Diana stay on the upper floor of the Swannanoa mansion, a privilege granted to few.

We can only speculate on the impact the Russells and Swannanoa had on Jim. Here were two men, Walter Russell and Jim Goure, who had grown up in circumstances of very modest means. Both had gotten jobs at relatively young ages and traveled far for those jobs – Walter Russell walking six miles to the dry goods store and Jim riding his bicycle six miles to the Western Union office. Both had an interest in science and both believed there were scientific underpinnings to their spiritual experiences. Both believed in the unlimited potential of every human being.

Although Jim himself clearly was an original who was not easily impressed by others, he might well have been inspired by Walter Russell. Here was a man who said he had tapped into the same source of Divine creativity that Jim believed in, and, having done so, had become a portraitist and sculptor to presidents and an advisor to corporate executives. Here was a man who said that there is an unlimited abundance in the universe that each one of us can tap into, and, after apparently having done so himself, was living in large marble palace surrounded by gardens. For the boy from Pueblo, Colorado, whose family of seven had lived in a small adobe house, this may have been heady stuff.

Later in life, after Jim had left government to dedicate his life to prayer, there would be similarities between some of his ideas and behavior and those of Walter Russell. Both Jim and Walter would decide that the demands people were placing on them and the cities in which they lived were not conducive to a life of spirit, and both would move to rural parts of the Blue Ridge Mountains. Walter Russell had a Van Dyke beard. Jim grew a goatee of similar appearance. Jim talked about creating a sculpture of Jesus that was four-sided and included a quote on each side, such as "Ye are the Light of the world." Walter, at the request of Franklin Roosevelt, had created a four-sided statue of the Four Freedoms. Jim would talk about creating a tall hologram of Jesus along with the words "Ye are the Light of the world" that could be seen for long distances. Walter and Lao Russell's plans for Swannanoa included creating a 300-foot illumined statue of the Christ of the Blue Ridge or Christ as *The Light of the World*. Walter had estimated that it would be seen for fifty miles at night and that "*The Light of the World* expresses the central theme of our work here. As an example of the marriage of science and religion – shown by using light with Christ – we hope *The Light of the World* will become a symbol to unify man for peace and happiness, as against war and oppression." A central theme of Jim's lectures for years would be the line from the Sermon on the Mount, "Ye are the Light of the world," and the importance of using that Light to bring peace and joy for all.

After Walter Russell passed away, Jim would make a very special request of Lao Russell, which she would turn down. It is just as well that Lao did so. Jim eventually shed his goatee, developed his own cosmology, and had considerable influence in the design of a structure that, far from being rooted in the architecture of the past, is still one of the most unique spiritual buildings in the country.

But, we are getting ahead of our story. First, there would be more Goure children, more years of government service, and the wild ride of the 1960s.

Jim (on the far left) with Lao and Walter Russell and, on the far right, Grace Faus

Jim, holding Gloria,
and Diana; Sri Sukul
and Walter Russell
in the foreground

Swannanoa (© University of Science and Philosophy)

Lao Russell
(© University of
Science and
Philosophy)

Walter Russell (© University of Science and Philosophy)

Jim in one of the early years after having left government to establish a prayer center

THE 1960s

For Jim and Diana, the 1960s began with the birth of a new child and ended with the birth of a new life, a life dedicated entirely to the Divine.

In between, the U.S. and the Soviet Union almost engaged in nuclear war, America appeared to be coming apart at the seams, and there was a new spiritual awakening in the country.

Life in the 1960s for Jim and Diana was largely about raising a family and about living in the Washington, D.C. area. They entered the decade with six children and soon added their seventh, Will, in January, 1960. Roger, the eighth, was born in March of 1963, into the hands of his father, who delivered him.

With eight children, family life had its chaotic – and humorous – moments. Diana remembers that, "When we lived in Potomac, [Maryland], Jim was teaching Sunday school and Paula and I were in the choir at Grace's church. Because things were somewhat hectic on Sunday morning, we generally went to church in two cars. So, it was not until we were sitting down to Sunday dinner that we realized Gloria was not with us. Sure enough, there she was, sitting on the church steps. Each of us thought the other had her in their car!"

At that church, Grace's Church of the Healing Christ, Jim taught Sunday school. Much of his material for his classes came from what had been revealed to him and Diana as they wrote from their Higher Selves.

Jim evidently felt invigorated with his life in the Washington, D.C. area. He later said of those times, "I love Washington. I love the Government. I love this particular country. Being in Washington was like champagne all the time. It was fantastic. The people there are the most advanced people on the planet because all the governments of the world send their very best people to our Washington, D.C. And it was a great joy for all of the family and for myself especially to associate with them."

Jim was employed by the Atomic Energy Commission (AEC) at that time. In the course of his work for the AEC, he had access to information and had discussions with knowledgeable parties that would be instrumental in his decision to dedicate his life to prayer and to helping others. Before getting to that point in the story, it might be helpful to remember the context in which he made that decision.

The 1960s was one of the most turbulent decades in American history. Within three months of his inauguration, the first president of the decade, John F. Kennedy, authorized a Central Intelligence Agency-run invasion of Cuba at the Bay of Pigs, which occurred in April of 1961. It was a fiasco.

Cuba would prove to be an ongoing source of challenges for President Kennedy. Two years after the Bay of Pigs invasion, the Soviets were discovered to have begun placing missiles with nuclear warheads in Cuba. Thus began the Cuban Missile Crisis, a five-week period during which the U.S. and the Soviet Union came within a hair's breadth of engaging in nuclear warfare. Those who were in elementary school in the early 1960s still remember the duck-and-cover drill: students were trained to duck underneath their desks in case of a nuclear attack by the Soviets.

There was not only superpower sparring, but a major war in the Middle East. In June of 1967, Israel launched a preemptive strike against Egypt and destroyed the Egyptian air force. During the same day, Israel neutralized the air forces of Syria and Jordan and by the end of this Six-Day War, Israel had gained control of the Gaza Strip, the Golan Heights, the West Bank, and the Sinai Peninsula. With the exception of the Sinai Peninsula, which subsequently was returned to

Egypt, these remain areas over which there is intense dispute.

The international conflicts were only one side of the chaos and tension of the 1960s. The United States also had to contend with internal violence. For many, it was a scary, anarchic time. In November of 1963, the first of several assassinations of prominent U.S. political figures occurred. John F. Kennedy was killed on the twenty-second of that month and five years later his brother Robert and the civil rights leader Dr. Martin Luther King would also be assassinated. Another well-known leader of African-Americans, Malcom X, was assassinated in 1965.

In the week following the assassination of Martin Luther King, riots occurred in 110 cities. Forty-six people were killed and 3,500 were injured. These riots capped what had been a decade of civil rights-related violence. Civil rights workers had been murdered in the South. During the 1965 Watts riots, which occurred over 50 square miles of southeastern Los Angeles, 34 people died and 600 buildings were destroyed or severely damaged. And in 1967, a peak year for civil rights-related violence, at least 90 people died and 4,000 were injured in more than 120 riots.

Civil rights-related riots weren't the only form of domestic violence. The U.S.-based Weather Underground Organization, describing itself as a "revolutionary organization of communist women and men," advocated overthrowing the U.S. government and doing away with capitalism. Toward that end, it bombed government and corporate facilities and engaged in rioting. During its most active period, from 1969 to 1975, the Weather Underground was linked to twenty-four bombings. Among the facilities bombed were the United States Capitol, the Pentagon, the Harvard Center for International Affairs, the New York City Police headquarters, and the corporate headquarters of Gulf Oil and ITT.

That doesn't complete the story of civil unrest during the 1960s. The Vietnam War has been the most internally divisive foreign war the U.S. has ever fought and it became a major source of hostility towards the government for many young people. Demonstrators against the war at times numbered over 100,000 protestors. In November of

1969, 250,000 people joined an anti-Vietnam War rally in Washington, D.C.

The war would touch the Goure family directly. Over two-and-a-half million U.S. personnel served in Vietnam between 1965 and 1973. More than 57,000 of them would lose their lives in Vietnam. One of those who served in Vietnam – and lived – was Jay Goure.

As Diana remembers it, "When he was 17, Jay ran off to California to join the Marines. It broke my heart. I felt that of all the services, the Marines was the most brutal and of all the children, Jay was the most in touch with Spirit. How could this be? What an awful thing to have happen to such a one as he.

"I even called Joseph Murphy, a Divine Science minister in California whom Jay knew, thinking he could get Jay out of the service. I was so afraid of what would happen to this boy. But, Murphy said to me, 'Your fear draws to him all that you are afraid of. Change your own thinking! See God's perfection in all of it!'

"What a lesson! And boy, how we straightened up and prayed right!

"And sure enough, even though weathering many storms in boot camp, Jay found the I AM group there, studied many of their books, and grew even taller spiritually."

While serving in the military, Jay did more than survive the Vietnam War. After Jim and Diana and the family had dedicated their lives to prayer and to serving the Divine, Jay would, literally, help *them* survive. (More on this, later.)

In the midst of warfare and scary international tensions and raging domestic disturbances, there was an enthusiastic faith that a new, better world could be built. It was a time of optimism and experimentation, and this enthusiastic experimentation extended to matters spiritual. A revolution in consciousness had begun that would help set the stage for the spiritual work Jim would do in the 1970s and 1980s. Young people in particular were searching for meaning and inspiration and had an openness to exploring new approaches to spirituality. Many of them sought meaning outside of traditional religious institutions and had an interest in new types of community.

Those who went beyond mere seeking and experimentation settled into a spiritual practice. These practices typically included prayer, service to others, a desire to deepen contact with the Divine, a new definition of the self, a sharing of spiritual experiences with others, and an emphasis on ethics.[4] All of these would be characteristics of the approach Jim would advocate.

Among those who believed that in spirituality lay the answers to the dilemmas man kept creating for himself was a woman named Juliet Hollister. Over peanut butter sandwiches in her kitchen, Juliet told a like-minded friend, "The world is in a mess," and she resolved to do something about it. Her vision was to establish a forum in which the wisdom of various religious traditions could be cultivated to promote positive social change. She approached former first lady Eleanor Roosevelt, who recognized the power of the vision immediately and who wrote letters of introduction to religious and political leaders around the world. With those introductions, Juliet set off on a round-the-world trip, meeting leaders such as Anwar-el Sadat, Pope John XXIII, and Dr. Albert Schweitzer.

In 1960, Juliet established the Temple of Understanding, an organization whose mission was to promote understanding among the world's religions. The Temple got a boost in 1962 when *Life Magazine* featured an article about Juliet's "wonderful obsession." Over the years, the Temple of Understanding focused on summits that brought together leaders of the worlds religions. One of its board members was James V. Goure.

But, Jim evidently felt the need for something that went beyond what the Temple of Understanding could accomplish. In a March 21st, 1973 session with their Higher Selves, Jim and Diana received this: "The Temple of Understanding has many projects afoot and many changes in the offing. They are all connected to the material and intellectual

---

[4] Adapted from *After Heaven: Spirituality in America Since the 1970s* by Robert Wuthnow.

levels. Jim's idea is the only spiritual idea, and he may be the one to carry it forward."

The turbulent decade of the 1960s seemed to close on a more hopeful note when U.S. astronauts landed on the moon in July 1969 and when, a month later, the Woodstock Music and Art Fair attracted hundreds of thousands of young people to a music festival in Bethel, New York.

The tragedies and hopes of the 1960s had laid fertile ground for what Jim would do next - dedicate himself to a life of prayer and service to others. Of all the things he witnessed during this decade, the international tensions and what he was hearing from others about the imminence of World War III would have the greatest impact on his decision. He felt there was a great need for him to do something. And in the first year of the next decade, he made his move.

The Goure family in Potomac, Maryland in the 1960s:
back row, left to right: Liana, Jim, Diana, Jonathan;
front row: Roger, Will, Gloria, Paula, and Chris

Jim receiving a plaque for his service to the Atomic Energy Commission

THE DECISION

H ere, in Jim's words, is how he came to his decision to dedicate
his life to prayer and to serving others.

"Being in government [in the Atomic Energy Commission], I was
privy to intelligence information. It became apparent in 1968 that the
world was heading towards World War III.

"The only thing I knew that could alter that direction was effective
prayer on a continuous basis for the planet and for the peoples of the
planet.

"I was less than 50 years old at the time, and I felt the only way we
could do it as a family was to move to a remote spot somewhere on the
planet and go into prayer on a one hundred percent basis for the planet.

"I was deeply involved in government, which took a lot of my time,
my mind, my capabilities. So, I really felt we should get to a remote
spot."

In one of the communions Jim and Diana regularly had with their
Higher Selves, on June 10th, 1970, a few days after Jim's forty-ninth
birthday, Jim wrote, "Light fills the world. Retire from government.
Move away to the high country. Peace will come to all. Peace is in
you. Maintain Peace. Man needs Peace. Man needs Light. Man
needs Love. See Man filled with Peace, with Light, with Love. Yes,
you need to work in a different way now and in a different area."

Jim continues his story, "I was too young to retire from the government. But, the president at that time [Nixon], two weeks after I'd made this declaration, issued a special proclamation that anyone who wanted to retire who had a certain length of time in government could retire. Well, I had two weeks more than the required time, and I was first in line."

Not too many wives would have gone along with a decision like this. But Diana's experiences with her mother and father, Grace and Charlie Patch, and their time in the mountains of Colorado, must have given her a disposition that would accept such a radical proposal.

It had all come together. From his mother, Lenora, had come a confidence that God's goodness would prevail, and the courage and commitment he had learned about at the Naval Academy would now be turned towards a courageous plan to commit his life to God and prayer. Jim had a vision of what he wanted to do. His retirement was in place. His wife was on board. His prayer and his approach had matured. He was ready.

To a turbulent planet that he loved and wanted to help save, to a God that he worshipped, to a nation that he loved, to the people of Earth, all of whom he loved, he brought a dedication to help, to love, to heal. He was ready to commit fully to prayer for the planet.

SWANNANOA

J im continues his story, "The remote spot on the planet then was next on the program. We got together with ten other people who knew how to pray effectively. And we simply asked, 'Where?' And the answer for all twelve of us – my wife Diana and me [and the ten other people] – was, 'Swannanoa.'"

"The only Swannanoa we knew at the time was in Virginia [Walter and Lao Russell's place], and it was an ideal spot for us. The perfect spot, we thought.

"We went there immediately, Diana and I, to the people who owned Swannanoa [Lao Russell]. And they said, 'I'm sorry. Whatever your prayers are, we still want to remain here, and this is our business. That's too bad.'"

"It was quite a shock to us. When twelve people get 'Swannanoa,' that's pretty powerful stuff. So, we looked at every house, every possible place to live. We even looked at churches that had been vacant and schools that had been vacant. We looked at everything in the mountains of Virginia.

"Eventually, we crossed the border into North Carolina on a Saturday night, and I found a motel right next to the Blue Ridge Parkway near the Virginia border.

"The next morning, which was Sunday, it was total fog. It was the thickest fog yet. I was feeling, 'O.K., God. I'm tired of looking. You find the place.' And , because of the fog, I thought, 'O.K., the Lord doesn't want me to look. Today is the day of rest.'

"So, my idea of rest was to drive around the mountains of North Carolina. Just get lost in them and enjoy myself. I got in my car and started to drive in the fog. I got off the main road onto a gravel road and rode around a bit. Eventually, I saw a sign that said, 'Stone Mountain, North Carolina.' I thought that might be interesting, so I continued driving through the fog and eventually came to Stone Mountain. That was the only place the sun was shining and there was no fog.

"Stone Mountain is one stone about twenty-five hundred feet high and about four miles around the base. It was a super-fantastic thing to see. I'd never seen a stone like that. It was impressive.

"So, I climbed it. You must remember, I was from Washington, D.C., and that's a flat land. The Boy Scouts were just coming down Stone Mountain as I was beginning my ascent. I asked the last Boy Scout down how long it would take and he said, 'Oh, about fifteen minutes.' Well, two hours later I got to the top!

"And on top, the wind and the rain had eroded the stone and it looked like an alter with many seats around it. That impressed me. That was like the Lord said, 'Sit down.' I did. I went into really deep prayer and immediately it filled up with some really great beings. To give you a feel for this, one of the beings was over two hundred thousand miles in height. So, they were pretty first class.

"They wanted to know what we were going to do about the world situation. They wanted to see how we were going to do it.

"You don't talk much to these kind of beings, so I showed them exactly how I was going to work on the planet. And that took only about three minutes. They're pretty quick. They saw that it would work. And they left – before I could say, 'Hey, I need a place.' They just left! I thought that was dirty pool.

"But I had a strange feeling that was still with me, so I climbed down Stone Mountain, got in my car, and drove one hundred fifty miles non-stop to the entrance of this place [what became the Goure house in Black Mountain, North Carolina]. There was a gate and it was locked. The road up to the house was full of weeds higher than my head. I climbed over the gate because I had this feeling, 'Go up there.' And I did.

"I went up to the house. Walked around it. Three times. It was obviously vacant and the curtains were drawn so I couldn't see inside it.

"Underneath one of the doors [to the house] was a newspaper sticking out. So, I pulled it out. It was dated three years before and it had a woman's name on a label.

"I got in my car and drove the back way into Asheville. I got into a motel and looked in the phone book. There was her name. I called her and said I was interested in this place. She said, 'Well, it's not for sale, but if you're that interested, I'd be glad to show it to you. Come out Monday morning at 10:30.'

"Monday morning I drove from Asheville towards her place in the town of Black Mountain. In doing so, I passed through the town of Swannanoa. I almost had a wreck when I saw the sign, 'Swannanoa.' That made me know: this was it.

"Then I convinced her we were going to make the house a prayer center."

The original owner of that house had been Lawrence E. Brown, sheriff of Buncombe County, North Carolina, of which Black Mountain is a part. Mr. Brown had been sheriff a total of thirty-four years - from 1926 to 1928 and from 1930 to 1962. The house had been built in 1958 towards the end of his time as sheriff and twelve years before the Goures arrived. Jim purchased the house from his descendents.

The house was outside the main part of the town of Black Mountain, North Carolina, eight miles up a mountain road. It was large - it had more than six thousand square feet (half of that in an unfinished basement that was later renovated). Over the years, the Goures would need every bit of that space, and more, as scores and then hundreds of people came to see Jim.

The house had stone walls and a sunken living room with a stone fireplace, and the living room became the scene for many a talk that Jim gave. This upstairs area had an open floor plan – so people could be in living room, dining area, or breakfast area and see each other, which helped as Jim gave talks to packed audiences.

The property also included nearly 24 acres of hilly, forested land that was filled with rhododendron and through which the Broad River flowed.

The house was indeed in a remote spot, as Jim had wanted, and its lovely, peaceful setting was conducive to the concentrated prayers for peace that Jim had dedicated his life to conducting.

BLACK MOUNTAIN AND BUCKMINSTER FULLER

B lack Mountain, the town outside of which Jim and his family moved, is in the Blue Ridge Mountains of North Carolina. These are among the oldest mountains on Earth and they include the highest point in the eastern United States, Mount Mitchell, which is 6,684 feet (2,038 meters) above sea level.

This area, previously known as Gray Eagle, was originally inhabited by Cherokee Indians, who believed it had special healing properties. The Cherokees also believed that nature was infused with a powerful spiritual essence. Local beliefs are that no war has ever been fought in this area, contributing greatly to the spirit of peacefulness that many feel there.

With all of this pleasant history, Black Mountain, North Carolina, at first blush, was an improbable place for Jim to have established a center providing an alternative approach to spirituality. It is known by many as the "Buckle of the Bible Belt." In terms of religion, it is a highly conservative place. In the greater Asheville area, of which Black Mountain is a part, there are over one hundred Baptist churches and nearly 150 churches of other Christian denominations. Particularly in 1970, when the Goures moved to Black Mountain, there were virtually no other alternative approaches to spirituality in the area and the greater community was somewhat hostile to alternative ways of viewing God and spirituality.

But there has been another, lesser known feature of Black Mountain's history involving a hotbed of creativity that indirectly would have a substantial impact on Jim and the prayer center he founded. This was Black Mountain College, an experimental college owned and operated by its faculty. The college was guided by principles of democratic governance and subscribed to a belief that the arts are central to the experience of learning. The college also operated along somewhat communal lines, and all members of the college community participated in its operation, including construction projects and kitchen duty.

The college's founding in 1933 coincided with the rise of Adolph Hitler and the closing of the Bauhaus school of art and architecture by the Nazis. The first teacher at Black Mountain College, Josef Albers, was a refugee from Nazi Germany and a former professor at the Bauhaus. When Albers and his wife, Anni, left Nazi Germany and crossed the Atlantic by ship, he spoke not a word of English. But talent he had in abundance, and he ran the painting program at Black Mountain College from the college's inception in 1933 until 1949. He was the first of many world-class talents who came to the college.

Over the 23 years of its existence, the college attracted some of the most well-known and influential artists of the twentieth century. Among the college's students and faculty members were John Cage, Merce Cunningham, Willem de Kooning, Francine du Plessix Gray, Paul Goodman, Walter Gropius, Franz Kline, Jacob Lawrence, Robert Motherwell, Arthur Penn, Robert Rauschenberg, M. C. Richards, Ben Shahn, and Cy Twombly.

Another individual who came to Black Mountain College was to have a significant, albeit indirect, role in the life of Jim Goure. His name was Buckminster Fuller, and he came to Black Mountain College for the summer sessions of 1948 and 1949, during which time he worked on the creation for which he is best known, the geodesic dome.

There were several parallels between Buckminster Fuller's life and Jim's. When both were twelve years of age, their fathers died. In early adulthood, both worked in mills – Jim in a steel mill, Bucky Fuller in a textile mill. Both served in the Navy as radiomen and both were commanders of small Navy ships. And both men dedicated their lives to the betterment of humanity.

Jim and Bucky Fuller also shared some common beliefs and attitudes. Both were optimists who believed that utopia was within reach. Both spoke of Earth as a spaceship – Bucky Fuller would say that Earth is a spaceship traveling fast (67,000 miles per hour) around the sun. Both believed that man's nature is inherently fantastic. Fuller said, "Man is designed to be an extraordinary success."

Both Jim and Bucky Fuller believed that scientific advancements had freed people's time so that mankind could address the most important questions. Bucky Fuller noted that, for the two million years man had been known to exist, he had been so busy with protecting and feeding himself that he had had little time to ask, "Why is man in the universe?" But now, with so much of the environment under control and with so much time freed up, Fuller thought we finally had the opportunity to address the most fundamental issues of existence. The question of whether man has a function in the universe, he believed, is the most important one.

Bucky Fuller's transforming moment came in 1927, when he was 32 years old. He was bankrupt and jobless and living in less-than-desirable housing in Chicago. That winter, his young daughter Alexandra died of pneumonia. Bucky felt responsible, began drinking heavily, and seriously considered suicide. But he pulled himself together and decided to conduct "an experiment, to find what a single individual can contribute to changing the world and benefiting all humanity." He wanted to determine what he – a man without money or corporate or government backing – could do to help mankind. He wanted to discover the principles that govern the universe and apply them to basic issues that confront humanity, such as shelter. During the next fifty years, he became a visionary architect and inventor as well as being a professor and a prolific writer.

One of his driving principles was the intelligent use of the earth's resources to gain the maximum return for the minimum of material and energy expended. He wanted to achieve "the effective application of the principles of science to the conscious design of our total environment in order to help make the Earth's finite resources meet the needs of all humanity without disrupting the ecological processes of the planet." He was also keen on creating environments in which man's inherent genius had the greatest opportunity to flourish. He wanted to shift mankind's focus from fear, war, and weaponry to what he called "livingry" – the deployment of resources for the betterment of all people. He believed he could accomplish this by changing the environments in which people lived, traveled, and worked.

It was with these guiding principles that he developed the geodesic dome. A geodesic dome is a sphere-like structure that encloses the largest volume of interior space with the least amount of surface area. Its concave interior facilitates the even flow of hot or cool air throughout the dome and helps prevent radiant heat loss.

In 1979, the spiritual organization Jim would found would build a Light or prayer center in the shape of a geodesic dome.

So, by following his inner guidance, Jim had landed in Black Mountain, this unusual center of conservatism and creativity, which would be the birthplace of one of the twentieth century's most unique structures, the geodesic dome, and birthplace of a new approach to spirituality that Jim would create. It was a place where the oldest of mountains were a breeding ground for the newest of creations. It was a place of peace for prayers of peace. It was a place of healing mountains for a man who would become known as a healer.

EARLY YEARS AT THE HOUSE

J im and his family moved into the house in the mountains outside of Black Mountain on October 10th, 1970. The day they moved in, a rainbow formed over the house, causing Jim to say, "We're in the right place."

From the beginning, they prayed. As Jim recalled, "We as a family started praying. Four times a day: nine, noon, five-thirty, and nine. We never missed. We did it. For at least fifteen minutes each time. In addition to that, during any spare moments, we were praying for the planet."

Jim had wanted to be in a remote spot so he and the family could focus on prayer. He said that, "We wanted the place we selected for our prayer center to be remote for one reason: in Washington we'd had people into our home *constantly* from all over the world, and we were pretty fed up with people. They can be pretty tough sometimes. So, the only thing we wanted was a remote spot, and this was remote." They had come to a peaceful place to get away from people. That wouldn't last.

"In two weeks people started coming. People we hadn't previously known. Rather than kicking them out, which was the first thing that came to mind, we gave them the prayer to help pray for the planet.

Then it was like a floodgate opened. People started coming from all over the planet."

Indeed they did. They came because they had a dream of Jim. They came because they had heard that there was a man in the mountains who was a healer. They came because they had had personal tragedies. They came because they wanted to get off drugs. They came because they had heard that there was this man who was talking about the most extraordinary things – and he was not talking about theory, he was talking as if he *knew*. They came because he had a way of making each person feel special, Divine, holy.

Jim welcomed them all. He captured his extraordinary generosity and the depth of his commitment to living a genuinely spiritual life when he said, "My concept is that we cannot own anything on planet Earth. Everything that is belongs to God. My home, that I call my home, isn't mine. It's God's. I am a tenant. And people from all over the planet, if they want to come, it's their home, too."

Things had come to Jim that "required proving Jesus' words for man to see and know. The first thing to prove was 'Love thy neighbor as thyself.' Loving thy neighbor as thyself means one hundred percent love. Nothing less. That meant that we must, as a family, open our door to everyone." This large heart and this giving benefited thousands.

Living Jesus' words was not always easy: "We opened our doors to everyone from the lowest that you can get to the highest. We've had IQ levels very close to zero and IQs way up into the super-genius level – those belonging to Mensa. We've had people that weren't able to walk in here at all. They were so far gone on drugs that they were totally incapacitated. We even had a man that came to kill me. He and I started talking. He began to change. He began to practice the Seven Steps prayer. He stayed overnight, and the next day he was a new man.

"And so, they came. All types. Every creed. Hurt, sick, dying, near suicides, people who were drugged out. Every type of human being. Every type of disease and sickness.

"And the prayer worked. If you see a person totally drugged out, carried in by four people, and in an hour that person is totally normal, you know prayer works. It's kind of mind-boggling, but in reality it's the normal way."

A common memory of those times was that Jim had an extraordinary ability to anticipate when people were going to arrive, even total strangers who had not called or written in advance. Knowing when and how many people would be arriving, he would ask that food and bedding be prepared for them.

Many of the first groups of people to arrive at the Goure doorstep came from Virginia Beach and were associated with Edgar Cayce's Association for Research and Enlightenment (A.R.E.). One of the very earliest arrivals remembers, "It was great being at the house. Living with Jim's family was pure delight. And the land was, of course, beautiful. Jim was upbeat, energetic, fun-loving...a man with much passion and a mission. He was a kick. Lots of fun. So much energy. So optimistic. Jim was like a young kid in an old man's body. We, as family (and as extended family) joined together four times a day to pray...Jim leading, of course. I was young. I should've helped Diana more. Poor Diana: always doing laundry and cooking. I stayed about two months. I know Jim had hoped I would stay on indefinitely, but I'm afraid I was too young – a free spirit who didn't want to get more deeply involved at the time. As it was, the time I spent with Jim and his family in Black Mountain will remain two months I'll *never* forget.

"Soon after I left, I'm afraid the word got out, and the hordes starting flooding the Goure family. Everybody I knew from Virginia Beach and folks that knew these folks came to Jim's. It was like the flood gates had opened. Folks were thirsting for the truth, for direction, for hope. Jim's mission had begun.

"Unfortunately, none had any money, and it had to have been a stretch for the Goure family to handle such an influx of humanity. Times were tough in the beginning, I'm sure. But, somehow, I doubt Jim and the family ever turned anyone away."

It was indeed difficult for Jim and the family. Speaking years later of his experiences, Jim said, "It has been years of testing for the family. Sometimes it strained even me. It was a strain because I have learned that very few people know how to live with one another. But one thing I can assure you of: the family that prays together can do anything. If your family (and if you are just one, you are still a family because you are never alone) will pray, you will hang in there through thick and thin, and it'll be fantastic.

"We have all gained from the people who came because there is something of the Christ in everyone. That Christ was in some cases difficult to find, and we had to dig, but we gained from the experience. We advanced. They advanced from the experience of this family.

"The second of Jesus' words that we had to prove was the statement about the lilies of the valley. If God will take care of the lily of the valley – water it, feed it, give it sunshine – how well and how much more will he take care of you. That one was tough. I can tell you that the Divine will supply your every need. It may get hairy, but you will come out of it."

For guidance on how to contend with the challenges before them, Jim and Diana continued to connect with their Higher Selves and ask questions. In one session in the early 1970s, they asked about some of the young people who had come to them from Virginia Beach and got this message: "This group of children needs a little more time here on the mountain top so they may become better established in the Light and so they may be able to carry it back into their lives with them.

"This has seemed to be a drain on you because there was so much darkness concentrated in some of them, which had to be disbursed. Yet, the Light is here and it is strong and ye shall not see it go out but it shall shine forever and it shall be strengthened more and more as you continue in this way. It is as though a part of you is being torn away – but realize that you are not you but the Larger Light that shines far and wide and brings healing and Light to these who seek.

"It is as though they came seeking – some to become clear, some to help, some to look - and they were helped tremendously and they were filled with Light and now they are taking it with them. But know that this is the lighting of the candle within each and this lighting does not take anything away from the first one. This is a growing process and an expansion and it is good."

A drain on him or not, Jim welcomed all comers. But this created a practical problem in the first months of the Goure family living in Black Mountain. He had no money. His retirement checks from the government had not yet arrived.

Jay Goure, who was serving in the Marines at the time, stepped in with help. As Diana remembers, "Jay was sent to Vietnam as a cook, which meant he had all of the duties of a fighting soldier as well as the responsibility to cook for his unit. What is so wonderful is he signed up to send part of his pay home each month. How did he know we were in desperate straights financially? It came at a time when we had just moved to North Carolina and Jim's beginning retirement pay never arrived for six months or so. Jay also instructed and paid for Walnut Acres to send us 100 pounds of brown rice and 100 pounds of whole wheat flour. This tided us over some lean times. In January, 1971, three carloads of young people from Virginia Beach arrived at our door. This gift of rice and flour enabled us to feed them. We had every imaginable rice dish. And one of them used our huge punch bowl to make six to eight loaves of bread each day of their stay."

Diana remembers yet another solution to feeding the masses that arrived: "One time we were fixing dinner with a young chef from Atlanta when two carloads of people drove up. I said, 'What can we do? This is not enough for everyone.' He said, 'Don't worry. Just a few shakes of hot pepper and no one will want seconds.'"

Food wasn't the only practical issue. There was also the problem of space. Including Jim and Diana, there were nine Goure family members in the house, half of whom were teenagers or younger: Roger was seven, Will was ten. Gloria, thirteen. Paula, sixteen. Chris, eighteen. Liana was twenty and Jon and Jay (who was in Vietnam) were twenty-two. When visitors showed up, they were given rooms. When the Goures first moved into the house, only the upstairs had been finished, and there were only four bedrooms. The basement had not yet been finished. Although the house was a relatively large one, 3,100 square feet upstairs and a similar amount of space downstairs, much of that was open space – a large living room, dining area, and kitchen. With all of the guests who were arriving, people were practically hanging from the rafters.

To help with the not-insignificant matter of funds, Diana worked for the YMCA Blue Ridge Assembly. At one point while she worked for Blue Ridge Assembly, she invited her bosses, Frank Washburn and Allan Robertson, and their families to join the Goures for dinner.

The Goures had prepared Twelve-Boy Curry, a dish that had been popular in the officer's mess when Jim served on a Navy destroyer. (The Royal Navy had introduced this Indian dish to the U.S. Navy. In addition to rice, Twelve-Boy Curry includes curried lamb, beef, chicken, or turkey with small side dishes to sprinkle on the top. Each side dish is brought in by a different "boy." The side dishes can include things such as chopped egg whites, chopped egg yolk, chopped peanuts, raisins, shredded coconut, chopped onions, grated carrots, pickle relish, etc.)

The food evidently was a hit, but then, as so often happened at the house in North Carolina, the unexpected arrived. As Diana put it, "Here I was having a dinner for my bosses when who should appear at our door but Judy Needle! Now, she's a great gal. I really like her. Because she knew all the closet metaphysicians in Asheville, she actually was the 'open sesame' for all of Jim's work in the area – Friday classes and all. But she began to talk of her psychic abilities and all the famous people she had helped through them. This was all so weird I thought I'd probably lost my job right there. But, Frank Washburn said, 'That's the most interesting evening I've ever been to!'"

When it came to cooking, breakfast was Jim's meal. Diana remembers that, "Since I was out the door early every day to work at the YMCA Blue Ridge Assembly, Jim became the breakfast cook. He cooked pancakes every day for years…for all of the family and for whomever else was in residence at the time. It became such a tradition that eventually he received a bronzed pancake award from Lu Whitaker." Although Jim and Diana were sharing the cooking responsibilities, the guests were not. That soon changed. Diana: "It became Gloria's turn to cook after Liana got married, Chris was in Colorado, and Paula went to work in Greenville, South Carolina. We had a houseful of people, so there were ten to twenty at each dinner table. Gloria and I came home each day and got dinner ready but the strange thing was, we were the only ones who worked in town. That soon changed when Jim realized it. Then different ones began vying with each other for Jim's praise as the best cook. Part of that may have been due to the time Gloria almost fed us dog food!"

It wasn't all seriousness and hard work. Diana remembers that, "In the early 1970s, we all had great fun at the pond [that was on the Goure property]. It was spring-fed, about one acre in size, and 18 feet deep. Someone had attached a rope with a tire high up on the huge oak tree at the edge of the pond. The point was to see how far out one could swing on the tire and then drop into the water. Someone from Virginia gave us a surf board and that was the best way to swim out into the pond because only the top two inches of water ever got warm.

"Each of us had our own style of entering the water. I liked to walk in but Jim liked to dive in. One day I was inching along about waist deep when Jim came by and said, "How is it today?" I could hardly catch my breath [it was so cold, but managed an] 'Ohhh kayyy.' [With that,] Jim dove right in and was so shocked by the cold that he could hardly wait to get out!"

It became Diana's turn about six months later. "We were driving to Charlotte, North Carolina, where Jim was going to give a lecture. We stopped at a restaurant for some chili. Jim was the first to try it. I asked, 'How is it?' He said, 'Ummmm.' So I took a bite and it was RED HOT!!! Jim said, 'Gotcha!'"

Although he had dedicated himself to a life of the Spirit, Jim was still quite capable of stepping in to resolve a practical matter. Diana remembers that, "Carol Parrish invited Jim to give a weekend workshop at Long Boat Key, Florida. Carol is a New Age teacher and minister [who now lives in Arkansas]. Jim brought Diana, Rosemary Crow, the singer, and Marianne Satterstrom, the angel lady. It was a good workshop, well received. After it was over, all four of us were invited to go on her (new) husband's sailboat across the bay to eat lunch in Sarasota. He had been living on the boat but had just moved off. So we all piled aboard and were out in the middle of the bay when suddenly the sky darkened and a huge storm blew up, wild winds, large waves rocking the boat. The captain asked all the women to go below. Just he and Jim were in the cockpit. Apparently there was no compass, no life jackets, and he had no idea how to get back to the marina. Jim said, 'I can get us back.' So, the helm was turned over to Jim and his Naval Academy training came to the fore, his knowledge of the way the wind was blowing and the way the waves looked. He brought us right back to the shore we had just left. He was thrilled with sailing again."

After the original groups of people from Virginia Beach in the early 1970s, the people kept coming and coming. For seventeen years they came. Saints and criminals. The retarded and the geniuses. The crippled and the healers. All were welcomed.

Because so many of the early visitors were young people – many of them hippies – Jim worked on finding an angle that would get them interested in God. Initially, he thought that opening would be through extrasensory perception and he felt it was important to make college students aware of extrasensory capabilities. In the early 1970s he wrote to colleges and universities within a 100 mile radius of Black Mountain offering a lecture on extrasensory perception. The only college that replied to Jim's offer was Guilford College in Greensboro, North Carolina. A Quaker friend from Virginia Beach, John Brown, was on the board of the college and the Goure's daughter Chris was a freshman there.

In connecting with their Higher Selves, Jim and Diana received this about the Guilford venture: "Guilford is a precious and beloved place of learning. Great strides are being made there. Great good is already coming forth in this place. A small beginning may be good…but walk softly…and bring in the completely sincere teachers, not the magicians – the pure, not the loose-moraled."

Although Jim was eager for young people to be aware of what was happening on inner levels, the ones who proved to be the first stable group that joined Jim's mission were women who were closet metaphysicians in nearby Asheville, North Carolina. They already had been primed by being in an Edgar Cayce "Search for God" group, and *they* were the ones to catch fire with his teaching. They were the catalyst for what came to be known as Friday Class.

FRIDAY CLASS

During the late 1960s and early 1970s in Asheville, there was an Edgar Cayce A.R.E. Search for God group meeting every Wednesday morning. The women in this group were closet metaphysicians. They wanted to know how to become more psychic, but in that conservative Buckle of the Bible Belt area, they generally kept quiet about their intentions.

Four of these women approached Jim in the early 1970s about learning how to be psychic, and he told them, "Oh, I can teach you that in four weeks. Just come at 10 a.m. on Friday." So, at their request, Jim, in early 1972, in the living room of his home, began what came to be known as Friday Class. Although he had assumed that he could teach the four women everything they needed to know in four weeks, Jim continued to give those classes for the rest of his life.

Despite what the women had requested, Jim's focus was never really on the psychic. He did not say it during the first classes he gave, but in later years he said the psychic could be a trap: you could get stuck on being psychic and that would retard your progress in knowing and worshipping the Divine. In the early days of his time in North Carolina, though, he felt that teaching the psychic might be a way to attract young people to the spiritual. He had observed the protests and the anger of the young during the 1960s and felt this was not doing them much good. That which would help them was God. But how to get them interested in God? The psychic, he thought, might be a way, and with it he did have some success with the young. But the first students in his Friday Class were not the young and angry but a group of calmer, middle-aged women.

The notes that were taken during the first year of Friday Class show these early sessions to have been more informal and personal than the classes of later years. They also involved longer periods of prayer. At these early classes, Jim spoke for awhile, but then the group would pray for about half an hour. In later years, the prayers tended to be briefer, perhaps so that the class, with a much larger and probably more restless audience, could be kept to about an hour or so in length.

The first thing Jim is quoted as saying in a Friday Class is, "First of all, we must recognize that there is Divinity within each of us. It is also within all other people and within everything on Earth." That was it. That would be the core tenet of his teachings for the next fourteen years: you are Divine and so is everyone and everything else.

Other aspects of his early teachings centered on finding the Light within, extending that Light to others, protecting oneself, and working with colors. Jim put particular emphasis on experiencing the Light within the solar plexus. He said, "There is no other thing as important as becoming one with this Light. The Divinity never intended our way should be anything but one of simplicity. And what is important is that we give this Light to others. When you pray, try to get out of your brain and into the solar plexus area. The Light is in your solar plexus area. Take a deep breath and feel the Light from your solar plexus flowing through your lungs and throat and taking out everything negative. Feel the Light expanding, radiating out into all. The Light shines into your past and it heals the past. The Light begins to heal all of your previous incarnations. The result: you begin to truly love. You begin to experience true joy."

He also said, "In prayer, let Love open your heart to the needs of others, and start by loving yourself. This may seem difficult at first. If you can't feel your Light, then imagine it. If that is difficult, don't worry. This is not an intellectual process."

In the early Friday Class teachings, Jim also emphasized the need for protection: "As you get more and more into Light, you need more protection because the Light attracts its opposite. Some negative forces may gather around you and try to distract you. While there are evil entities using negative forces, the rest of us must use protection from evil. A good method of protection is this: say, 'I am the center of a big bubble of Light and Love and nothing can enter but Love and Light.' Say this over and over until it becomes part of the very fiber of your subconscious. *Know* the bubble is there. As soon as you wake up in the morning, *know* that your home is in the center of a bubble with the Divinity present. Say this over and over, morning, noon, and night. In three days your problem is over. You have protection. Do this also with your car. Love your Divinity and all life around you with mind, soul, and spirit, and don't worry. Put bubbles of Light and Love around yourself, your children, your husband, and family. All will be protected."

Releasing the past, holding to the Light, and giving thanks to God were also themes that Jim introduced during the first year of Friday Classes, and they were to be themes that he would return to continuously over the years. He told the Class during the first year, "Release the past! Know it is in God's hands! Know that all relationships are now good! The past is rectified! Never accept the negative! Accept only Light and Love! Create true Love! Maintain the Truth! Give thanks for the Divinity in action in every big and little thing! This is one of the fastest ways to increase your own Divinity. Give thanks for air, water, husband, no husband, children, no children – everything."

He also, during that first year of Friday Classes, fingered the issue that, to the very last lecture he gave, he felt was the major thing holding back people's spiritual development: "The ego is one of our greatest problems. The 'I want' and 'I'm going to' - when they come from the ego - are just to satisfy yourself. When your desires are higher, they come from the Divinity within you. And as Christ said, 'If I be lifted up, all be lifted up.'"

To get beyond the ego, Jim said, "I can't stress this enough. It is very important that you go beyond personal results in your prayers. Pray for our country and for present and future leaders. As a member of the Christ Party, the government rests upon your shoulders."

In the early years, he also talked about colors and their therapeutic powers. "Red vibrates at the base of the spine and affects the natural world. It is warm and stimulating and strengthening. It helps digestion and gives power and a positive outlook. The red planet is Mars. Orange vibrates in the spleen and gives vitality. Orange is the sun color. Yellow affects the nervous system and emotions. It causes optimism and gives a cheerful outlook on life. The yellow planet is Venus. Green is the color of the heart area. This color gives harmony and balance. It helps the blood in every way. It stimulates sympathy and kindness. The green planet is Earth. Blue is a cool color. It begins the area of higher consciousness. Spiritual healing becomes possible and serenity is achieved. Peace, truth and harmony are achieved through the use of this color. Saturn is the blue planet. Indigo is a purifying color. It is good for the nerves. It is also good for the mind, hearing , and psychic and spiritual growth. The indigo planet is Jupiter, the greatest planet. Violet is the highest vibration visible to us. It is inspirational. Neptune is its planet and is a New Age planet.

"Colors affect your whole being, not just the body and mind but your soul. They can help you to overcome karma. The New Age colors are lavender and pastels of all colors. Violet vibrations are very helpful for the whole system. Remember, Light dispels darkness! Being out in the sun is good for you. Let it flow into you, over you, through you."

Jim's overarching purpose in everything he was teaching during the early Friday Classes – everything he was saying about Light and colors, ego and releasing – was to get people into a state of consciousness where they were more concerned about *giving* than receiving and where this giving enabled Earth to be a more peaceful, beautiful, Light-filled place. During that first year of Friday Classes, he told the group, "Remember! We are here to help! We are here to save this Earth, to help our fellow man! And there is no burden too great! You know you are about your Father's business. Know it with all your being! We are here to heal ourselves and to get on to doing greater things. We need to go now into the greater things. Heal the Earth – assume it is like a person. Imagine it before you and say, 'The earth has released all its past. The earth has released all its negatives.

The earth has released all its fears. The earth has released all its relationships (to the planets, the sun and all other galaxies).' There is no end of your capability. Move into a bigger spectrum. Don't be afraid to take on the big world. Then the little worlds will be automatically taken care of."

Jim continually admonished people to use prayer to create on a grand scale: "Create a new world! Create it now! A world that is a creation of beauty, peace, harmony, and joy. That Which Is is *the real you*. Give thanks for your oneness with the Divinity. We must do this kind of praying to make it possible for our children to live in peace. Living here on Earth will be wonderful. It will be a good time with everyone helping everyone else. Great things are happening. Personally, I don't think we will have to go through a cataclysm. All things are possible with Divinity. It is a joyous and beautiful world. This is a new age," Jim said emphatically. "A new age of Light, of Love, a new and peaceful age."

While Jim was emphasizing the need to pray for the planet, the questions he received in the first year of Friday Classes – and for much of the rest of his life - showed that people had more narrow, more personal concerns, which, despite his grander vision, Jim was quite willing to address. Question: "Do you think it is wrong to eat meat?" He didn't. Question: "When somebody comes to you for advice and help about a problem, what is the best way to handle it?" Answer: "First, pray. When the person comes to you, listen! Let the problem come out. And *know* the Divinity is there in that person. Know that Love is present, that Light is healing. If the person asks what to do, say, 'Let us pray together.' Know the prayer is being answered." Question: "When people want to talk on and on negatively and you just wish they would shut up, what can you do?" Answer: "Many times people need a release. You might just let it go right through, but let them release it. You can always try changing the subject if it gets to be too much."

Showing a way to bring the spiritual into the physical, Jim also had advice for the early Friday Classes about how to start a day and how to prepare for the day's events. Regarding the morning, he said, "Begin each day with prayer as soon as you wake up. Give thanks for Light and Love and Joy and for being in the right place at the right time. Give thanks that all things are working out well for you and your loved ones."

He also advised Class members, "Whatever you are involved in, make right preparation. Make preparation for a PTA meeting. Prepare for going shopping. Prepare yourself to be sensitive to the objects you are going to buy. Try, if possible, to buy what has been made with loving care. That working world also needs Light. Send Light to the whole company or organization you're working for. Pray and know there are right relationships – right relationships between parents and teachers, between your children and their teachers, between your children and other children. Even if you don't have children, pray for the children, for the teachers, and for the whole school system. Whenever you go to the theater or to a movie or wherever there is a crowd of people – like attending church – this is an opportunity to change people. With elections coming up, pray that the right leaders will be elected. Try to go within you as you look at the ballot. If possible, get a sample ballot ahead of time and *feel* within. Hold to the Light and after the elections hold to true government coming."

What he had to say about dreams showed that in that first year of Friday Classes, Jim may have been more open about his personal life than he was in later years. In a comment about nightmares, he revealed one of his own: "There are no nightmares just as there are no accidents. Painful dreams usually have a meaning for you. I'll tell you about one of mine. Long after leaving the strict regimentation of the Naval Academy and Annapolis, I had what could be called a nightmare. I thought I was called out for duty and was not dressed properly. I had on one white sock and one black sock and my uniform was all wrong. The dream meant that I must understand both the black and the white qualities in people and must bring my life in tune with modern times. My main mission is to be here at home praying, and I had been running around doing many other things. The dream helped me to see this."

This willingness at the early Friday Classes to talk about his personal side, ever rarer over the years as people either idolized him or used personal information to attack him, led Jim to say this about one of his brothers at a May, 1972, Friday Class: he quoted the Bible, "Judge not that ye be not judged," and then, evidently speaking of his brother Richard, he said that his brother while on Earth "had experienced all the negative side of life and was criticized for living such a life. One day while at the San Diego Zoo, he saved a child from drowning. A week later he died. He appeared [to Jim] in his astral body and explained he had been a priest or holy man through many incarnations, giving counsel to people who were living negative lives, but he had never experienced evil. He asked permission to have a life in which he would experience the negative side of earth life. His karma had been cancelled when he saved the child. The lesson for us is that we should never judge anyone under any circumstances."

The more personal nature of the early Friday Classes also showed itself when in November of 1972 the Class notes state that, "One of the group members asked Jim to say something about the funeral of Peggy, someone most of us knew. Jim and several of the group had attended. It was most unusual, they said, because it was a happy, joyful occasion instead of being sad and doleful. As one of those present commented, 'It was the first happy funeral I ever attended.'"

In speaking of Peggy and her funeral, Jim would articulate a perspective on why it is difficult for spiritual people on Earth, a viewpoint we shall see him return to in the forthcoming chapter *Advances*: "Many people on this Earth have come from other planets where people truly love, where there are no wars, where there is no hatred, where everyone tries to help others. Here, in this plane, they run into the dog-eat-dog world where the negative dominates, where people have not been loving each other. They find it an extreme condition that sometimes gets to be overwhelming. It is just too much for them. But in their short time they accomplish a lot. Their very presence here is a Light. Peggy went on to a higher plane. There was great healing present at this funeral. It was truly a joyous occasion, a great experience. And a beautiful thing happened during this service. A rainbow formed to bless everyone there."

A woman in the class asked Jim, "Did our prayers for Peggy help her – really?" (Peggy had died of cancer.) Jim's response: "Whenever you pray for healing for someone, your prayers help. They help to overcome the negative beings who are present. Your prayers are used. They make a greater Light."

Although he later suggested to people that maybe they would be better off if they stopped reading spiritual books and simply went within to get the Truth, in the first year of Friday Classes he had recommendations of books to read, and those recommendations showed that he had found inspiration from different religions and from various perspectives on life. His first recommendation was to read the King James version of the Bible, the most important books of which he said were Genesis 1 and 2 and the New Testament. (In later years, he would narrow that recommendation to reading only the words spoken by Jesus.) He also recommended *Kinship with All Life* by Boone; *Ye Are Gods* by Skarin; *The Aquarian Gospel of Jesus the Christ* by Levi; *Autobiography of a Yogi* by Paramahansa Yogananda; *Jonathan Livingston Seagull* by Bach; and *Dreams, Your Magic Mirror* by Sechrist. He also read to that first year's Friday Class from the *Bhagavad-Gita*.

As for becoming psychic, the primary reason members of the Friday Class originally had come to see him, Jim didn't say much during the first year of Friday Classes (and in later years said virtually nothing). But in that first year, he did give this advice: "Become still. Relax. Imagine Light expanding from your toes all through your body. The method of opening the third eye is this: First pray for an hour and feel Light and Love permeate your whole being. With your eyes closed, pray for yourself and concentrate on trying to see from the center of your forehead. Imagine the vibrations of Light and Love focusing from there. The third eye has been dormant, so it must not be opened suddenly or you will experience a severe pain in your forehead. Do this for only a short time – not more than five minutes at first. Then ask to see clairvoyantly from the third eye. Do not try to force your third eye open. Let the Light within you open it gradually. You will see – not with your physical eyes – but on a wavelength of Light. After two or three weeks, you will begin to see those who have 'died.' You will also see angels, devas, and other beings."

In giving further advice about the psychic, he said, "Do you want to communicate with loved ones here, those in Eternity, and with superbeings? Select someone you really want to see and focus your attention on that person. Those on the Other Side will look different from the way you remember them. They will seem to be between eighteen and thirty years of age. Try to bypass the brain and make the communication a primary act of feeling. Do not try to argue. Become aware of Divine Light being and aware that your vibrations have become higher. Feeling is the key to right communication. Keep it cool."

Other perspectives Jim imparted during the first year of Friday Classes:

- "Man now needs the Spirit of God to help change wine back into water. There is too much drinking in the present age."
- "You will eventually find your mate. When you put God first, all other things necessary will be added. Finding a soul-mate is not the important thing."
- "Do not seek hither and thither for the Christ. Turn to the Light within."
- "Flying saucers do exist. Ninety-nine percent are here to help us. About one-tenth of one percent are not here for that purpose. They have advanced scientifically but not spiritually."
- "Anytime you have a 'down' period, giving thanks is the best and the fastest way to get centered back into the Light. If you can't do it by yourself, ask for help. Call on your prayer partner or any friend."
- "It is your conception of life that matters. Enjoy life to the maximum."
- "Decide on a world problem as a prayer project."
- "Light equals Love equals God."

Jim also told the early Friday Classes, "Make sure *you* take control of your life. *This Light knows and answers all things.* You should not have to ask anyone else what to do. You have only to turn to the Light within. Examine all you are looking at. Is it controlling you or are you the master? Don't look outside of yourself. Everything you need is within. Send Love to everyone around you so your life will have love and joy. If you think that you love someone more than others, remember that all have Divinity and all are equal in that respect. Do not give in to what other people think. Rise above earthly conditions, all that appears to be negative. You be the Master."

For all the confidence with which he taught and for as emphatic as he could be, Jim did not insist on blind faith in his words. He told the class, "Don't worship Jim Goure. I'm no different from you. I'm a human being, losing my hair and having to wear glasses at night. Don't look for a Master. Always test things – all teachers – including me. *You* are Divinity. Truth is not what Jim Goure says nor what the Bible says. It is what you find within yourself. Grow in response to what you *know* is true. When working with Divinity all ego and self-righteousness leaves you. There are many ways up to the top of the mountain. Each way is different, each expression of Divinity differs from the others, but in some ways they coincide. Recognize Truth as you go along and apply what you know."

As broad-ranging as his topics at Friday Class were, Jim wanted to give more. At one of Jim and Diana's Higher Selves sessions, the question was asked, "Why is it that Jim feels like crying after each Friday Class?" And the answer that came was, "Because there's so much more he'd like to be doing, so much more he'd like to to be giving, so much greater a number of people he'd like to be teaching, so much more Light he'd like to have received by these people, so much more transmutation he'd like to be taking place, so much more power he'd like to see these people being able to handle and receive and give and use, so much better a world that could be, should be coming into being now."

Jim showed early on that he had a vision for how he intended to bring about that better world. At the June 16th, 1972 Friday Class, Jim said, "Why are *we* [the Goure family] here? Why did God lead us to this place at this time? Because: 1) This place is to become a Light Center to change negative forces in the world into Light. Experiments are being made with the effects of colored lights in the frequencies of the rainbow colors showing a tremendous effect on mind, body, and soul. Things of the past and physical ills can be changed by correct exposure to these lights. 2) This home is open to all beings who may come – no matter who they are – who need it to be healed and strengthened." And, showing that he wanted to do what Walter and Lao Russell had first talked about doing, "3) A statue of Christ sixty feet high called The Christ of the Blue Ridge will be built as a center on which the Christian world can concentrate its consciousness. Other projects radiating from this Center will deal with improvements in government, in medicine, and in education."

In a further articulation of his vision, on February 23rd, 1973, he spoke of a Light Center. "We want to build a Light Center up here. The purpose of the Light Center is to change the destructive negative force. We want to build a two-story, eight-sided building. Each room will have a different color light and the center room will be for effective prayer. There will be seven rooms and an entrance. People for an area of 150 miles around will be affected. Hopefully we can build a chain of these Light Centers on mountains near population centers. Mountains give out high vibratory rates."

Although he clearly focused on the spiritual, Jim never saw himself as being in competition with churches. He purposefully did not hold Sunday services or have a Sunday lecture series so that he would not compete with them. He even invited ministers to speak at his Friday Classes. Going a step further, he told the early Friday Class members, "We should all attend church or churches. Pray for the minister and the congregation. Know that all are filled with Love and Light. This will affect persons who are open and bring about changes. We go to church to worship God. That is our primary reason – not to hear the minister. We should begin by preparing ourselves. We should go feeling that it is something holy. We give thanks for His presence, His Light, His Love. We give thanks that the congregation is also filled with His presence, His Light, His Love. We pray and we *know* this is so. Then we proceed to church where we become still – that we may hear the Word of God. And the Word will be in *your* voice. You will feel such love and Light as you never felt before. The worship of God is an experience. We need to begin – to worship the Holy One. We need to bring about changes in the churches, not physical but spiritual changes."

The signature prayer for which Jim would be remembered, The Seven

Steps to Effective Prayer, was something he developed over time. In reading the notes of the first year of Friday Classes, you can watch him begin to put together the pieces. First, he talked about the Light from the solar plexus, and he talked about the importance of protecting oneself with the bubble of Light. It was a piecemeal approach, but by the end of the first year, the prayer, in rough form, had begun to coalesce. Jim began to speak of steps in prayer on December 1st, 1972. And on June 22nd, 1973, the last day for which there are notes of the early Friday Classes, Jim for the first time gave a seven-step prayer. Step one was a step of releasing, "I release all my past. I release all my fears. I release all my negatives. I release all my relationships." The second step was what he called a mantra: "I am Love or I am Light." The third step was "to know this Light that Thou Art is radiating through thy being." The fourth step was to "radiate this Light out in all directions – to everyone – but especially to your loved ones. They are there for a reason. They are there for your growth, for your greater understanding of life." The fifth step was, "We radiate out not only to all beings but to all things – everything." Included in this fifth step was asking: "You can ask any question and you can receive an answer. Or you can ask for a Great Being, a Christed Being to come and help you, to assist you in any program, any project you have at this point." The sixth step involved "becoming the bubble": "I am the bubble of Light and Love. Only Light and Love are here." The seventh step involved being grateful for this Light, being grateful to the Divinity for what has been done. "Be thankful. 'In all thy ways, be thankful and praise the Lord, O my soul.' If you can just go about saying, 'Thank you, God, for this that I do,' if you will do this, you won't believe how great your day of love can be."

This prayer would eventually be streamlined and condensed into seven easily memorized steps. This streamlined prayer, along with Jim's teachings from the 1980s, are summarized in the next chapter, *Teachings*. Those wanting an expanded version of Jim's teachings should see the final section of this book, *Part III: Teachings*.

Jim had not intended for the Friday Classes to be a long-running show. He said in one of the early classes of 1972, "I want to get you through this training and out of this class as soon as possible. The world is at a very critical time and needs you. I *insist* that each of you must spend an undivided hour every day in prayer." Embedded in this comment was Jim's vision of what he was – and was not – aiming to accomplish. He *was* providing people with tools they could use to help improve their own worlds as well as the world of planet Earth. He was *not* trying to build an organization or a following. He had made that clear when he said, "I want to get you...out of this class as soon as possible."

But from the notes of the first year of classes, you could feel the excitement among class members, and perhaps it was this enthusiasm, coupled with a flood of new people wanting to be taught, that encouraged Jim to continue the classes long after he had thought they would end. In her notes of the October 13, 1972 Friday Class, one class member wrote, "Jim gave us a report on the retreat that he and Diana had conducted at Chesapeake, Virginia. He said the place was an old estate near the water, beautiful and quiet. There were twenty-seven persons who participated in the prayer and discussions, and Jim said the results were 'great.' We hope that sometime he and Diana will conduct a retreat for us – take note, Jim!"

Jim reciprocated the feeling of enthusiasm and affection: "You people are very special and prayers from this plane are very effective. What you do is important. What you do affects the whole Earth. So, keep in balance by thinking all of the time about Light and Divinity. Take care of yourselves. You are very special people."

The first Friday Class had started in early 1972 with four or five women meeting at the Goure home. Then about a dozen came. Then the crowds overflowed from the living room into the dining areas and beyond, with about fifty to one hundred people in attendance.

To accommodate these crowds, in 1979, seven years after the Friday Classes had started, they were moved to the Light Center that Jim had spoken of. The classes still began at 10 a.m. every Friday morning. Jim would sit in an elevated, multi-colored, swivel chair and would start by asking people to close their eyes and take a deep breath. Then he would pray, "Thank you, God, for bringing us together in Thy Light and Thy Love that we may be aware of Thee in all Thy ways.

Open our hearts and minds and souls to Thee. Amen." As he had with the early Friday Classes, Jim would then lecture for a half hour or so and finally open the session up to questions. The topics he spoke on were wide-ranging - from Love to War to Peace to Tragedies to Healing to Creativity – but the underlying themes always contained his optimism, his faith in the Divine, and his recognition of the Divine in each individual.

Although the timing – every Friday at 10 a.m. - and the format – lecture, questions, and prayer – were the same, there were subtle differences between the earlier and the later classes. The later classes were somewhat more formal and less personal, and the message was simpler and more focused. For example, whereas in the first year he had recommended books that spanned several different religions and perspectives, in the later years he talked almost exclusively about the teachings of Jesus. And as time went on, you sensed that Jim had concluded that the only thing that really changed people was a feeling that they were loved. It wasn't the words. It was the love. It may not have been the teachings even. It was just the love.

Jim in front of the stone fireplace at the house, giving a Friday Class

Jim with Hawk Little John at Camp Elliot, North Carolina; Jim
had high regard for the spirituality of American Indians

TEACHINGS

For the seventeen years he was in Black Mountain - at Friday Classes, workshops, Advances, and in other venues - Jim taught people about the Divine. He basic message was this: "You are It. You are the Divine. Recognize who you are. Be Divine. In recognizing who you are, use that Divinity to create Good for everyone and everything."

The Foundation

If there were one central inspiration for the Light Center and for United Research, it was what Jesus said on the Sermon on the Mount: "Ye are the Light of the world." Jim took this to mean that each of us had a responsibility for helping Earth. The part about "Ye are the Light" meant that each one of us is Divine. And the part saying, "...of the world" meant that we had a responsibility to do something with this Light, to use it for the betterment of the planet and everyone on it.

Jim also frequently cited the quote from Jesus that appears in the Book of John, "The things I do you can do and greater". He interpreted this as meaning that, if we can do the things that Jesus did and greater, then that same Christ spirit that was in Jesus is in us, too. And the very nature of the Christ spirit is in knowing your Divinity and doing something with it for the betterment of all.

Jim also quoted from what has come to be known as the Lord's Prayer, that the Father is in heaven and, from another part of the Gospels, that the kingdom of heaven is within. He drew a link between the two, saying that if heaven is within and the Father is in heaven, then the Father, or God, must be within – within each one of us.

Jim felt there was no higher teaching in the Bible than what Jesus said and he told several people to read only the words of Jesus. But at times he would quote from the Old Testament also, and in support of his contention that each one of us is Divine, he would note that in Genesis it says that God created man in his own image and likeness and that God saw that his creation was good. Jim's take on this was that, if God created man in His own image and likeness, then man himself must be Divine: being made in the image of God must mean that God made man Godlike. And Jim further deduced, what kind of God would stop creating? What kind of God would have a once-and-done approach to creating? It was inconceivable to Jim that this would be the case. So, God must be creating on an ongoing basis, meaning that each one of us has been created by the Divine, in the image and likeness of the Divine, as in the beginning.

Jim taught that in knowing the Divinity within ourselves we would know the Divine Love that is within. In knowing this Divine Love, in being one with it, in being one with this magnificent, never ending Love, we would have no desire other than to give and give and give of this Love to everyone and everything.

Recognizing the Divinity within self, we would also recognize it in others. We would see them as our well-beloved brothers and sisters. Knowing that the Divine is in others, we would have total respect for them, and we would know that we must give and give to them of the Love within ourselves.

"All man is crying out for this Love that you are," said Jim. He saw a lack of love as being the cause of every problem on Earth. Every illness, every crime, every war was the result of a lack of love.

The answer to every problem was for us to access the unlimited supply of Divine Love within and, through prayer, allow the Creator within each person to heal them, to have this Divine Love transform their hurts and to change their past to Light.

Jim taught that the only limitations were those in our concepts of self. He said that, because the Divine is in each one of us, in putting down ourselves, in condemning self, we were condemning God. "Stop condemning self!" he would say emphatically. "Know you are Divine!"

And then, he said, get on with doing something with this Divinity. Create more Good than there was in the beginning, because obviously, according to Jim, there was not enough Love in the beginning, otherwise, why would Earth be such a killing planet?

Divine Mission

Another aspect of being this Light of the world that Jesus spoke of was that each one of us has a Divine mission. There are Divine missions that all of us have, such as prayer for planet Earth. But each individual, according to Jim, also has a unique mission. Discovering that mission and then doing it is our whole point in living. You get your mission by praying, "The Creator within me reveals to me my Divine mission" and by declaring, "The Creator in me accomplishes my Divine mission."

Prayer

Jim paraphrased Jesus and admonished people to "Pray without ceasing." Not that he saw prayer as an end in itself, but as a way to enter Divine consciousness and get about being what Jesus told people they were, the Light of the world. To get your consciousness firmly anchored in that of the Divine, he said you needed to "Practice, practice, practice." Practice saying "I am Light" five hundred times a day was one of his recommendations.

He said you did not need to close your eyes to pray. You could say, "I see Light" while you were driving or scrubbing the floor or answering the phone – any activity that does not take a fully concentrated mind was an opportunity to pray. One could also program the Divine Self to pray while one was asleep, so the totality of one's being was continuously involved with prayer.

Jim's enthusiasm and his unshakeable belief in the power of prayer was infectious. And the results were spectacular. There were simply too many people who had been healed – healed of illnesses so severe that physicians had sent them home to die, healed to the extent that the diseases never returned. People were healed of physical ailments, of drug addictions, of suicidal tendencies. The healings went on and on and on. And the people came and came and came.

Jim's Prayer Background

So how did Jim come by this emphasis on prayer? He revealed a great deal when he was asked, more than forty years after his father, Raymond's, death, how he got involved in spiritual matters. His response: "After my dad died in an accident, I wanted to know the answer to life and death. Beginning at the age of twelve, I *really* studied the Bible – inside out and backwards – to get an answer. It did not answer. Scientifically, it did not answer.

"So, I studied the rest of the Bibles of the planet. And they didn't answer my questions about life and death. Then, I really studied the great masters of the planet and what they said. All of them said, 'The things I do you can do and greater.' All of them said, 'The great guru is within you.' All of them said, 'The kingdom of heaven with within you.'

"But, they didn't give us a technique, a how-to. It was a vacant spot.

"I finished this study about the time I was twenty-one. I was at the Naval Academy. I happened to be reading a book by some yogi, and this particular book said – he was a great guru, by the way, a really great guru – 'If you follow my system, my technique, I'll guarantee you that you can do the works I do in one million five hundred thousand years.' I threw the book away. To me, God never laid that kind of trip on anybody.

"The idea I had was that God was available now. It was a question of a technique of finding God. If the Kingdom of Heaven is within, how do we find Him? How?

"If all of these masters and great beings could get information and say, 'The things I do you can do and greater,' and also that 'I and the Creator are one,' and 'The Creator doeth the works,' then there had to be some way of getting to that.

"The only way I could find was to come up with a prayer that would really work. I spent a couple of years studying people who had effective prayer, people who healed and you could see the healing. I asked them, 'How do you pray?' People all over the planet are praying, but very few prayers are answered. If all the prayers were answered, nobody would be sick. Everybody would be well and wealthy. But prayers weren't being answered.

"In studying these common, ordinary people who got results from prayer and how they got those results, I myself tried to come up with *a* prayer that would work for everyone. I was getting results. Really good results on my own. But I was dissatisfied because there was a sense of ego, of personality, that was involved with it, a feeling of, 'Look at me. I can heal.' And I did.

"But I felt right then that that was a trap. That was really, literally Satan. This personality, this ego that wanted recognition was Satan.

"Then, the idea was to come up with something that *anybody* could use and get results. I went into prayer to get that. As soon as I made up my mind, immediately, the first thing that came was one of the steps of the Seven Steps of Effective Prayer. This first step that came, which was while I was at the Naval Academy, was, 'I am in a bubble of Light and only Light can come to me and only Light be here.' I equate Light and Christ as one. Because John [the Beloved] said Christ and Light are synonymous.

"So, the idea of being protected was paramount. Influences from the outside world were interfering with prayer, interfering with capabilities. Lots of times when I went into prayer, prior to using the bubble of Light, strange thoughts would come in from the outside world, interfering with the prayer that I was into. These thoughts and even visions were beautiful, but they were a distraction. Even seeing great beings is a distraction from God. I don't care how great they are.

"This bubble of Light protected me from other people's thoughts and emotions. That allowed the additional steps to come over a long period of time."

Those additional steps became…

<u>The Seven Steps to Effective Prayer</u>

Jim wanted to develop a short, simple prayer that anyone could use and that could be memorized easily. Above all else, it had to be effective. It had to be a prayer that got results. Over the years, this prayer acquired several names: The Effective Prayer, The Seven Steps to Effective Prayer, the Light Prayer, and oftentimes simply "the prayer." Here it is:

1. I release all of my past, negatives, fears, human relationships, self-image, future, human desires, sex, money, judgment, communications, and loved ones to the Light.
2. I am a Light being.
3. I radiate the Light from my Light center throughout my being.
4. I radiate the Light from my Light center to everyone.
5. I radiate the Light from my Light center to everything.
6. My whole being is in a bubble of Light and only Light can come to me and only Light be here.
7. Thank you, God, for everything, for everyone, and for me.

The Light that is referred to in this prayer is the same Light that is referred to in the Bible – and indeed is referred to in all of the bibles of the world. In the Sermon on the Mount, Jesus said, "Ye are the Light of the world" and "Neither do men light a candle and put it under a bushel, but on a candlestick, and it giveth light unto all that are in the house. Let your Light so shine before men, that they may see your good works and glorify your Father which is in heaven."

Jim's background was predominately Christian, and his references to Light were all Biblical in nature. But it may be worth noting that other religions have also spoken of the Light. The Mundaka Upanishad of Hinduism tells us that "In the effulgent lotus of the heart dwells Brahman, the Light of lights." In the Adi Granth of Sikhism, it is said,

"God, being Truth, is the one Light of all." The Dhammapada of Buddhism states that "The radiance of Buddha shines ceaselessly." The Holy Koran says that "Allah is the Light of the heavens and the earth." A verse of the Song of Kablaya of the American Lakota is, "The light of Wakan-Tanka is upon my people." A tribal African saying is that, "God is the sun beaming light everywhere." And Lao Tzu, whose philosophy became the basis for Taoism, said, "Following the Light, the sage takes care of all."

In the Seven Step prayer, the first step is a step of releasing – where we release all that is holding us back from knowing and being the Divinity that we are. In this step, Jim attempted identifying all of the core blockages he saw people having – and providing a technique for being relieved of those blockages. The first of these blockages is the past. Most people are consumed with what has happened to them in the past. From the past has come all of the other of the hang-ups: negatives, fears, troubled human relationships, self-image, concerns about the future, an image of self as being inferior, distracting human desires, problems with sex, being consumed with concerns about money, constant judging of everything, problems with communications, and the frustrations with loved ones. All of these hang-ups are to be released to the Light.

The second step is a positive declaration of who we are: "I am a Light being."

The third through the fifth steps put this Light that we are to work. The center of Light within ourselves from which we radiate the Light is located in our solar plexus area. The third step calls for radiating the Light from our personal Light center for the good of our own being. In the fourth and fifth steps, we go beyond self and extend the Light for the benefit of everyone and everything.

The sixth step is the step of protection that Jim developed while at the Naval Academy: "I am in a bubble of Light and only Light can come to me and only Light be here." We can put not only ourselves but the cars and planes we travel in in the Light. We can place those traveling with us in a bubble of Light. We can place our children in bubbles of Light before they go off to school. And so forth.

The seventh step is a step of thanksgiving. "Thank you, God, for everyone, for everything, and for me." In praising God in everyone and everything – and in ourselves – we find that we love all of creation, including ourselves. Jim would say that, if you wanted superconsciousness, simply repeating this step a million times a day, every day, would bring you superconsciousness. Because if you thank God for everything, then eventually you come to see God in everything, which is the very definition of superconsciousness.

Although the steps, as written, use the word "I," the prayer can easily be adapted if one wants to pray for others, simply by replacing "I" with "The Creator in [whomever one is praying for] releases all of his/her past to the Light," etc. The reason for using the words "The Creator in…" is so that we put things in the hands of the Divine, rather than having our egos try to impose a solution that our human minds and emotions think is right, but may be entirely inappropriate.

The prayer, Jim said, could be used for anything – for groups of people, for nations, for the planet, for all of creation.

Jim promised people that if they used this prayer 15 minutes twice a day for two weeks straight, they were guaranteed a miracle. Those who gave it a try invariably experienced a remarkable, wonderful, fantastic change in their lives.

ADVANCES AND WORKSHOPS

In addition to Friday class, Jim conducted workshops and Advances. In the early years, the workshops were predominately out-of-town events sponsored by individuals or organizations such as Spiritual Frontiers Fellowship (SFF), where Jim was a popular lecturer. Jim had been introduced to this organization by the Reverend William Asher, a Methodist minister from Virginia, who, along with his wife, Charlotte, became one of Jim's strongest supporters. Jim's lectures at SFF events in various parts of the country were for many their first introduction to him. From that experience, several came to hear him in North Carolina, then came to live at the Goure house, and finally settled in the Black Mountain area to be a part of the community that was joining Jim in the greater United Research mission.

Jim's generosity extended to other organizations, prominent among them, the World Unity Forum (WUF) and the Spiritual Unity of Nations (SUN), both which have been headed by John Davis. These organization, similar to the Temple of Understanding on whose board Jim had at one time served, sought to bring together various religious leaders.

At the World Unity Forum meetings, Jim was remembered as asking, repeatedly, "What are we going to do when the hundredth monkey of man arrives?" He was trying to get these leaders to see beyond their parochial interests and recognize that there was a revolution in consciousness afoot, and that if organizations such as WUF were not prepared to help these people, then the full potential of the changes in consciousness might not manifest.

At his workshops, Jim had a basket where you could anonymously drop a question and he would pull the questions out randomly and answer them. Many people felt he had an uncanny ability to tune into who asked the question and what was really behind the question they were asking. As one person remembers her experience, "At one of Jim's workshops, I put a question in the question basket. My question was deep, troubled. When Jim read the piece of paper with my question, he stared off into space for awhile. Then, he said, 'Come to the mountains.' It didn't mean anything to the others, but was meaningful to me. I did come to the mountains. I stayed at the house for two-and-a-half months."

Advances were United Research-sponsored events that were held at the YMCA Blue Ridge Assembly in Black Mountain. This conference center is situated on 1,200 acres and is on the National Register of Historic Places. (The name for these events, "Advance," was a pun on the word "retreat," which is the name many religious organizations give to multi-day events that they conduct. Jim's perspective was: we're not retreating. We're advancing. We're advancing in the Light.) The Advances were more informal than the workshops and involved much sharing – of experiences, of music, of humor, of fellowship. The musicians and singers who performed at the Advances included Light Center regulars such as Rosemary Crow, Bill Mason, and Judy McFadden. Performers would also include, on occasion, well known artists such as Metropolitan Opera star Marguerite Piazza.

The first Advance occurred in May of 1977, when about three hundred people gathered "to accomplish the awakening of humanity to Light." The feeling from this Advance was that, "It was an experience which reached far beyond the physical boundaries of the Assembly. Change was created in the world and a time of new opportunity in communication, of sharing, of knowing was brought forth. We are among new times. We have witnessed the marriage of the new heaven with the new Earth. It is time to release the old, the past, and concentrate on the now of your life. The Light within radiates from you to each one you meet. You are an example to the world. This is a new age, a new Earth."

More than almost any other type of event that Jim lead, the Advances had some very moving moments. One of these was when Jim had a love song played for everyone in attendance. It was Debby Boone singing *You Light Up My Life*. With the song being played at Jim's request, the lyrics had the added meaning of the aloneness that oftentimes accompanies the life of the spiritual person and the love and gratitude that person feels for others who also have engaged themselves in the life of Spirit. The lyrics to that song are, in part,

So many nights,
I'd sit by my window,
Waiting for someone to sing me his song..
So many dreams I kept deep inside me
Alone in the dark.
But now you've come along
And you light up my life.
You give me hope
To carry on.
You light up my days
And fill my nights with song.

Rollin' at sea, adrift on the water,
Could it be, finally, I'm turning for home?
Finally, a chance to say, "Hey, I love you,"
Never again to be all alone.
You light up my life.
You give me hope
To carry on.
You light up my days
And fill my nights with song. [5]

---

[5] The lyrics are © Universal Polygram and Curb Records

And then there was that moment on November 1st, 1981 at the *New Insights* Advance when, consumed with love of the Divine and love for everyone attending the Advance, Jim spoke as the living Bible. A woman had just shared with the audience a healing that had occurred in a young person who had been so ill with rheumatoid arthritis that she couldn't walk. She was brought to the Light Center three or four times by friends. Not long afterwards, her recovery was so advanced that she entered a Race for Your Heart marathon in Chattanooga, Tennessee, and finished seventeenth out of 1,000 runners. This person had told her friend that if she had to liken her Light Center experience to a song, it would be *Love Lifted Me*. The woman relating the story said, "Not only did it lift her, it set her in motion. As Jim would say, in a paraphrase of one of his words, 'Fantabulous.'" Jim then came up front and said, "You are fantabulous. Thank you very much."

It was the last session of the Advance, and he began to speak to people's thoughts about going home. "The inner sight that you've all had here has been beautiful and wonderful. We all enjoy this togetherness. Many of us have experienced merging. We have merged, and it's fantastic.

"But, in the back of our mind is another world. It's the world we're going back to. In that part of the back of our mind, as it comes forward, is, 'Do I really have to go back? Can't I stay just a little while longer? Can't we expand this?' We are already beginning to look at it as we looked at it before we came: with our human eyes. With these outer eyes, we have a seeing that is not true. We see a loved one that has problems – mental, emotional, physical problems. It's a real trial for us because we know that if we had done our job perfectly, they wouldn't be that way. We all are dreading going back to that condition. We know *we* are better for having been here.

"Now, how to go back – whether you are going back to a loved one or you are going back to a lonely room, a lonely home, a college campus room – how tough can that get – or whatever you are going back to. – you are thinking about going back. Do not think about going back. Ever again. You are going forward now. Remember: you are *advancing*. You are advancing from now on. Not going back. You are advancing the Light with you. You are advancing the Love you have received with you. And it is advancing before you. *Lo, before you arrive, I Am there.* You are advancing the Love and Light into that. And that lonely abode becomes an abode of Light. A place of Love. Welcoming you with the warmth of Love. The so-called loved ones are now *Divine* loved ones. And they radiate Light and Love and *give you* Light and Love. Because they're not any longer what you have seen with your eyes. The true eye of you is seeing the Inner Being. The Inner Being is now manifesting. The Inner Being is coming forth to you. The Inner Being is surrounding *you* with Love. That Creative Source is filling you so that you no longer can see with these two eyes that of negativity in any way or any form.

"Every day you strengthen and advance – more and more. The advancing tide of Love and Light, waving and passing over all things. And the Passover has begun. The true Passover has begun. Passing over of Love and Light, changing all as it goes. You are increasing this wave of Love and Light, passing over and around and through planet Earth. Through everything and everyone. It's a new way of in-sighting, seeing the way it really is. You have heard these reports from you, from the center of the Earth out, the living waters are passing over – you're not just handing a glass anymore to just one – you are handing over the wave of living waters, passing over and through and around and in planet Earth."

And at this point Jim went into another state of consciousness and declared to everyone at the Advance, slowly, working to control his emotions, "You...are...the...Light...of...the...world." You could feel Jim overwhelmed with his experience. And then, the living Bible, what felt like the Voice of God spoke,

I have been wanting to speak to you in a new way, all of these years, all of the eons of time. I shall try.

I am in you.
I have been in you since before the world was.
I am...that Light in you.
It is filling you,
And there never has been a time I am not with you.
There never has been a time I am not centered in you.

I center you.
I expand you.
I am you.

I am Love in you.
I am that Love in you that is in the world.
Before world, in the world, and now.
I am the Love in you of the universe.
I am the Light of you in the universe.
I am in the stars and the rolling wave.
I am you.

You cannot separate me from you, ever.
Speak, and I am there.
There never has been a time I am not there.
I am you.

And I love you.
I love you.
I love you.

Thank you for letting me speak.

With a moment to collect himself, Jim went on, "This inner world you have come to know. You have heard of what it does. You have heard of miracles, impossible miracles, the changing of the tide has taken place. Earth is saved...because You Are. Because You Are Love...and you are loved. There never is a time now that you will not be loved.

"The new mission of the Heaven and the Earth joining together, that means the merging of the Christ dimension, alive, with the two eyes you see with, in and through planet Earth. That merging is being done now, because of you. There is no greater mission, ever, for planet Earth. Ever. This is the new newness of all time. This is the beginning of the new Heaven and new Earth, and the old Heaven and Earth will pass away. This is the fruition of the prophecies. All of the prophets. The prophecies have all been misunderstood. It is simply the merging of the Christ dimension into this dimension as one. So that all will see, just as you see now with these eyes. And that's the way it is.

"Your joining in, merging this now, and carrying this out is absolutely essential for you. You all know you have come to this planet this time, that you have come here to this room this time, you came for this mission to come here, to be here just now. You…could not escape being here. Beause you, before time began, agreed to be here, to carry on and bring this mission into existence, so that all of man will no longer be the hue man crawling on his hands and knees, looking for the footsteps of the Christ. He stands up as God-man, totally loving.

"You have designated yourselves in your souls to do this thing. You feel it in you. It has been stirring for some time. When you feel the beauty and the wonders of this happening, you know you cannot stop. You know it is the most important thing in your whole millions of years of existence. Your whole life has come to this point. To do this one thing. It's fantastic.

"The joy of accomplishing this mission is beyond the beyond.

"You are doing it for your fellow man. Because you love your fellow man with your whole being. You are doing it because there is nothing more important in all of existence up until this time. Because it is more important than life. You would lay down your life to accomplish this, with great joy. It won't be necessary. But that's the kind of dedication you have now. To accomplish this great mission.

"And I foresee the accomplishment within twelve years. To be a part of this is greater than being one of the twelve disciples. It is being the Christ. Living it every moment.

"And being the Christ is not caught up in self. Not caught with self. It lets go of all things and becomes and stays true, creating the oneness, total oneness of the Christ and man, together. Knowingly so. The power of the Creator is you, in this group, if you really go to work at it, it can be accomplished long before 1993. It means cessation of war. It means cessation of killing. It means a flow of love. It means doing everything to help one another. It means for all of you…you will say,

'I have arrived.'

"Many of you have come from planets where people loved one another. And the ache in you has been with you all these times...for that oneness that you had. Well, now you have that oneness. And that oneness is home, here. And it's a home of beauty, joy, fantastic greatness.

"Your names in the Book of Life are beyond the Book of Life. They have been removed from the Book of Life. All of your names. You...are the chosen ones. And thus you stand tall...for all to see. And that's the way it is.

"Thank you, God, for these Thy loved ones. Amen.

"Thank you very much. Thank you for being. It has been a great experience for me, and thank you so very much.

"You all are in my heart. I want you to know that we are all family and we're all together. There is only love between us because that's true family."

THE VOICE

W hat was it about Jim's voice? What was it about that voice that touched people so deeply?

What was it about that voice that caused such an ache in the heart, not an ache of missing someone, but of feeling so fulfilled and so full of love and of finally being home and of wanting that feeling to never end?

For some, Jim's voice carried them into a different state, a meditative state. They would attend his lectures and then leave, not being able to remember a thing he had said, but feeling that they had just heard some of the deepest insights into life and into God that they had ever received. What was it about that voice that could so transport people?

For others, the voice was something that calmed them, made them feel secure, made them feel it was all going to be alright. What was it about that voice?

What was it about the way he said the verse, repeated lo those many times in Psalms, "Praise the Lord, o my soul", that made you feel, as his voice suddenly softened and became deeper and deeply loving, what was it that made you feel at that moment, *This man truly loves God. He truly is a man of God* – what was it about his voice that made you feel that?

From the voice alone, people felt. *This is a man who loves, who truly loves, who loves each one of us, who loves everyone.* The love, always the love, the voice conveying the love and a feeling that you were loved, no matter who you were and no matter what you had done, you were loved, you were loved deeply.

You never wanted it to end, this voice of love. You wanted the feelings you felt listening to it to go on forever. You never wanted to leave it, that voice of love. You only wanted it to stay in your heart forever.

As he began a lecture, Jim tended to start slowly. Since he spoke extemporaneously, there would be several minutes in the beginning where he would be translating into words the overall sense of what he wanted to say. The thoughts always came, but oftentimes deliberately and with feeling.

But as he got into his subject, the pace quickened. He had found the words he wanted and they would start tumbling out and then the sentences would run into each other and sometimes not even complete themselves as he dashed through his thoughts using speed to lay emphasis on the truths he was speaking.

And then, not often, but often enough to have created memorable moments, he would stop. The eyes would fill with tears. From some great indwelling, an experience of the Divine would have welled up in him and the power and the emotion of the moment would overwhelm him and he would pause, not long, but long enough to collect himself. And then the voice, now deep, struggling to control its emotions, would do all it could to convey, one more time, the beauty and the wonders of the Divine.

CHANGED LIVES

There were over thirty interviews conducted for this book. The most frequent theme of those interviews was, "He changed my life." The lives of thousands were changed. The drug addicts cleaned up their acts. The suicidal got their lives back on track. Those terminally ill with cancer were healed.

But there were other kinds of changes. Less dramatic ones. People came to believe in themselves more. People changed their lives...for the better. People opened up more. They became more loving. Family situations improved. Resentments against fathers and mothers were transformed. Antagonistic relationships were changed to loving ones.

All of this came about through hearing Jim and applying what he had to say about Light and prayer and love. It worked! It worked over and over and over again.

Some of those who were healed or those who didn't require much healing to begin with got on with discovering and living their Divine missions. They went into prayer and got their missions. These missions often were surprises. A young woman, when praying for her Divine mission, heard, "Politics." She resisted, "No. Ot's dirty stuff." The answer that came back was, "That's why. More people of Light are needed in politics." She went on to become a professor of political science and has been appointed as a human rights advocate by the governor of her state. An accounting teacher reversed course and, following her inner guidance and that of another spiritual teacher, founded a day care center, using the prayer and Light principles that Jim taught. Another woman determined that her mission was to provide holistic education to children and she now teaches AIDS orphans in Kenya. (These and other experiences with prayer are recounted in the *Part II: Remembrances* section of this book.)

In each instance, the people who dove into prayer for their Divine mission came up with something that had to do with helping people. And they got about doing exactly that.

So, not only did Jim change *their* lives, but, through them and their good works, he continues to affect the lives of thousands.

UNITED RESEARCH

On December 30th, 1975, Jim and Diana signed the articles of incorporation that created United Research, Inc., a nonprofit corporation. The board members, in addition to Jim and Diana, included lu Murphy Whitaker and Barbara Frogger, both of Virginia Intermountain College in Bristol, Virginia.

Jim and Diana chose the name "United Research" because it characterized a community effort: "Together (united) we search again (re-search) for God in our lives." The name reflected the community nature of people using prayer to promote a greater good for all. It also was meant to imply an organization that searches for ways to eliminate differences, to find more oneness, and to pray effectively for the good of the whole world, that all may live in peace and joy.

The establishment of United Research created a vehicle for the receipt of donations towards education in prayer and the building and maintenance of a prayer center. But, to be a nonprofit organization exempt from federal corporation taxes and allowed to accept tax-deductible donations required a 501(c)3 designation from the Internal Revenue Service (IRS) of the United States government. The IRS, with its signature lack of imagination, resisted granting United Research that designation. "The Service," as the IRS likes to call itself, in an Orwellian twisting of the reality most Americans confront, kept asking, "What religion is this? What denomination? What type of research are you planning?" Jim's responses about research physicians might conduct that could validate whether prayer had a positive impact on health fell on deaf ears. (Jim was simply too far ahead of his time: in 1991 the federal government *itself* established the National Center for Complementary and Alternative Medicine to explore the effectiveness of various alternative healing modalities, and, lo and behold, one of the healing practices the Center takes note of is prayer.)

The not-so-small matter of United Research being granted its nonprofit status did not resolve itself until a bee emerged from the normally placid bonnet that is Diana Goure, who wrote the IRS, with a touch of sting, that prayer is not the sole possession of any one religion or denomination, that prayer is as free as the air we breathe, that United Research would not be bound or limited to one religion or denomination but must be free to all who wish to learn to pray more effectively, that Mr. Goure had given 30 years of his life to the U.S. government, loved his country and prayed for it daily, and, in so many words, who was the IRS to impugn his integrity and intentions, and that she looked forward to the IRS granting United Research its well-merited, nonprofit, 501(c)3 designation. Which, it did, in its own slow, lumbering way, nearly two years later, in September of 1977.

This was to be a most unusual organization that would confound more than the IRS. Jim Goure, the man who had been employed by one of the largest, most structured, most rule-bound organizations on Earth, the United States government, created an organization that had virtually no rules and no structure. The articles of incorporation for United Research stated that, "The corporation is to have no members." Not only did it have no members, but it did not solicit donations, did not advertise, and did not use organizational titles. Its organizational structure was a mystery to most people. Nobody knew who was on the board – or even if there were a board. This upset some people, but Jim simply wanted people focused on the Divine, not on personalities and organizational politics. Rather than having an organization with rigid rules, Jim wanted everyone to come from the Divine. He wanted people to be self-directed. People were told to go into prayer before making a decision. About the only rule was that narcotics were not allowed anywhere on the property.

At the time of its incorporation, United Research itself owned no property. Events were held at the Goure house or at another venue. The prayer center that would be completed in 1979, four years after United Research was incorporated, would sit on Goure property. The building itself belonged to United Research, but it was on land owned by Jim and Diana.

In the early 1980s, after that building had been completed, descendents of Sheriff Brown, the original owner of the Goure home, let Jim know that they intended selling the remaining land they owned that surrounded the 23.6 acres Jim had purchased from them when he and his family moved to Black Mountain. Jim was concerned that the land might be sold to developers and that the peaceful, pristine surroundings for the prayer center would be spoiled.

So, on November 1, 1983, United Research purchased approximately 75 acres from members of Sheriff Brown's family for $235,000. For a man who had never been in business, Jim certainly negotiated a sweet deal. He got the Brown family to agree to carry the mortgage, and United Research did not have to put any money down, did not have to pay interest on the unpaid principle, and was not required to make the first of 12 annual payments until one year after the deed of trust had been executed. The average price of approximately $3,100 per acre was in line with area land values at the time.

United Research was never large. For the fiscal year 1986 (the last year of Jim's life), it had total contributions and revenues of nearly $170,000. Despite the fact that Jim would not solicit funds and got angry when others did, about half that amount came from the donations of people who realized that funds were needed to keep the place running. The remainder of United Research's funds came from revenues generated from the workshops that Jim gave and from the sale of books and tapes and from subscriptions to the newsletter, *UR Light*.

This sum of money had to pay wages of the Light Center staff, utilities, professional services such as accountants – and make an annual payment of $20,000 for land that had been purchased from the Brown family. Except for a brief period during the 1970s when the prayer center was being built, Jim did not take a salary and for most years was not otherwise compensated for his services. In 1986 he did receive a percentage of proceeds from certain programs that he led. These payments totaled $9,338. For a man who allowed all comers to his house, fed them, and provided them sleeping accommodations, on whose land the prayer center was built and whose roads people used to get to that center, who gave tirelessly to those who came to him for counseling and to those who called him for help at all hours of the day and night, whose speaking activities generated funds for United Research, and who, on top of everything, had eight children needing college educations, it was remarkable that he didn't ask for more. He led an almost incomprehensibly generous life. Through it all, his driving motivation was to keep people focused on the Divine, to keep his approach pure, and to live the life that Jesus had admonished us to live – a life of love, of generosity, of prayer.

Although he had founded United Research and guided it with the purest of motivations, there were moments when Jim wondered if having an organization of *any* sort had been the right move. Jackie Boyce, who participated as fully in the activities of United Research as almost anyone, remembers, "Jim loved to go out to lunch. It was fun and sometimes something extra was said. He and I were driving into town one day to go to lunch some time after the Light Center had been built when he said to me, 'You know, I don't know if I did the right thing creating an organization.' He knew the true mission and vision get confused with perpetuating the organization – without remembering why."

But this United Research was a most interesting experiment in determining whether a group of people could live from inner guidance rather than from organizational rules. As we shall see, it had its moments of glory, and its moments of frustration.

LIFE AT UNITED RESEARCH

Life for those staying at the Goure home or helping out at the Light Center was similar to what it is like at many alternative spiritual communities – exhilarating, exhausting, maddening, and fulfilling. It seemed to be toughest on those who were trying the hardest, cared the most, and had the strongest strain of perfectionism in them. Like most non-profits, United Research relied heavily on the services of volunteers, and once people volunteer or contribute a sum of money to a nonprofit, they tend to think they own the place - or at least should be able to tell others what to do. It doesn't work that way.

Compounding the challenge was the purity of Jim's approach. The last thing he wanted was another rule-bound organization more concerned with its own survival than with accomplishing its original mission. He wanted people to go within and find that which they were supposed to do. Some did. Some didn't. Some worked hard. Some loafed and took advantage of Jim's generosity. Some appreciated his generosity in a limited way, but didn't appreciate the full magnitude of it, didn't appreciate the sacrifices he undertook to provide what he did, and left him anyway.

Other than Diana Goure, the steadiest among the volunteers were mostly middle-aged and older women living in the area and a small group of younger people in their twenties and thirties who lived at the house and had felt called to be with Jim and help him with the mission he had laid out for everyone. Among the younger people were Jackie Boyce, Mary Kaye Brett, Stan Dromey, and Sarah Gayle. They helped build the Light Center, maintain the property, edit the newsletter, and perform other tasks that kept the place running.

Most people loved the lack of structure at United Research. They felt it gave them freedom. But it could also be confusing. Said one woman who flew from California to spend time at the Light Center, "He told me Lavida would take care of me – and then he and Diana left on a trip, probably one of the international prayer missions. Nobody said anything to me about what I was supposed to do. I had no idea what the function of the place was. When I asked Jim what I should do, he simply told me, 'Come from the Creator.'"

But the experience could also feel liberating. This same person eventually came to feel that, "Those times at the Light Center were my happiest moments. Jim provided an environment in which I could flourish. I learned about prayer and meditation and how they can totally transform you. I went from being totally uncentered and shut down – I had been hurt – to having a mission of helping others. I totally changed.

"I had so much fun there. I liked his open-door approach and the fact that anyone could share their experiences or talents at Light Center events. He loved creativity. If you were a musician, you could perform at the Light Center. There were no committees to decide who could play. Jim said that whatever your gift was, it would be amplified at the Light Center."

At one point, Jim asked this woman, "How does it feel to live without having the expectations of others? How does it feel to just be?" It obviously felt wonderful – for her and for hundreds of others.

The only requirement for people staying at the house was they attend prayer sessions at 9 a.m., 12 noon, 5 p.m., and 9 p.m. As for other tasks – for doing things such as cooking meals and mowing the grass – Jim did not want rules and schedules. He wanted people to act from a knowing within themselves. This worked with some, but there were still large numbers who took advantage of him. There were people living at the house who contributed nothing towards cleaning or maintaining the place. Jim got so frustrated that, at one point, with the Navy commander in him coming out, he put a sign on the refrigerator that barked, "Once a week, swab the walls."

At times, the loafing and indifference of people to tasks that needed to be done got to be too much and the Janus head of Jim the Gemini would turn and his temper would flare. People who had been told they were special, that they were Divine, and who had felt they had a special, close relationship with Jim, suddenly found themselves on the receiving end of a cold stare or a blast of anger.

Those who were around Jim for long stretches – for months or years - came to feel that these outbursts always had a larger purpose and that love was always the motivation. He was perceived as pushing the buttons of those who had become complacent or as blocking the attempts of anyone who might be revering him. Woe unto the person who would try to put Jim on a pedestal. Jim did not want to be venerated. He did not want to start a church or religion. He rebuffed people when they tried to make a guru out of him. His message was always the same: Don't look to me, Jim. You are It. You are the Divine.

Whether his outbursts were always Divinely inspired or not, evidently, the Divine on occasion would have something to say to James V. Goure about his temper. On September 15th, 1976, in one of Jim and Diana's private prayer sessions, where one of them would go into a deep meditative state and the other would ask questions, this is what was received for Jim: *Your means of transportation must smooth out, as you begin to see the car deva helping you get places on time without worry and irritation. How are things different from [Washington,] D.C. if all is upset and turmoil in getting places or [if there is] lack of love for other people who are your brothers and sisters for whom you are praying at the prayer table but whom you curse when behind the wheel? Life must begin to be more balanced in EVERY aspect. Let there be a time of quiet so that you can carry with you that Peace which is so sorely needed out in the world and out on the highway. You are a person who can make your life beautiful in whatever way you want it to be. Use some of these suggestions that you are teaching. See your life becoming that which you want it to be.*

One of the young persons who stayed for years to help Jim may have put his finger on what was causing a great deal of the frustration. His observation was that, "The place became a revolving door: people came for healing, either got it or did not, and were out the door. But the place was not geared for people with emotional problems who thought it would fix everything. It was best for those who were already centered. It is very easy to retreat into the spiritual and run away from the emotional."

Whether they were all getting it or not, Jim certainly wanted everyone who came to have the best opportunity possible for getting it. He knew he could not be present for every newcomer, so he trained those staying at the house and volunteering at the prayer center to teach the Light prayer to newcomers, to mentor them, and to take them to a special place on the Broad River that had been named Meditation Rock.

Those that did get it included several people who found themselves opening to a new source of artistic creativity. Rosemary Crow was the first to break through and create her own music from her Higher Self. She had already been a fine pianist and in charge of the church choir at All Souls Church in Asheville, but the music she started creating after she met Jim was fresh, alive, inspiring. It was a sound that Jim, with his love of song that praised God, would always thrill to. After having composed several songs, Rosemary began recording her music and touring the country. Shortly after Rosemary Crow broke through, Mary Beth Buchholz began painting her wonderful renditions of words of Spirit. Judy McFadden started composing deeply moving piano music. Another pianist, Sunsurei, played a uniquely flowing music. People such as Bill Mason who developed their talents late in life started to create a simple music that touched people's hearts. Established artists such as the painter Arthur Douet and the Metropolitan Opera star, Marguerite Piazza, as well as the First Lady of Yoga in America, Lilias Folan, were also attracted to Jim.

The messages Jim and Diana were receiving from their higher selves were indicating that something wonderful was happening. From the Higher Self on November 21st, 1976, came this: "…boundaries are gone, chains are broken, slavish patterns are freed. Life is beautiful. And you are opening eyes, hearts, and minds to see and feel and know how to live in the Light! It is great joy to be alive now – great joy to let this flow be in you and through you to all you meet – and many you don't meet."

And from the Higher Self on January 29th, 1975, came this piece of poetry:

There is only ONE LIGHT in all manifested lights.
There is only ONE SPIRIT in all men.
ONE LIFE – ONE LOVE – ONE PEACE.
The goal of each is to search for this ONENESS within.

To help others achieve that Oneness, United Research itself was to become a creator, a creator of a new type of prayer center, which it called the Light Center.

THE LIGHT CENTER

Hundreds were now coming to hear Jim lecture and to seek his counsel. With the Goure home being continually filled with people, Jim felt that, "After twelve thousand people had passed through the home, we started to think in terms of – the home can't handle the flood of people that are coming in. So, we thought in terms of a building that would accommodate all the things we had in mind, including helping the planet."

Planning the Light Center

A great deal of spiritual energy went into the design and construction of such a building, which was to be called a Light Center. Jim invited people living at the house and participating in United Research activities to be on the building committee, asking them to go into prayer for guidance as to how the Light Center should be designed. The planning committee consisted of twelve people who met every week for several months to pray and get answers from the Source on different aspects of the building, such as the shape and placement of the windows, how the rooms would be arranged, and so forth. This planning occurred during the mid-to-late 1970s.

The expansion plan originally called for there to be three phases, which, to conserve funds, ultimately were condensed into one phase. The three original phases were:

- Phase I: A Light Center structure that was to be dedicated to prayer and prayer only. There were to be no bathrooms or offices in this structure. The intent was that this structure be dedicated solely to spiritual activities;

- Phase II: Another building with bathrooms, a kitchen, administrative offices, and bedrooms for those praying in the wee hours;

- Phase III: Offices and people to care for the holistic man: nutritionists, psychics, reflexologists; and rooms for representatives from each of the major religions (the intent being that these representatives would take the Seven Steps prayer back to their own religions, which would cause these religions to change).

Another aspect of the original vision, which also has not yet come to pass, was that there would be twelve Light Centers around the world: two in the U.S. and the balance in other countries.

There was a groundbreaking ceremony in May of 1975, four years before the structure was completed. On a portion of the Goure property that was a few hundred yards from the Goure house, a crystal was buried in the center of the spot where the dome was to be built. Songs and prayers were conducted at the groundbreaking with the intention of infusing the site with high spiritual energy. Construction began in the late 1970s.

Although legal requirements – such as having an architect and a licensed contractor - were met to satisfy building inspectors, to a great extent the dome was built by the Goure family and by members of the larger United Research family who were living at the house and were imbued with the spiritual energy that came with being in Jim's presence. These Goure and United Research family members included Jackie Boyce, Mary Kaye Brett, Liz Budd, Stan Dromey, and Franklin Kirby as well as Gloria, Jonathan, and Roger Goure. (Others who also helped requested anonymity.)

Finally, in 1979, the Light Center was completed.

The Building

The Light Center is a two-story building, the upper floor of which is a geodesic dome based on Buckminster Fuller's design, which he had worked on while at Black Mountain College. This domed ceiling has forty windows that, appropriately enough for a "Light" center," allow in a great deal of natural light. The windows are in the shape of triangles, trapezoids, and diamond-shaped rhombuses. These windows originally were to have been stained glass, each pane being one of the seven primary colors of the spectrum, but a shortage of funds meant that only clear glass could be used. The floor of this domed upstairs room, which is circular, has a diameter of approximately 40 feet and is covered with a purple carpet. This room is where prayers and workshops are conducted.

The number five, which some have deemed to be the number of the Christ, is repeated throughout this upper chamber: there are five groupings of five windows, there are five diamond-shaped windows, and there are five stanchions in the middle of the room, each of which is a pentagon

In naming the building a Light Center, Jim purposefully did not use the term church, with its connotations of an organized religion. He wanted it to be a place where people of any religion or of no particular religion tuned into God, into Light, directly – without ritual, without a priesthood, without any intermediaries – just a direct communion with God. There is no altar and there are no relics or pictures of saints. The basic concept is that, without anything external to focus on, there is no place to look except to the Divine within.

The one object that does exist in the dome, other than chairs and stanchions, is a globe, suspended from the center of the dome's ceiling, which is there to remind people of the mission given by Jesus in the Sermon on the Mount, to be the Light of the world.

A chamber downstairs features special lighting and music conducive to deep meditation and inner transformation. Also downstairs are a bookstore and an audio-visual library with materials devoted to spiritual life.

With the additional land United Research purchased from the Brown family, there were around one hundred acres of wooded hills surrounding the Light Center. This acreage includes trails through quiet woods and a mountain stream called the Broad River. It is, in effect, a large meditation garden, where the mountainous land and paths by the water help one find peace and inner renewal in nature's beauty and quiet.

Dedication

Symbolic of its mission of establishing a new kind of Light, the Light Center was dedicated on October 21st, 1979, the one hundredth anniversary of the invention of a commercially practical light bulb by Thomas Edison. There was a sense of excitement about the Light Center, a sense that something had been built that heralded a new and wonderful world. Four hundred people came to the dedication. So many came that all the chairs were taken and people were sitting on the floor and in the doorways.

Spiritual Energy

Through every phase of its planning and construction as well as its ongoing operation, the Light Center had been infused with high spiritual energy. It was Jim's vision that this energy would be so strong that anyone walking in the door of the Light Center would be instantly healed.

Jim was very aware of the energy at the dome. He may not have said much about it, but he *always* worked on it. When he would return from a trip and sense that the energy in the Light Center had faded or become discordant, he would pitch a fit, demanding to know what the people working at the Light Center had been doing or not doing. He would ask, "Why aren't you praying?"

Vision

Jim articulated his vision for the Light Center as being "to establish the universality of us, to knowingly establish this Light throughout the universe. The Light Center has been centered throughout the whole universe. There is a ray of Light through the center of the dome – from the center of the cosmos. We are trying to expand it to include more. You can tune into this Light wherever you are and spread it to one and all. The upper room of the geodesic dome is for giving Light and Love to all the universe. It is an impersonal Light."

Jim indicated that the mission of the Light Center was to help people with what he considered to be the greatest needs of mankind: the need to be healed, the need to be loved, the need to change consciousness, and the need to be freed of the constraints of identity. "What is needed is a change of consciousness and healing. The purpose of the Light Center is to free you from personality. The most important message of the place is, 'I love you.'" Jim believed that in having these needs met, "There is a sense of having come home...and having started. People get changed and go back into the world from the Creator consciousness."

He also said, "This place is Light. Everyone who walks in to the Light Center should be healed. Anybody who calls in to the Light Center should be immediately healed. The purpose of the Light chamber downstairs is to get the endocrine glands to function as they will in the new heaven and the new Earth. We will get to the stage where even criminals are changed within 15 minutes – and the change is enduring."

In being a place of Light, Jim believed that "The fundamental mission of the Light Center is to finish the drama of the Christ." That Light spoken of in the Sermon on the Mount, "Ye are the Light of the world," would be centered in the Light Center, and as people visited the Light Center they would find the Light within themselves and take that Light back into the world, bringing Divine Good to everyone and everything. It was to be a place where people could awaken to God-consciousness and then go out into the world and live that consciousness, thereby uplifting everyone and everything.

As grand as his vision for the Light Center was, Jim never saw it as an end in itself. He thought that, "Eventually people won't come here because they will be healed automatically, at a distance." He also believed that, "The Light Center should finish its mission in twenty years. People will take it within and become a Light Center themselves. The way to make it happen is continuous prayer."

Community and Growth

To support the establishment of continuous, twenty-four hour-a-day prayer at the Light Center – and to serve as a place where anyone wanting to pray at any hour of the day or night could do so – the Light Center was kept open every hour of every day.

Another part of the vision designed to support continuous prayer at the Light Center was the establishment of a community on United Research land. Jim said, "It would be great to have prayers here continuously for the people of the world. In order to do that, we need to have people who live here, who are willing, deep within themselves, to spend a part of their day in prayer here. One of the reasons we want a community here is to be an example of how a community can live in total peace. Total trust. Total love of one another. There is an urge in people to find such a community. Ever since the first commune, which was established by the disciples after Jesus died, there has been a thirst for communes, again and again. A place where you can love, where you can have trust. No locks on doors or windows. Where there is complete faith in each other. There is an urge in everyone to have this peace. I don't care who they are or where they are. They want it. There is a need for this to go on. Not only here but in every home. Be an example of peace where you are *now*. There is a need for prayer to bring about this trust and peace."

The Light Center

Jim speaking at the dedication of the Light Center on October 21, 1979

Stan Dromey's painting of the Light Center (© United Research, Inc.)

Jim in his office at the Light Center. Stan Dromey's
painting of the Light Center is in the background

The upstairs of the Light Center, where prayer is conducted
(© United Research, Inc.)

PRAYER MISSIONS

In the late 1970s, Jim received an invitation from the Reverend Wildorf E. Goodison-Orr to conduct a workshop at the Unity Church in Kingston, Jamaica. Jamaica at the time was a tense place. The government in power was committed to international socialism, nationalizing businesses, and maintaining friendship with Fidel Castro of Cuba. The opposition party favored privatization, foreign investment, and closer ties with the U.S. Both political parties became linked with rival gangs, which were armed. Recurrent violence combined with the nationalization of businesses was only increasing the impoverishment of the Jamaican populace.

In their prayers prior to the event, Jim and Diana had received from their Higher Selves, "This can be the eve of the awakening of man in this place. You have the right people to go to Jamaica. They will grow a lot during this trip and will begin to see what must be done to help the world at large."

From what could be seen simply by paying attention to news reports on Jamaica and from what their Higher Selves had told Jim and Diana, Jamaica seemed just the kind of place that could use a dose of effective prayer. So, Jim accepted Reverend Goodison-Orr's invitation. As Jim remembers it, "The date was chosen. It so happened the date they selected for us to come was quite traumatic: they had to bring the tanks out and they were in the streets and it was near riot. The person who made the date called and asked, 'Are you going to come?' And we said, 'Yes. We wouldn't let a little thing like that stop us.'"

Five people would accompany Jim to Jamaica: Ray Amundson, Rosemary Crow, Rose Davis, Susan Flannagan, and Rubinelle Friedman. Along with Jim, they would spend much of their time in Jamaica praying for the country.

When in January of 1979 Jim spoke before the Unity School of Christianity in Kingston, there were one thousand, two hundred people in attendance. They were hungry for hope, for a belief that there was some way they could engage God on their behalf, on behalf of helping their country. Jim remembers that, "We taught them the Seven Steps. It was a tremendous experience for us and for them. Afterwards, they all came up to us and said, 'You have given us hope. You have given us something to do that can change our government.'

"The last week in October this year [1980], after five hundred people were slaughtered by the Communist government, the government was voted out. Within five hours, the Cubans were moved out. This was the first Communist country to become democratic. The results of this trip convinced us that the way to help bring peace on Earth is to pray around the clock for at least three days in each country."

If prayer could work for Jamaica, why couldn't it work for all the nations? The experience inspired Jim to start what he called World Prayer Missions.

Jim felt that the United States had tried every approach but one to achieve world peace. It had tried wars, diplomacy, military aid, financial aid, and people-to-people visits. None of these had worked. The only thing the U.S. had not tried was prayer. The World Prayer Missions were an effort to redress that situation.

Jim further articulated his reasons for conducting the prayer missions as follows: "People say to me, 'Why don't you just pray for those countries where you are?' We have been! And are! But the results are slow. Our being together there is a healing that takes place faster. And when you leave behind your past and your traditions, you let go and you begin to merge with the peoples of these other countries and there are great happenings that take place within you. After one of these prayer missions, you never come back to what you were. You know the mission of Earth and you know your own Divine mission.

"There are enough of us here, now: we're the hundredth monkey, right here. We can alter the whole Earth because the Creator in us is not limited. There is sufficient Light.

"Jesus wasn't afraid to get right down there amongst the nitty gritty. Why didn't he sit up on a throne and zap everybody? That would be an easy way to do it. OK, Jerusalem, bang! But, it didn't work and it doesn't work. We just have to get right down in there and lift that veil that is covering man.

"We are implementing the Tree of Life in the Book of Revelation, the healing of the nations. Our idea is that we go to each nation, to the capital of each nation, and pray three days nonstop for that nation. Healing does work through prayer.

"We are going into Columbia. We know it will change. The power of Light is beyond the power of darkness. And we welcome the opportunity to face darkness and to change it. To know the Creator is present.

"And then we are going to Ireland, Northern Ireland, and London, England, to change where Christians are killing Christians. That must stop.

"Then we may go to Egypt and Israel. That is one of the key areas on the planet. It is probably the only area on the planet where World War III could start. Because of the way people are in that area: an eye for an eye and a tooth for a tooth. That type thing must *stop*! The Creator is present, and knowing it will make it so. And there will be change."

So, late in 1981, United Research formally committed to conducting World Prayer Missions. The first was to Columbia in South America in February of 1982. Three more Prayer Missions were conducted to countries in 1982, some of which were, like Jamaica, experiencing considerable violence and civil turmoil. In June, United Research traveled to Mexico; in September, there was a mission to Northern Ireland, the Republic of Ireland, and England. At the end of the year, there was a mission to Egypt and Israel.

There also were four Prayer Missions in 1983: to China and Japan in April; to Eastern and Central Europe – Finland, Poland, and Russia – in June; to the Indian subcontinent – India, Nepal, and Sri Lanka – in September; and back to the Middle East in December with a mission to Jordan and Syria.

There were only two missions in 1984 – to South America (Argentina, Brazil, Chile, and Peru) and Europe (France, Greece, and Italy).

The pace picked up again in 1985 with four prayer missions: Central America (El Salvador, Honduras, and Nicaragua); Africa (Ethiopia, Kenya, Nigeria, South Africa, and Zaire); Peru (for a second time); and, towards the end of the year, Switzerland (to pray for the Reagan-Gorbachev summit) along with Northern Ireland and England (for a second time).

In 1986, Jim conducted his last Prayer Missions. The first was to Asia (Hong Kong, Japan, Philippines, Singapore, and Thailand in Asia), Australia, and New Zealand. And then, in September, there was one last trip to Peru.

While Jim was alive, United Research conducted 21 prayer missions to 40 countries on six continents (Antarctica was the only continent not visited). Many of the countries visited were ones that had had a troubled past or that had troubled relations with other countries, or that felt threatened by other countries.

In addition to the international missions, domestic prayer missions were conducted to Washington, D.C. in 1982, New York City in 1983, the Hopi Indian Reservation in 1984, and the Cherokee Nation in 1985. Jim also wanted there to be prayer missions to every state capital and to every city in the U.S. with a population of at least 200,000.

While the emphasis was on traveling to nations in need, United Research also visited places with unique spiritual energies and histories, such as the pyramids in Egypt, the city of Jerusalem in Israel, Machu Picchu in Peru, and the Hopi Nation in the U.S.

On its international prayer missions, United Research people would go to a country and spend a minimum of three days in the capital, praying for the country, its people, its government, and its relations with surrounding countries. Prayers were conducted around the clock. By breaking into four groups, each of which was responsible for six hours of prayer a day, two hours at a time, twenty-four prayer was maintained for the country. This could be demanding. Imagine arriving in a country after having traveled for several hours – or, in the case of the Far East, having traveled a full day – and being asked to pray. Your group's schedule required you to pray for two hours, then be off for six hours. Much of the free time could be taken up with meals and sleep. With a two-on-six-off schedule, one might pray from, say, 7 p.m. to 9 p.m., then nap for a few hours until the 3 a.m. to 5 a.m. shift began. The twenty-four hour prayer cycle would finish with prayers from 11 a.m. to 1 p.m. This was not your typical vacation.

It was United Research's intention that everything it did on prayer missions was to honor people, no matter what their nationality was, no matter what their religion was, no matter what race the people were. The basic perspective was that all people want God and that United Research's prayers were to facilitate people finding God, finding the Divine within themselves.

The prayer missions were open to all – whether the individual was new to United Research or had been associated with it for a long time. The prayer missions typically included groups of 20 to 60 people.

Jim said there would be changes and change there has been. Jamaica was freed. The Berlin Wall came down. The Soviet Union dissolved. The warring parties in Northern Ireland have worked hard to bring about peace. Large numbers of Mafia members in Italy and the United States have been jailed. The number of wars around Earth has dramatically declined.

And there were changes not only in the countries that were prayed for but in the people who went on the prayer missions. People returned feeling they had experienced something fantastic. A not-uncommon reaction was, "This was the peak experience of my life." One person's experience was that, "I went on prayer missions with an attitude of,

'What can I do for the country we're going to?' I went with a giving attitude. But I felt that I received more than I gave – in terms of spiritual growth and inner joy. It's fun working for God." Jim's perspective on the value of the prayer missions for the individuals that went on them was, "The rewards for those who go and for those who partake at a distance will be fantastic. It's like the granting of a thousand, thousand lifetimes for you. That's the way I see it."

Jim also felt that, "In our trips to countries, almost universally, there is a tremendous feeling of accomplishment. There is a tremendous feeling that Light has been anchored, that Light has been established, and that this anchored Light is causing changes. For example, two days after we left Northern Ireland, they announced on the radio that the Catholic and Protestant churches were thinking about getting together and trying to solve the problem of Northern Ireland. It is interesting to see that this is volunteered – after 400 years of killing. It is really amazing to see that it works – the Water of Life that you have to give works. It is for us to begin and do and stay with it.

"We feel that we are secure here in this country. We are secure in our homes. And we feel that we don't have a responsibility for the invasion of Lebanon and the murders that took place there. But, everyone is our well beloved brother. Every person. They are our responsibility. Countries are our responsibility. When you look at all the nations, you tend to think of them as a nation, as a government, as something like that.

"But, they are people, and people in those countries are our responsibility. The land. The Sahara Desert – people dying from a lack of water – is our responsibility. Food is our responsibility. Because the Water of Life produces all of that. We need to take up the gauntlet and make it our responsibility.

"Rather than condemning. That is easy. The media do that constantly. Rather than fighting against. That doesn't make sense. That doesn't make sense to a person who can give Life, to fight against. It's amazing how we get trapped. Everyone wants to fight against, because we think it's wrong. What's wrong is not fulfilling the need."

A group picture from the prayer mission to Southeast Asia. Jim and Diana are in the back row, towards the right. Roger Goure is also in the back row, in the center, with sunglasses.

THE LAST YEAR

At the time Jim and his family came to the Black Mountain, there wasn't much in the area in the way of alternative approaches to spirituality. But, by the mid-1980s, the New Age had arrived in America. There was an avalanche of spiritual alternatives: Zoroastrians, Rosecrucians, Tibetan lamas, Native American shamans, Hawaiian kahunas, channelers, mediums, astrologers, yoga instructors, Tarot card readers, re-birthers, healers of all stripes, and scores of gurus from India. Shirley MacLaine would appear on the cover of *Time* magazine holding a thicket of crystals in the palms of her hands. That cover of *Time* would be entitled, *Om...The New Age - Starring Shirley MacLaine, faith healers, channelers, space travelers, and crystals galore*. New Age books suddenly were the fastest growing category for booksellers. Amidst all of this, one of the more improbable changes was that the greater Asheville, North Carolina, area, heretofore known as the Buckle of the Bible belt, had become a New Age mecca.

The Great New Age Show, with its exotic gurus and all manner of promises, was too tempting for some who had been with Jim, and they became guru-hoppers – moving from one guru to another, staying only as long as the entertainment lasted or until the exotic wore off or until they discovered the guru's faults or until, heaven forbid, they were asked to show some discipline.

With all of this churn, and in a sense competition, attendance started to decline at Jim's events. And yet, he pressed on. During 1986, the year in which he reached 65 years of age, the typical age in his generation for retirement, Jim conducted 18 workshops and prayer weekends at the Light Center and was on the road for nearly 50 days where he conducted an additional 10 workshops and two international prayer missions (to Peru and the South Pacific). Jim also continued to teach his weekly Friday Class at the Light Center and to counsel people who came to him for help.

Diana had been hoping for something different: "Over the years, Jim worked very hard – seeing people, teaching, lecturing, traveling. I worked hard also – keeping records, getting information out to the public, giving up the privacy of our home so Jim could invite all sorts of people to come and stay anywhere from overnight to several months or years. And in addition, there was the family of eight children, the house, the garden (some years), and my job." She had hoped that this might be a time when "we might quit working so hard and have some time to relax." It was not to be.

In the early part of 1986, Jim created the Intensive, a participative workshop that was by far the most powerful spiritual event most participants had ever experienced. This was his parting gift, his one last attempt to get people to break through and stay centered in the Divine. It was his last attempt to get people to do what he had been pleading with them to do all of these years.

At the Intensives, people opened up as they never had before, and many people did break through, at least for a time. They began to know things about other people they could not possibly have otherwise known. Through prayer, they began to use this knowledge to help others. They began to know the enormity of Divine Love, and they began to use prayer to bring this greater Love to everyone and everything.

What Jim was doing was training people to do was what he had been doing for years – prayer readings on people, healing people them through prayer, healing the planet through prayer, and worshipping God from a deep, deep knowing.

Despite the effectiveness of these Intensives in getting people to open up, Jim was exasperated. An impatience had been building in him that is common to many self-realized beings. Because they have worked strenuously to achieve what they have spiritually, they expect others to do the same. And they can run out of patience when they see that others are not willing to work as hard.

About two thirds of the way through the very first Intensive, Jim expressed his frustration: "I have a question....All of you said to me when we started...that you wanted to be One, knowingly so. Tonight you are beginning to experience that. This [material that I am using for this Intensive] is exactly what I taught sixteen years ago, fifteen years ago, fourteen years ago, thirteen years ago, twelve, eleven, ten, nine, eight, seven, six, five, four, three, two, one, zero! It has not changed! Why the hell haven't you done it?! You all have been hearing this since you came here. Why did you wait? Now, I need some answers! Why did you wait?!"

Answers started pouring in from a stunned and unsettled group of participants: "We don't trust ourselves." "Fear that we can't do it right."

But Jim was not accepting of those answers: "Everyone has had this experience [of oneness with the Divine] somewhere in...time. But you don't want it because you don't feel you'll be acceptable."

One woman said, "I've experienced being one with the universe." But Jim quickly asked, "Why didn't you stay with it? Why didn't you continue that effort?" To which the woman responded, "It just happened when God did it. I can't say, 'God, now I want it.' God tells me when to do it." Which elicited this from Jim: "Wrong! Wrong! Wrong! You are Divine! *You* must declare [your Divinity]! You are the authority!" The woman then said, "The experience just took over." Jim: "Yes, but it wasn't someone up there. God isn't up there, damn it!"

Jim went on: "As I asked in the beginning, 'What do you want out of life?' All of you said, 'To be God.' Well, then, why in the hell didn't you do it? If you wanted this, why haven't you always wanted it? Why in the hell haven't you done it? I don't understand why you guys don't desire with your whole being. What the hell is wrong with you?"

Another person suggested this answer: "When we do it together here, the experience is possible. But if you talk to us each night and say, 'Now, go home and do it...'" Jim interrupted her, "You won't do it. None of you would do it." And the woman finished her sentence, "...surrounded by our conditioning and beliefs....but now that we've experienced that it's possible..." Jim cut her off again: "It's incomprehensible to me that you would say such a thing. It's incomprehensible. All of you have to desire God because it's in you. It's an automatic thing."

Jim wrapped up his message by saying, "I was taught a more fundamental belief than the Baptists. But, I'm eternally grateful for it because I remember hearing what Jesus said, 'The things I do you can do.' And I kept saying, 'I gotta have that.' He said, 'The kingdom of heaven is within.' No God up there. You all went to church. You heard that 'The kingdom of heaven is within.' What the heck is the matter?"

And then, calming down, he said, "Alright. I've satisfied my curiosity. We've got a tough job in the universe. All of man is like this. This week has been good for me. I've been pretty angry at all of you. It's been a very tough week for me. It was so hard for me to understand. Why have I got to do this [Intensive]? But now I know...it must be an experiential thing. All of you have experienced the Creator. All of you have. And you know the mission of the Earth and the mission of the people is to come up into that [experience of being the Creator]. Earth *must* become just as you have become this night – the Creator in Action. I've been talking about being the Creator in Action since...but, talk won't do it."

And after that, Anne Boyce, a woman who had been with Jim for years, and who had been one of his strongest, gentlest, and most gracious supporters, said, "We've grown a little bit in sixteen years." At which point Jim softened and said, "You've grown fantastically." And with that, he invited everyone to join him for refreshments.

Over the course of the year, there were little signs of...something. The man of endless energy, the man an early visitor had described as "a little kid in a grown man's body," sometimes seemed to be a little tired. Even so, he certainly did not cut back on his schedule.

But, there were intimations that something was going to happen. On the trip to Peru that year, one participant remembers, "I knew he was leaving. I think he thought it might have been then. He was really quiet. He told the group he would be leaving.

"People were pretty upset. They were wondering if space ships were coming to get him. People were actually up looking for one.

"There was a ceremony in the meadow at Macchu Picchu: we were in a circle. Walking back to the hotel after the ceremony, Jim was quiet and sad. It was not like Jim at all."

Another person had a similar sense of foreboding: "I knew Jim was going to pass away shortly. I was at the Intensive two weeks before he left. If Jim were having trouble, I knew it when he would hug me or shake my hand. He avoided me at the Intensive. I told my mother in the car ride home that Jim was leaving."

To another person he talked about his sense of completion, that United Research had visited forty countries, that there were forty windows in the dome, that this signaled a fulfillment, a completion.

So, Jim was giving brief, indirect signals, so brief that if you weren't listening carefully, you would have missed them. On September 19, 1986, almost three months to day before he died, Jim, in talking about the last trip to Peru and the decision of beings in Macchu Picchu to leave that area, said to a group attending the *Your Place in the Sun* workshop, "Long before I left here for Peru, I began to feel a sense of accomplishment of a life, the end of a long span of life here on planet Earth. In one sense, it was like a sense of the end for me, too. It was a sense of sadness. There were many days here when I felt an extreme emotion of love, of joy, and an end."

Jim's evolution was subtle over the years and was not something he explicitly talked about. But, one senses in the young James Goure the unbounded optimism and enthusiasm of youth, an unshakeable buoyancy about the power of prayer to change things for the Good. He never stopped believing that or talking about that, but as you listen to a continuum of his lectures, you begin to feel that, after years of teaching people how to pray effectively and watching them enthusiastically use the prayer and get results and then slip back into their old ways of seeking acceptance from others rather than getting into God, he recognized that something more was needed.

The very last lecture Jim gave, which spoke to this problem, was entitled, appropriately enough, *The New Life*. As he was transitioning to his new life, he gave the keys to a new life for everyone.

If you listen carefully to his voice on the recording of this lecture, you can hear him breathing harder and faster than he normally did, the shortness of breath a telltale sign of what was to come.

He began the lecture by expressing some of the same frustrations that he had had at the first Intensive. But then he moved quickly to a diagnosis of the problem and a solution.

"I've been giving several Intensives over the past year. People who have attended these Intensives, on a scale, go up very rapidly and then level off. It's been very difficult for me to understand why people level off and why they don't continue on being what they can be.

"So, I've made additional studies of what's been delaying people in being who they really are. Each one of us thinks we are not the reality all of the spiritual people have been talking about. We do not accept what the gurus have been saying for thousands of years – that every person is God. Jesus said it. But we reject it.

"What is holding us back from accepting the reality that we indeed are God? *The* God. The one and only.

"What is keeping us from accepting this? It is our concept of identity. That without an identity we are nothing.

"It would be great if we didn't have names. These names are limitations. The very concept that you are a woman or a man is a limitation.

"You are Divine! There is no male; there is no female in the Divine.

Why don't we get into this concept?

"A year ago it was presented to you to name very organ in your body 'the Christ' or 'Light.' People experimented with it, went up a little ways, and then leveled off.

"For some reason, we are caught at the level of not being able to progress, of not being able to be all that we can be.

"Therefore, we need to reevaluate what is going on inside of us. Why don't we accept the reality that we are God? Why don't you? I hear people say, 'We accept the fact that we are an identity.' The hell you are. You are not an identity. That's a concept you are trying to present to people – that you are Mary or Joe or Pete or Jane. That's not reality. You are Divine!

"You saw the demonstration proving that you are Light. But, the first thing we think is, 'You are a male' or 'You are a female'. People are locked into the identity crisis of male or female because we each are trying to become male or female. We're working at it – to express manhood or womanhood to the ultimate. That is not the way it is. The way it is is that you are Divine.

"People go to an Intensive, accept that they are Divine, and then level off into their personal problems again. Rather than seeing that this is not a personal problem. Everything is the Creator in Action.

"We reject that reality because we think this identity is not perfect. We are holding back the reality of ourselves because we cannot accept that we can be God and also be bow-legged and have something missing from our body and snore. Well, you can be God and have these problems. In reality, there are no problems. There is only God, God, God.

"But, we can't accept that reality. We accept that we are not perfect. We accept that we can't be God 'til we're perfect. We say we weren't dealt a perfect body and therefore in this lifetime we can't be perfect and we can't be God.

"Well, Jesus said to those dummies in those days, 'Ye are gods.' Even though they were barefoot and stinking, he said, 'Ye are gods.' But, they didn't accept it.

"So, once again, I've been doing research and finding out what the heck is keeping people from reality.

"The way I'm going to suggest now is to name each organ in your body male and female, man and woman, father and mother, messiah and goddess merged together. This will offset the unbalanced condition in everyone. The unbalanced condition is that you think you are a man. You think you are a woman.

"This technique will be of great assistance to you. It will help you attain the reality that you are God, that you are Divine, that you are the beginning of a new life.

"Sometime down the pike you realize that you are not male, you are not female. You are Light. You are God. You are Divine. And only Divine. That's the way it is!

"In praying for the male-female, do the same thing for the planet that you've been doing for yourself. The planet is a living entity. If you can change the planet the way you change yourself, you will speed up development of the planet and the people of the planet. The reality of God is that people are changing into a new type person.

"It is essential that you do this so that people don't have to go through trauma. When Light hits you, all the yuck that's in you has to go somewhere. And the going out of you will be a sickness of some form. You will say that you are not what you should be. You are again denying God – saying that you are sick, that you are not Light, that you are just human.

"There is a tremendous change going on and this change is going to be speeded up. There is going to be a tremendous showering of Light on the planet soon, and if you have some yuck inside of you this yuck will cause interference and you will go into a difficult period.

"But it is not necessary to go through a difficult period. It is necessary for each one of us to realize that we are indeed God. It requires our accepting this. It requires our working with this moment by moment. As God, you are in everyone and everything and you have a responsibility for everyone and everything.

"If you only work on yourself, you will not make it all the way. The way to make it is to help all of mankind – not only on planet Earth but throughout the whole universe. God is in everyone and everything. Therefore, since you are God, you are in everyone and everything. You are incomplete until you help everyone and everything attain to the consciousness of God.

"Break into this new life by helping the whole planet.

"In this evolutionary jump, individuals are being held back by their concepts of themselves. Everybody's concept of reality needs to be changed.

"The technique for doing so that Jesus gave was: pray without ceasing. It's a wonderful technique.

"Eventually, as you pray without ceasing, these other things will drop away.

"So, we need to get going. We need to get with this program as quickly as possible. And not to hold back anymore. Not to get caught up with our own little problems. Once you start working on the world, your own little problems will dissolve. Once you start praying for the planet, your own teeny problems will dissolve. Because that's the way of God. That's the way of Life. That's the way of man attaining God.

"It is time we get into who we really are. Not Jane, Joe, or Mary or any of that.

"It's a time of change, of tremendous change. It is a time of change for the planet. It is a new life for each individual.

"The way to break free is to say, a million times a day, 'I am Life.' A million times. Do it every day.

"You have the time. You have so much spare time. To say, 'I am Light' or 'I am Divine' is a prayer. You can say it while you're walking or while you're working.

"Peace comes from Love. Peace comes from Light. Peace comes from people realizing they are Light."

And then he concluded with a prayer: "Thank you, God, for this togetherness with Thee. Thank you, God, for the Light guiding us and filling our beings. Thank you, God, for the world being filled with Light. And a new life is begun in the people of Earth. And so it is. Amen."

And there it was. The essence of his message. Get beyond your personality and your identity. Know your Divinity. Do something with it. Do as Jesus admonished us to do: pray without ceasing. You can do that. Saying, "I am Light" is a prayer that you can have going on inside of you at all times. But don't stop there. Pray for the planet. Help Earth give birth to its new life. And in doing so, you will give birth to the new life within you.

A few days after giving this lecture, Jim was scheduled to travel to California, where he was going to visit people who had told him they were in need of healing. In another sign of completion, one of these individuals was Cheryl Lee, who was one of Jim's first recruits from Virginia Beach to the place of prayer he was establishing in Black Mountain. Diana and Jim left the house, with Diana driving. The roads were slippery. They stayed at the Holiday Inn near the Asheville airport. In the morning, Jim knew he was not well and asked Diana to call the Light Center and have people there pray for him. But it was too late. He died of a heart attack that morning, December 18, 1986. He died as he had lived – on his way to help people.

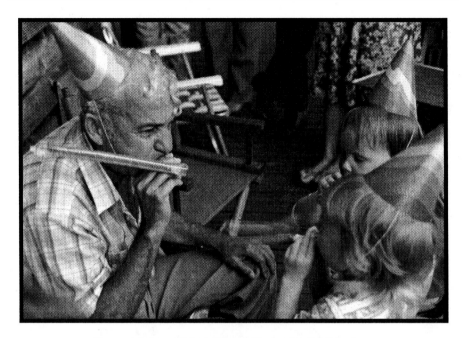

Jim with granddaughters Crystal and Lindsey

The family at Blue Ridge Assembly after an Advance: from left to right,
Diana, Jim, Grace, Liana, David Wilson, Paula, Will, Jay, Roger, Gloria,
Jonathan, Sue Daniels Goure, Chip, and Chris

Diana and Jim at
Machu Picchu
in Peru

Diana and Jim at Machu Picchu

EVERLASTING[6]

Except for the few who had picked up on the intimations that he would be leaving, none had anticipated that he would die when he did – or, for some, that he would die at all. Most were shocked. They had seen him only the day before or a week before or a month before, and he had seemed fine to them.

But dead he was, and people began to collect themselves and face Life without Jim. Some confronted it in a traditional manner, by writing condolences to the widow. One of those who wrote Diana was Lao Russell, Walter Russell's wife and the person who had turned down Jim's request to use Swannanoa as a spiritual center. In a letter dated Christmas 1986, she wrote not only condolences to Diana, but a testament of the oneness with another that virtually all strive for but so few achieve:

> Dear Diana,
>
> I was grieved to hear that Jim re-folded. The love and loyalty of a husband is truly our greatest gift on earth. I was so very sorry to have this news. Please know that my love and thoughts are extended to you at this time and always.
>
> My beloved and I were and *are* truly one in our work just as I

---

[6] The poem, letter from Diana, and quotes from the memorial service that are contained in this chapter are © United Research, Inc.

know you and your beloved Jim were – and *are*. The love that I knew with my beloved – and still know – sustains me and I know you will find this same strength, as I do.

Again, please know that I shall hold you in my love and thoughts, and I hope one day to again see you on God's mountaintop.

Lovingly,
Lao Russell

Some wrote poems:

He's gone home, our friend Jim.
He touched many souls and brightened our lives when they seemed dim,
He worked so hard serving his fellow man.
He taught us things of Love and Light,
How to take a stand for what is right....
We'll miss the humor and that smiling face of his
And that closing line, "And that's the way it is!"

Diana herself wrote a note to the larger United Research community the day after Jim died, saying, "Jim Goure loves this earth and all people everywhere. He loves being more in touch with everyone of us than he ever was before. His being has expanded greatly and he is drawing us all with him into a higher consciousness than was ever possible before. Give thanks and rejoice!" Diana also said, "Most of all I thank you for your love and prayers that continue to uplift and support me."

For the greater United Research family, a memorial service was held for Jim in the Light Center on Sunday, December 21st, three days after he passed away. It was unseasonably warm that day as the sun shone through blue skies. The Light Center, as it had been on its dedication day, seven years earlier, was filled to overflowing. All seats were taken and people sat on the floor or stood in doorways and aisles. Carl Falb and Bill Asher presided over the event, asking people to express their thoughts about Jim. The remarks were often humorous. Family and others spoke. Singers Rosemary Crow, Serenity, and Sue Daniels

Goure sang the songs Jim loved.

Diana and her mother, Grace, spoke. Diana said, "Jim always knew I wouldn't say much. But I feel like he gave each one of us everything he could give us, and now it's our turn to give it all out to the world." Grace said, "Jim bringing out a truth and making it so easy for us with his Seven Steps. It really is the stepping stone, and he's on the eighth step."

Another who spoke said something similar to what Diana had said, that "the awareness that we must be for ourselves and each other what he was for us: our link to Divine Knowing, our hotline to God and the Ultimate Healer."

Others had memories of help and humor. Among those who spoke was a minister who remembered asking Jim, "Mr. Goure, what do you do for a living?" And Jim had responded, "I help other people help themselves."

Sue Daniels Goure, Jonathan's wife, sang her signature *The Christ Within,* a cappella, in her sweet, arresting soprano:

Now I know, the Christ has come
I can feel it deep within my heart
Now I know, the Christ has come
It's in you - It's in me -
When you spoke, I listened
When you looked at me, I saw
When you touched me, I felt the universe
The day that you were born in me.

When you came, I knew you
Even though, 'twas long ago
I remembered the love that we once lived
The day that you were born in me.

You gave to me a golden light
It shines for me all through the night
Deep inside me, a newborn baby cried

The day that you were born in me.

When you spoke, I listened
When you looked at me, I saw
When you touched me, I felt the universe
The day that you were born in me.
The day that you were born in me.[7]

Jim indeed had touched many who, when he did so, "felt the universe" and "remembered the love that we once lived." Among those who had been touched was a woman who stood up at the memorial service and talked about how, "When I came here 13 years ago, I was a drug addict and a very sick soul, and Jim and the Goure family, they showed me what love was and they turned my life around. It took nine months for that process of turning my life around to really gel in me. The day things began to change for me was in a mental hospital in upstate New York, June 2, 1974. That was Jim's birthday. Six months prior to that I had taken my life. I took an overdose of drugs. I died. I went out of my body. I asked Jesus to bring me back. That day that I died was December 18, 1973 [13 years to the day that Jim died]. Jim and I used to love to pun together, but I think he got the last one in on me."

Another who stood up and spoke was Judy McFadden, whose compositions and piano playing at Jim's lectures and workshops had moved so many. Her most poignant memory of Jim evidently had been her last: "The last time I saw Jim was on Tuesday. He took my hand to pray with me and then he opened his eyes. When I saw what was in his eyes, I knew for the first time that I was seeing total joy. The reason there was total joy was because he was seeing God and that's why whenever you looked into Jim's eyes you felt love like you never felt it anywhere else, because he was seeing God in you and that turned him into total joy. For me, that was the key to Jim's life – beholding God in every face."

The most cosmic summary of Jim's life came from a Shinto priest, Hideo Izumoto, who had this to say: "I know Jim since 1983. I feel

---

[7] © Sue Daniels Goure, reprinted with permission

this my home. Earth more advance for New Age mission. My first teacher say Jim special angel for New Age. His guiding angel is Joseph and Maria and also Jesus Christ. Three days ago when I pray, Jesus Christ came out and say he [Jim] did the mission on this Earth at this time. So, his relationship with Jesus Christ was very special. My second teacher, Mr. Furia, he say he never met such a special person like Jim Goure, who is very much built up in God. That means he is very, very honest to God. He doesn't care about money and owning things and power, which other people seeking. All he want is to be honest to God and work for God. He doesn't care other things. Even maybe his family needs. He is most true, honest to God in doing his mission for Earth change, Earth's evolution. So, he is very special person and he accomplish mission very well."

And then, as if Jim were present in the room and he was speaking directly to him, Hideo said, "Jim, thank very much for your work, for us. I know why you must leave this dimension at this time. So, please do new mission for God for advance of this universe, for Earth New Age. So, then we can be happy. Thank you very much for God and for Jim, for what you are doing now.

"Most important teaching is advance. As this universe is advancing, people inside Earth need to make advance. That's what we are here for."

And in a prelude to that advancement, Helen Carson, filled with what she felt was the spirit of God, said, "I love you. I love you all. For the first time, I really know when Jim looked at another being how he loved. We're going to do it, and it's going to be O.K. We have got the ball in our court, and the greater works we will do from this day on. This world is going to be different. Each of us today is going to leave here and go to our homes and we're going to begin to love the way we are meant to love. I love you."

George Goure speaking at his brother's memorial service. To
George's right are his wife Kathryn (mostly obscured), Roger Goure,
and Diana Goure. Immediately behind Diana and Roger and to
George's right are Jonathan and Will Goure. To George's left are his
sister Helen and Grace Faus.

PART II: REMEMBRANCES

REMEMBRANCES

*P*art II: Remembrances provides first-hand accounts of people whose lives were affected by Jim. Jim always had people talk about the Light and how it had changed them, and this section of his biography provides you with remembrances of those who knew Jim and experienced putting his techniques into practice.

Over thirty people were interviewed for this book. Everyone had distinct memories of Jim. Over half of these stories, representative of different types of experiences with Jim, are included in this section of the biography. Other stories, ones that were told at United Research events or that appeared in the United Research newsletter, *UR Light*, have also been included. Some of those interviewed requested anonymity and the exact whereabouts of those quoted from tapes or the newsletter are not known. Given the large number of the responses that were going to have to be on an anonymous basis, it seemed best to simply make all of them anonymous.

Some were healed of physical problems, some were healed of mental problems, some took his admonition to find their Divine missions – and get about doing those missions. All were touched by his love. Here are their stories.

Growing Up Goure
    He Was a Great Man
    The Love
    He Brought the Universe to Us

REMEMBRANCES:
GROWING UP GOURE -
HE WAS A GREAT MAN

T he 1950's was a very conservative time. People just wanted to blend in. It was a cookie cutter age.

Jim was reading to us from books about flying saucers and angels. It felt right. But I didn't want others to know I believed it. I was scared of being different.

He tried to have us [the family] pray once a week. We'd go around and do out-loud prayer. Sri Sukhul [the Indian teacher who had helped Grace Faus and whose workshop Jim and Diana had attended] was into colored lights. Jim got a light projector and used the lights on the family three or four times. [This was a precursor to the Light chamber that now exists at the Light Center.]

He wasn't afraid of being out there, stirring up the pot. He gave a lecture at the University of North Carolina at Asheville in the early 1970's that might have sounded outrageous to people living in the area. He talked about UFOs and negative entities.

At the first Spiritual Frontiers Fellowship conference where Jim spoke, he was the only speaker who did not have his picture in the conference brochure. So, the first time that he spoke, only twenty people showed up. But word got around the conference because at his next session there were fifty people. By the end of the conference, more people were coming to hear him than any other speaker. People hadn't heard the kinds of things he was saying.

The main thing he did was teach people how to be empowered and find the Light. Others were talking about love. No one else talked about Light. He gave people a vision. You as one person can change what is happening for humanity on Earth. It's a very empowering message. His legacy is that people make a difference on Earth through the Light and letting go of limiting beliefs. We are empowered to make a difference on Earth in a major way.

In every country we went to [on prayer missions] we anchored a column of Light.

He loved the questions at Friday Class. He said it helped him know the answers the Divine wanted him to communicate. People left Friday Class with such a spiritual high.

The earlier way the Seven Steps was taught was better than the later way, which was just words. In the earlier way, he had people visualize an image of Light on the inside.

Some of the people at the house were tough. He learned not to trust people because they would take personal things he had said and make them public. So, he couldn't share personal things with people. Some people were just taking and he would pop [get angry]. But the energy at the house would be balanced by people who came and were givers.

He was having his own or family challenges. One of my siblings was an angry young person. Other family members resisted having people in the house all the time. Sometimes it was hard.

He's the best I've seen at getting rid of possessions. There was a woman staying at the house who could hardly move. At the prayer table, Jim inwardly took a look at her. He found that this woman's grandmother had died of cancer. The grandmother dearly loved her granddaughter and was hanging around the granddaughter with her energy of cancer. [After Jim prayed for her,] the spirit of the grandmother left agreeably. The next day the granddaughter was full of energy.

He was *very* clairvoyant and knew whether someone was speaking and acting in a truthful way or not. Some people came and prayed with us. One of them fell asleep during the prayer. Silently I judged the guy as a jerk. Jim tuned into that and after we came out of prayer he said something directly to me.

He'd work with everybody, even drug addicts. Jim told people to stay away from drugs – saying they create holes in your aura and leave you open to attachments or possession. A woman who had been wasted on drugs came and stayed at the house. When she first came she couldn't talk. She became empowered. She reclaimed herself. She went on to get her PhD.

There was a commune nearby named Lake Eden or something like that. Some of the commune members came to hear Jim speak. Some of them got off pot because of what Jim said at Friday Class.

One guy came who was a drug dealer and angry because Jim was telling young people not to do drugs. The dealer told people he was bringing a gun to shoot Jim. Jim told the guy to come on up to the house. He stayed at the house. Jim was very good at facing darkness with Light.

He was very powerful at facing down fear. He was very strong. He did awesome bringing Light into darkness.

He was true to the Light. He was a great Light. He'd get up at three or four in the morning and pray for an hour. He was very, very good at expanding Light.

Jim had no spiritual tradition. He did it by growing his own experience. I remember he had headaches when his third eye opened.

Jim's enduring legacy for me was that he got me on the spiritual path early. I never did drugs, which I totally appreciate. I feel as though through watching him I gained ten or twenty lifetimes. He gave me ten or twenty lifetimes the nine years I was there [at the house in North Carolina].

But, it was hard. I didn't know how to integrate it into life – getting a job and so forth. Integrating the physical and the spiritual was hard. So what if you make a million dollars or a billion dollars. How much Light and Love you're able to give and connect with - that's basically it. What else has value? *He* learned how to be successful in the system [working for the government]. Then he totally shifted gears and taught Light.

From the perspective I have now, his interpretation of love might have been over-born. Also, he had a tendency to exaggerate.

I tried telling him I loved him but he couldn't open to it. He had a very strong bubble all the time.

I would go up and over emotions rather than go through them and come out the other side. [The Light approach] can be an avoidance technique.

One of the things I did after Jim left was that I always sent Light to people. It finally came to me, send Light to Christ, to someone who didn't need it. I did this for about two days. After three days, it was like Jesus was in front of me, face to face. It became a game of who could send more love.

I have huge respect for Jim. He was a great man. He still is empowering for a lot of people.

REMEMBRANCES:
GROWING UP GOURE - THE LOVE

Before the move to North Carolina, Jim was pretty much absentee. I'm sure I saw him at dinner. I saw more of him in North Carolina. Still, there was not a lot of parenting going on.

I came home once I when was 17 after having had some alcohol – the legal drinking age for beer and wine was 18 at that time. He was waiting for me inside the door. He had a five minute chat with me while I was holding up the wall. He didn't say anything about the alcohol, he just made sure I knew he knew.

How did I deal with living in the house? Not having had other experiences, it's hard to say. There were always lots of people in the house, even when we lived in Washington, D.C., because there were lots of kids. It was just more of the same when we moved to North Carolina.

Some of my behavior has been shaped by having lots of people around. I'm more cautious of my privacy. I learned to put up walls. It's taken me a long time to start using people's names. There were a billion people around. I had the attitude of, "If you're here for more than one week, maybe I'll remember your name."

I developed a mix of tolerance and frustration from living in the house. I became more tolerant. But I also became more frustrated. The whole New Age thing of hopping from one thing to the next drives me crazy. Get a clue for what you want and go for that!

The most personally significant of the prayer missions was the South Pacific trip. I had an interesting experience through prayer and he knew about it without my telling him, which was kind of annoying.

Jim certainly had a temper. A few people got mushed under that. It wasn't that often.

Diana was the best at standing up to Jim. He realized he needed to back down if she got her back up. She'd get tired of whatever it was and she'd let it be known and we'd stop…for awhile.

What do I most admire about Jim? His ability to love. That's why people wanted to see him. It wasn't to hear him speak. They came early or waited until he was finished speaking to talk with him because they wanted to feel the love.

What I appreciate among the things he taught is the Tree of Life – the ideas, not necessarily the booklet. I didn't understand any of it while he was alive. I think I know now: It's all God. There is no good and evil. There is no outside of God. The outcome is unalterable, so it's not broken. There's nothing to fix. That can either scare the heck out of you or give you freedom, depending on how you choose to act. You can't do it wrong. There's no such thing as doing it wrong. How is that possible? You don't think the Divine Plan will allow you to do something wrong, do you? It kind of takes the sting out of consequences.

All the other things Jim taught were gimmicks: the Seven Steps, the lights. They're something to get you by for now. He got stuck on muscle-testing.

All pain and suffering is of our own creation. Stop creating that pain and suffering if you don't want it anymore. If you're not seeing abundance, you're looking with the wrong eyes. Look with your heart. Whether you make money or don't make money, who cares? How's your love going? Jonathon Livingston Seagull is my favorite book. I only take one thing away from it: Practice love.

If there's nothing to fix, there are only two things you can do: 1) Follow your guidance; 2) Practice love. And if you haven't got guidance, don't worry. You can still practice love.

I can't think of anything else to teach anybody. The rest is irrelevant.

REMEMBRANCES:
GROWING UP GOURE -
HE BROUGHT THE
UNIVERSE TO US

I t's quite an experience being in the Goure family. I grew up with prayer, of course. It was unusual to hear about other children who didn't have prayer.

It was kind of a peer pressure, guilt trip – I prayed and that was different and I didn't want to be different. Mainly it was when we moved here – with the hillbillies – I thought we were moving to hee-haw or something. To pray was unusual for them. I tried to hide it. I wouldn't talk about it. I tried to be accepted.

But as time went on, I realized that the acceptance was within. There is nowhere else to go but within. It shines out to everyone else, so it's within you. You bring everyone else inside of you. And you are accepted.

If I had a problem, I would just go up to Jim or Diana and we'd all get together and pray about it and everything would work out. So, it was easier going to them instead of going within. But, we all learned from that.

Jim cut the ties by bringing the whole universe in to us! [By allowing anyone to stay at the house in North Carolina.] But that was good because growing up with that I met people from everywhere. It wasn't just the family. I got being single-minded out of my consciousness. I learned how to get along with people.

It's real important to pray with your family. It shows.

REMEMBRANCES:
ONE OF THE FIRST PIONEERS

W e first met in Virginia Beach when a mutual friend brought Jim to my house – which had been nicknamed the "Mildew Manor" - to join our regular meditation group. I had spent the previous three years in Virginia Beach with many soul friends, all connected in some way with the Edgar Cayce Foundation (A.R.E., the Association for Research and Enlightenment). Jim was on his way to his new home in Black Mountain, North Carolina, as he had just retired from his work at the Pentagon.

Jim came to me after the meditation and asked me to come to North Carolina and join the family and help build the Light Center. I had quit my job as a medical technician that very day. I was only too delighted to enter into this new adventure.

It was great being at the house. Living with Jim's family was pure delight. And the land was, of course, beautiful. Jim was very excited about his dream of bringing about a center for healing and psychic research/work. He had a whole world he had created – like a god.

We, as family (and as extended family) joined together four times a day to pray…Jim leading, of course.

Jim was upbeat, energetic, fun-loving…a man with much passion and a mission. He was a kick. Lots of fun. So much energy. So optimistic. Jim was like a young kid in an old man's body. Jim was a powerful individual, a person who will always remain vibrant in my memory.

Jim was a traditionalist. He was all man. Jim would lead *everything*. This is probably why I did not stay. He had such a strong ego. He was always in charge. It was going to be too wrapped up in his ego for me, for my creativity.

I remember his driving. He cut the corners all the time on the winding mountain roads in North Carolina. He was wild.

I was young. I should've helped Diana more. Poor Diana: always doing laundry and cooking.

I'd been there one-and-a-half months before I went down the mountain. I almost threw up. I had to turn around. I told myself I needed to get prepared before I left.

I stayed about two months. I know Jim had hoped I would stay on indefinitely, but I'm afraid I was too young – a free spirit who didn't want to get more deeply involved at the time. I think he was not used to people picking up and leaving. He hadn't thought I wouldn't stay to build the Light Center. He acted shocked that I was leaving.

As it was, the time I spent with Jim and his family in Black Mountain will remain two months I'll *never* forget.

Soon after I left, I'm afraid the word got out, and the hordes starting flooding the Goure family. Everybody I knew from Virginia Beach and folks that knew these folks came to Jim's. It was like the flood gates had opened. Folks were thirsting for the truth, for direction, for hope. Jim's mission had begun.

Unfortunately, none had any money, and it had to have been a stretch for the Goure family to handle such an influx of humanity. Times were tough in the beginning, I'm sure. But, somehow, I doubt Jim and the family ever turned anyone away.

His legacy for me will be that he would drop everything and come see me in California. Years later (1986, if memory serves), I called Jim, asking for his prayers for me. I was between two serious surgeries and wanted his spiritual strength in my court. Mind you, I'd only been in touch with him a couple of times over the years. Without hesitation, he assured me of his support, not only in spirit, but that he was about to leave on a lecture and healing tour that would take him to the West Coast, and he would add my home to his travel plans, to visit me in person. Now *that* was the promise of a special person! After all those years, I felt the same strength in his commitment to humanity, one person at a time, that I had felt in those early years.

Jim never got to fulfill that plan on the physical plane, however. He died shortly after our phone conversation and just before leaving on his trip. I've always suspected, however, that he somehow kept that promise to me.

REMEMBRANCES:
BUILDING THE
FOUNDATION

In the year of 1971, I was part of the first group of young people to live with Jim and Diana Goure and their eight children in Black Mountain. For many months, in between the daily chores and also the part-time jobs we had in the nearby towns, we joined in shifts with Jim and his family in praying for world peace four times every day.

I lived there with my brother, David Dane, and my boyfriend, Nigel Perrow, and we found our way to the Goure's doorstep following a dream I had while staying in Virginia Beach with my brother. The dream was about a very special man standing in front of a large stone house in the mountains and calling out to me. When I told my brother the dream the next morning, he said, "I have met this man. I journeyed to his home once before with my friend Jimmy Stivers, and I have been wanting to take you there."

The dream seemed such a strong calling that the very next day the three of us packed our bags and headed off to hitch[hike] all the way to North Carolina. When we arrived in Black Mountain late in the afternoon, we phoned Jim Goure from a roadside [phone]box, and he welcomed us, saying he had been waiting for our arrival. He then drove into town to collect us and that night we were eating dinner around an enormous table with his family. After several years of following the hippy trail around the world searching for the meaning of life (our home country was Australia), we felt like we had found our true home! We didn't leave to go anywhere for several weeks. Then we needed to travel down to the town to look for some part-time work and I distinctly remember that it felt like we had been in heaven and we were traveling down to earth again!

There is so much I could say about our time with Jim Goure. He helped me to build such a strong foundation for my life and work. Most importantly, in all the hours spent in meditation at his home, I was able to truly focus on my life's task, which, ever since that time, has been working with holistic education for young children (body, soul, and spirit; hands, heart, and head).

I am now in my mid-fifties, have founded and run a Steiner kindergarten for many years, and raised three boys of my own. I am remarried and my husband and I are living and working in Kenya where we are helping with schooling for AIDS orphans.

REMEMBRANCES:
HEALING NATURE

In 1971, T. J. Davis, Edgar Cayce's protégé, told us, "There's a guy in North Carolina doing healing." From Virginia Beach, four of started driving to North Carolina in a Volkswagen convertible. We had no address other than we knew it was on Route 9. We drove up the driveway that led to the Goure's house. Jim greeted us by saying, "I've been expecting you," and asking, "Which of you was driving with his left leg up out the window?"

I stayed a week at the Goure's. As a hippy during the 1970s, I thought it was great to eat brown rice and bake bread. Diana later told me the reason why they ate those foods was because Jim's retirement check had not yet arrived.

While I was there, a bird flew into the picture window of the Goure home. Jim, Diana, and the four of us prayed and healed the bird's wing. Jim picked up the bird and took it outside and it flew away.

REMEMBRANCES:
A PICTURE OF WHAT A MAN CAN BE

Jim was a picture of what a man can be. My experience of men had been of them walking away. I grew up on the streets of Chicago. My mom was a waitress. My father left us when we were young. My husband passed way when I was 30 years old. I was a widow with five children. I went down to 98 pounds. There was a great need in my life at that time. I was physically, mentally, and emotionally ill. Jim and God got me through it.

Jim helped me get physically better and spiritually better. Jay, Jonathon, and Jim in a sense saved my life. Jim put me in Jay and Jon's care. I had a stroke. Jay and Jon put me through the lights. They prayed with me. It was better than if I had gone to the hospital.

My daughters worked at a Shoney's restaurant. Jim used to go to Shoney's to see how they were doing. He also used to come by the house and we went out to dinner lots.

Between my two sisters and myself, there were seven daughters. The seven girls sang. Jim called them The Seven Steps. He was a grandfather and a dad to them. They loved him.

I went to Jim's Friday Classes, which were attended by 80 to 100 people. I also went to Wednesday evening lectures by Jim at the Sheraton. Sometimes I went to see Jim on Sundays also.

I liked it better at the house than at the Light Center. There was more togetherness. It was homey. It was more real. We were more family at the house.

I felt like he was telling the truth. He was talking in a way I understood. It was not hellfire and damnation.

Diana is a strong woman. I have a lot of respect for her. She took a lot of stuff on other levels so he wouldn't have to take it. If you were psychic, you could see the doubters and those who thought he was crazy and needed to be killed. Diana would sit in the back and meditate and guard him.

Too many people clamped on too hard to him – rather than the message. That's the reason Jim left. The thing is the message. They were making the man the message.

When he died, it was too soon.

REMEMBRANCES:
THE TRUEST FRIEND

When I was 25 and started meditating I had recall of a dream I'd had when I was seven years old. It was a Heidi dream: I lived in the Swiss Alps with my grandfather. He had great love for me. The dream had foretold my meeting Jim. It definitely was my destiny to know him and share the mission of the Light Center.

I went to an early SFF conference in Charlotte. I guess it was in 1975. Jim's was one of the workshops I had signed up for. When I heard him, I felt I was hearing the greatest thing since the Sermon on the Mount. This man had universal knowing. It was the greatest knowing since Jesus. He spoke from knowing – not from theory or from a spiritual tradition.

Around 1976 I started visiting the Goure home. Every time I came I knew it was the center of the universe for me. There was nowhere else I wanted to be.

I moved to the house in 1976 and lived there for around five years. Prior to the Light Center being built, the Goure home was the Light Center. Jim had been told through Divine guidance to open his house to the world.

The house was quite a training ground. Jim delegated responsibility. He told us that when people came and visited, we were to take on responsibility for teaching them the Light Prayer and for praying with them. He also asked us to take newcomers to Meditation Rock.

There could be difficult moments with this approach. I was 26 years old. A man in his fifties came who had marital difficulties. I prayed with him. But afterwards, he more or less said, "What do you know? You're too young to know about my marital issues." It was either this man or another one whose wife had told him never to come back, after the man and I prayed, his wife called that night and told him to come home.

We young staff members were moved around a lot. You got moved from your bed so the latest newcomer could be accommodated. There was no stability.

Jim preferred to talk with newcomers after they had been around for about three days. They were more receptive then.

There were different phases. There were periods when he saw almost no one.

Jim told us to learn the Light Prayer, be the Light of the world, and pray for self and others and for all of creation.

He told us to follow the Divine within. He didn't want to create schedules as to who would fix dinner or vacuum the house. He wanted it to come from the Divine within as to who would do what.

We had 30 days to get ready for the Light Center dedication during the October 1979 Advance. We were in such a rush to get things ready for the dedication that Jim decided we could do prayer without ceasing and could break the routine of praying four times a day at the house. This was a mistake. The times around the table praying were very profound. We prayed four times a day: 9 a.m., 12 noon, 5 p.m., and 9 p.m. The prayer created community. Anybody with a need could tell the group what their need was and we would pray for them. The prayer smoothed over the personal differences. We prayed for the world. If someone saw a need somewhere in the world, we would pray for that. It was very powerful. Something was lost in transition from the house to the Light Center.

Jim had a vision of the Light Center that healing would begin before a person had even arrived at the Light Center. He also had a vision of 24-hour prayer at the Light Center. He insisted that the Light Center should be run by God-conscious people.

We had an expectancy that the Light Center would be discovered and we had to be God-conscious by the time the masses came.

Jim kept telling us, "You need to do all-night prayer. Break into God-consciousness."

Jim shared with us the times he had prayed to see Jesus. One time he felt that spiritually he was at a point where that should happen was when he was in the Navy on a ship. He got up real early, found a part of the ship where he thought no one would see or bother him, and prayed, "I want to see Jesus." Instead of seeing Jesus, he saw a sailor who couldn't sleep and had come up to the deck where Jim was. Jim was annoyed. The second time he was on a beach and found an isolated sand dune. Again, someone came around. I can't remember what happened the third time. He finally got the message: Jesus was showing him that the Christ was in everyone.

A couple of times I prayed late at night, "I want to see Jesus." One of the times I did this a drunk fellow came in at around 1 to 2 a.m. I showed the drunk around the Light Center and prayed with him. Another time, it was winter, a guy from town came in a rattle-trap truck. He had not been to the Light Center before and was intrigued by what he had heard about it – but also afraid of it. I was getting the same message Jim had gotten: the Christ is in everyone.

In the early days, Jim said very casually that Jesus and Buddha had come to him at the same time and asked him to tell people not to worship them.

I went on all of the prayer tours except for the last trip to Peru [there were three prayer tours to Peru]. By virtue of going on the prayer tours, I came to appreciate parts of the world I had not previously thought much about. I loved China. Jim said it was where I had first incarnated on the planet. I loved Australia and New Zealand. I liked Syria and Jerusalem in the Middle East, and in Africa I liked Kenya and Ethiopia. In Poland, we were there just ahead of the Pope John Paul II. We created safety for his visit through our prayers. People saw in prayer several plots of the Communists to kill him or make his death look like an accident. Russia was the most difficult prayer tour. It was where the energy was the darkest.

Jim said there was a God-conscious person in every country and that Diana and he were going to connect with them. I wanted to be a part of that.

Jim said to me, "You're the number two teacher." He wanted me to direct prayer trips at the same time he was. For example, he would take a group to northern Russia and I would take a group to southern Russia, at the same time. That never happened.

Jim loved to go out to lunch. It was fun and sometimes something extra was said. He and I were driving into town one day to go to lunch some time after the Light Center had been built when he said to me, "You know, I don't know if I did the right thing creating an organization." He knew the true mission and vision gets confused with perpetuating the organization – without remembering why.

What one word or one sentence summarizes Jim? Truth and knowing. A presence of Divine love. He could be human. He had tantrums and got upset with people. People would feel a love they had never known. Then he would lose his temper over nothing. He was a Gemini for a reason. Part of his mission was to have people know that the love is within them.

After he died, so many people said, "He was my truest friend." He loved you and supported you from the highest level of your being.

REMEMBRANCES:
TRUST AND ACCEPTANCE

My reaction to Jim was more personal than cosmic. The thing for me was the personal connection more than the mission. I'm more interested in saving myself than saving the planet. I think less of him as saving the planet and cosmos than as someone accepting of me. I have a lot of unresolved father issues, and he was a father figure to me.

He had this uncanny ability to go inside and see what was cooking. It was amazing. What he could sense about my history and psychology was so on the money it was spooky. He would say things and I immediately knew what it was about. He could say things – not much – and get right at you. He would say things about my past that rang 700 bells and got me thinking about acceptance, forgiveness, understanding, and not carrying around baggage. Amazing that this was communicated in relatively few words. I really felt he was a Divine being who had the ability to get people right where they lived.

Those moments and his acceptance of me are the main things I remember. His trust and acceptance of me was very important.

On all the international prayer tours I went on with Jim, the really important times were sitting down with him and his looking into my soul or the two of us just talking.

I enjoyed the tours. Those were really amazing places we went to – and survived! We went to some places that really were challenges.

He was such an unlikely combination of people. He would drink Scotch. He could talk sensibly. He had none of the preacherly aura. He seemed remarkably human and un-preacher-like. He didn't rely on his status and what he knew.

I also remember the amazing humor. I liked that it was serious but not serious. You could laugh at things.

The central thing I had come to was the amount of creative power each person had and the Divinity of each person: the individual is the Divine creative force. Jim was driving to the same thing. One of the things I liked about Jim was that he agreed with me!

If you really listen to Jim and understand what he says, you don't have to convince people. Verbal discussions of truth are not necessary. You don't have to be perfect. You don't have to be in any particular place. You just have to sit down and do it. It is subversive in the extreme.

REMEMBRANCES:
HE SPOKE TO MY HEART

I heard about Jim from Allison Waugh. I was eighteen years old. It was the spring of my freshman year of college. Allison and I went out to dinner and started talking about God. Allison told me, "There's a spiritual center I'd like to take you to." My dad said, "You can go as long as it's not a cult."

So, Allison and I went up to Black Mountain for an event. I can't remember what Jim said because it was kind of surreal. Finally, I had met someone who spoke to my heart. I was blown away. When someone speaks the truth of God, your soul recognizes it.

Everything he said resonated deep in my heart. I loved the bubble of Light but loved most thinking you are God no matter what happens in your life.

After the event, Allison took me to the Goure house. I was in the kitchen looking at a picture on the fridge. All of a sudden, Jim was there. He smiled at me, that radiant smile he had, and said to me, "Will you come back?" And I said, "Yes! I loved it!" He beamed. I left there with a floating feeling.

The thing I remember most about Jim was the way he loved. You knew you were loved unconditionally. He was just pure love. Around Jim you felt that great flood and river of love, the love for us, so that we would become what we are meant to be.

I stayed at his house all the time. I'd go for one to two weeks. I'd be driving up and find he was already waiting for me outside the house or dome. He'd say, "I could feel you coming."

I just remember totally loving talking with him. We would sit around the kitchen table and talk. He would tell me, "Bubble up because men will be attracted to your light." He had a great sense of humor and loved to laugh.

He gave *so much*, all the time. People there were so needy.

He came to Atlanta for my wedding. He stayed in my parent's house. He danced with my mother. He had a good time. Mother absolutely adored Jim and Diana.

Once, Jim was visiting during a traumatic weekend for me. It may have been the weekend of my wedding. A friend had been severely beaten up by her boyfriend. I couldn't recognize her face. Jim took her hands and told her, "You're going to be OK. You know you have to leave him." It was wonderful the way people listened to him. He was such a presence – he truly had the voice of the Christ. It allowed the other person to hear the Divine within them. She felt better, and eventually she did leave the guy.

He was a man's man. That's why so many men liked him. He was just a regular Joe. Not what you think of when you think of a spiritual type.

His whole life was to get us to step outside the box. It's right before you – the Light, the Love. Everything you need in life is within you. "You are the Christ. You are Light. You are Love." Declaring everything within you the Christ – I love that. The Light Prayer and everything was geared towards us becoming the Divine. He gave us that wonderful idea – everything is possible, there are no limits with God. When he said at an Advance, "I've been waiting so long to tell you. I am Divine." I knew that's what I had to become.

Whenever I think about it, I'm still blown away. He gave me

everything. I know I can handle anything. Not what the world would regard as handling things or having things right.

He could get mad, fiery. He loved this planet, and he could get fiery about it. He'd be really fiery and tell us, "You've *got* to pray for this country." Then, we'd really get into praying for whatever he asked us to pray for and afterward he'd say, "You did it! It's changed!"

Yeah, he cared about world peace, but mainly he wanted us to become the Christ. He gave us the tools and practices to push us over the threshold to the Light. He treasured our Being more than he treasured the planet because if you change everything around you then the planet automatically changes.

How did you hear about Jim's passing? I was standing in the kitchen in Atlanta. Ken, my husband, answered the phone. My parents had called. He handed the phone to me.
When they told me what had happened, I collapsed on the floor and cried. I never believed he would die. I understand now why he had to go. People had put him on a pedestal. When people started worshipping him, he knew he had to go. But, at the time, it was very hard for me to believe he had died.

The memorial service was the first time the spirit of God spoke through me. We *have* to do the greater works, was the basic message I got.

You don't need anything but the Christ within. If you take the time to pray, you will be God-conscious. It's magnificent.

The Effective Prayer is still affecting people. It's a phenomenal prayer. Never has there been anyone who was given the prayer who hasn't benefited.

He still speaks to me, especially during Intensives. What he always says to me is, "Just Be."

We most honor him by living what he taught us. There is no greater gift to him than becoming what he wanted us to be.

REMEMBRANCES:
IT REALLY CHANGED MY LIFE

I heard about Jim from Doug Riehl's wife, with whom I worked. She told me about a group meeting being held on Wednesday nights in Atlanta, where I lived. I started going to these meetings – they were prayer meetings.

The people at the prayer meeting were talking about going to an Advance. But it was four hours away and I thought, "I'm not going to drive for four hours and sit for a weekend. I don't care who it is."

But Doug said to me, "Get in my van. I'm picking you up at 3 p.m. on Friday afternoon and you better be ready." We flew up to Black Mountain. The Advance had already started. Jim was talking. We went in the back door of the chapel. I'm listening to Jim talk about Light and I think, "Oh, my God, I've always known that, but I never heard anybody say it. Wow!" It was so neat to hear someone who really knew about the Light talk about it. I just loved it.

On Sunday afternoon of the Advance, we came up to the house where the Goure family and others were living. All these people were around. Jim says to me, "I want you to come up here and stay." I said, "I'm a college student. I can't do that now." Jim said, "You can think about it."

Well, I got back to Atlanta and I thought about it all week. By the end of the week, I decided, "I'm going." It was the end of the quarter. I call Jim and tell him, "I'll be there in a week." Jim said, "OK."

He gave me the best room in the house. One thing I liked about the room where I was staying, which was across the hall from Jim and Diana's bedroom, was his snoring. It was so loud it was like music. It was real comforting. I always felt really safe.

Sometimes, in the middle of the night, I would wake up and I knew that if he was not snoring he was praying. I would get up and pray with him in the living room.

He would get up early and make pancakes. I would put on the coffee and set the table. It was usually the two of us up early.

One morning he was fixing pancakes and he came over to me. He said, very seriously, "You want to tell me something? Tell me how you always have such a happy heart." He *really* wanted to know. I was shocked that he asked. I don't remember what my response was. It was the only time he asked me that question.

It seemed like I had always known him. It felt like he was one of my family members. *Was there anything he did to make you feel like family?* The way he always smiled at me whenever he saw me. He lit up. He was glad to see me.

Jim loved every minute of it. He loved every second of it. But, it was hard for Diana. She had a really hard time. I don't know how she did it. Diana was more quiet, shy, reserved, while Jim was more outgoing. I really felt for her. I don't know how she took it for that long. One time she made him eat in their room for a whole week.

How would you compare the beginning vs. the end of the three months? Like night and day. I believed in myself more and I wasn't so shy.

One night they talked about going to Rita Livingston's house. I thought, "I'm not going." I was so shy I actually hid. He came and found me. "It'll be all right. You'll be fine. It's only us."

So, it got me to open up more to people I didn't know. I never used to open my mouth to people I didn't know. I'd sit in a corner or go outside.

It helped me fit in. Everybody cooked one meal a week. They let me have Wednesday night all by my self. I don't think anybody had ever given me so much responsibility. That made me feel like I fit in. He *loved* my cooking.

This was the beginning of my path. I had not been into spiritual things. Even though I'd had experiences when I was young, those experiences were more of a dream. I didn't connect the dots.

He wanted me to have a session in his office. He told me, "I want you to say 'I am Light.' I want you to do it 500 times a day." I did it. I didn't have anything else to do.

About a month later, he wanted me to have another session in his office. He closed his eyes and was very quiet. Then he opened his eyes and said, "*What* have you been doing? You have so much Light." I responded, "Well, I've been saying 'I am Light' 500 times a day."

One thing that amazed me was how quiet he was when he was away from the crowds. What was he doing? Probably tuning in and getting really focused.

Give me five words you would use to describe Jim. Love – big time. He loved like nobody I had ever met. He was a big time lover. Light. Truth.

On the last Peru prayer mission, I didn't want to come back. I literally had to make myself return.

I knew he was leaving. I think he thought it might have been while we were in Peru. He was really quiet. He told the group he would be leaving. People were pretty upset.

We held a ceremony on the meadow in Macchu Picchu. Afterwards, walking back to the hotel, Jim was quiet and sad. It was not like Jim at all.

I was at work in Atlanta when Doug Riehl's wife told me Jim had passed. I boo hooed and boo hooed and boo hooed and boo hooed more.

I came to the memorial service. What was so amazing, I felt I could see his energy everywhere. It was a feeling. He always told us the Light is in everything. It was that feeling. It was pretty amazing. I don't think I've had that feeling again.

Since his passing, I have felt his presence. A good while after he left, one night I was cooking dinner and he called my name. He didn't say anything else, just my name. It felt like he was in the house. I turned to see if he was there. It sounded like he was in the room with me. Sometimes I feel him with me, but not like that.

What could he have done differently? I don't know. Stay alive. In the physical. That's what he could have done! "Hang around awhile." That's what I'd tell him! "I can't believe you did that. What were you thinking?" That's probably what I'm going to tell him when I see him! "What kind of a stunt was that you pulled?!"

It really changed my life.

REMEMBRANCES:
SMILING ALL THE TIME

The first time I met Jim, my mother-in-law insisted. She was living in Florida. Carol Parrish was doing a workshop with Jim. We had a teacher in Columbus, Ohio, where I lived, who said God is within. So, I had a background of seeing the Christ in everyone.

Then I got talked into going to Charlotte for an SFF [Spiritual Frontiers Fellowship] week. When Jim shook my hand, octagonal beams of light came out of his eyes. (I asked him years later about that and he said, "Oh, that was just light.") I had a reading with him. He saw things it was impossible for him to know. I cried all week when I went to his sessions.

He invited my sister-in-law and me to the house. We slept downstairs. It was just an open space then. We went to Friday class.

I went back to everyday life totally changed. I was doing the Effective Prayer. I was releasing my parents. People I did not even know would come up to me and say how wonderful my parents were. My husband said, "You know, you're smiling all the time."

Jim had said, "You could be married to a telephone pole and be happy." My own inner promptings and dreams were leading me to separate from my husband. Jim told me, "It's time." I needed that permission.

At one of Jim's workshops, I put a question in the question basket. My question was deep, troubled. When Jim read the piece of paper with my question, he stared off into space for awhile. Then, he said, "Come to the mountains." It didn't mean anything to the others, but was meaningful to me.

I did come to the mountains. I stayed at the house for two-and-a-half months.

At the house, I saw how people took advantage of Jim. People were living there and not contributing anything. Jim was frustrated. He put a sign on the fridge that said, "Once a week, swab the walls."

He was gone a lot. Everybody had to carry on when he wasn't there. He really inspired people to work from within. Although there were personality conflicts, he was expecting them to work things out.

He had a way of treating a person as if they were the most important person in the world to him. Then, if he did not treat them that way, they got upset.

Until I started working full time, I went to Friday class all the time. He had an amazing way of organizing his lectures. He talked off the top of his head. He seemed to be rambling, but it came together.

The way his voice was, it just took you off into some form of meditation. I didn't always hear what he said. But, I got just as much out of it.

He would show his irritation when people would try to pin him down. He made an allegory about God consciousness being like a ladder through clouds to the sky. He said, "My greatest joy would be if I were the last person to go through." A woman said, "I didn't get that. Would you say that again?" He said, "No."

So many people were draining him – or trying to - that when I would go to one of his workshops, I would try to reverse that or give him strength. At a meal, there was a woman I felt was behaving in a draining way. I said to Jim afterwards, "She really drains you." And

Jim said, "Like a vacuum cleaner."

Jim was invited to speak at a center in California where I heard him give a talk. The woman who ran the center was dressed all in white. She was sort of hanging on him and gazing up at him adoringly and said, "Oh, Jim, I just know we were together in a past life in a temple." And Jim said, "Or in a cave."

He had that capacity for expressing love in an extraordinary way. He had to be so careful. There were all kinds of women who needed love and they looked to him in ways that weren't always spiritual. My mother had a well-known minister in Columbus, Ohio come on to her. She thanked Jim for expressing love without making a sexual advance. He thanked her for saying that.

In some ways he had a terrible memory. He didn't remember people as people because he didn't take in anything judgmental. He didn't make judgments, so sometimes he didn't remember people at all.

He could let loose and have a good time when he wanted to. At the end of the trip to Peru, we all went to the lounge. I had too much to drink. He was telling people's futures or reading palms. I remember him saying to a young Peruvian waitress: "Has anybody told you lately they loved you?" She didn't know what to do. At one point in the evening, we all stood up and sang *Let There Be Peace on Earth* and everybody in the whole place stood up and sang with us.

How would I summarize Jim Goure in one word? Love. He was a gentleman, in the best sense of the word. He certainly had psychic capabilities. That did not seem important to me. He made you believe in yourself. He made me feel I wanted to be the best person I could possibly be – not because of him but because of what he believed and what he made you believe about yourself. He really did believe in the best in everybody.

REMEMBRANCES:
A BEAUTIFUL EXPERIENCE FOR MY FAMILY

You know, you can't ever see Jim and not know that he loves you, not know that he's tremendous. I knew that, right away.

I'm kinda slow. I've known Jim a long, long time. First time I ever heard him was at Queen's College. I wanted to believe what he said, but I really thought he was off his rocker. This was too good to be true, and I was a long way from realizing that there is *nothing* too good to be true.

But, the next year I went to the SFF [Spiritual Frontiers Fellowship] conference at Lake Junaluska [in North Carolina], and I was on the front row. Use the Seven Steps and Jim promised a miracle. So, on the way home, I decided to bubble up this automobile. It was just kinda something to do. Sort of like crossing your fingers. I drove through Atlanta traffic – from Junaluska to just south of Atlanta. I got home and parked my car right next to my husband's – same wind direction and everything. The next morning we were having coffee on the back porch and my husband says, "Hmmm. That's funny." And I said, "What's funny?" And he said, "Why is my car wet with the dew and yours just as dry as it can be?"

Somehow you get to saying, "Maybe that was a coincidence. Maybe that really wasn't the first miracle. He promised it in two weeks and I got it in two days." But, they've been coming along ever since. That's the first time it [the Seven Steps] worked, and I'm still slow, but it's done so much for me.

It seems like a long, *long* time that I've been using the Light prayer because that's when the *important* part of my life started. Sometimes I have to turn around and look back to see where I've been to really know what it's done for me. It's changed my life.

My husband died of cancer in 1976. He died at home in the living room, in my arms. If he had to go and if he had to go with a malignancy, thanks to the Light prayer – and I know that's what it was – it was a beautiful, growing experience for my family and for me. It was an opportunity for my daughters and me to show him how much we loved him. The cancer had metastasized almost all over his body, but he never took a pain pill. Not one. He wasn't hiding that kind of pain from me. I know he wasn't.

I was able to tell him what I knew about what to expect, making his transition, what I had heard other people say. And he lived about two hours after the talk. I was able to tell him all kind of things we very rarely tell our partners. That also was thanks to the Light prayer.

REMEMBRANCES:
THE LITTLE THINGS

I came up to the Light Center about a month ago [around September 1980]. Jim was talking about this Light stuff. I started down the road and decided I would focus the Light, as he had suggested. I was down the road about ten miles towards Chimney Rock when I saw a fellow who looked like he'd been on an all-night drunk.

So, I started feeding that Light towards him. I didn't look at him. Then, I saw in the rear view mirror, he stopped and turned around and stared at me 'til I was out of sight. And I thought, "Well, maybe there's something to this Light stuff."

Jim's response (laughing): Maybe there's something to it! It gets your attention! Sometimes the little bitty things are the ones that attract our attention, that say, "Hey, maybe I've got something here." Maybe it's the little things that get us into the realization, "That little thing was super-consciousness-in-action." Experiment. Do something with Light. As soon as you do, you are a Creator-in-operation. Heal. Do something where you know the Light has done it. When you do, you are the Creator-in-operation. You are into superconsciousness. That is the beginning.

REMEMBRANCES:
"GO TO FINDHORN!"

Around 1975 or 1976, I had graduated from college and moved to Asheville, North Carolina. Friends in Asheville told me there was this man, Jim Goure, speaking Wednesday night at the Sheraton Hotel. I've always been searching for truth, so I went. There were about 20 to 30 people there.

I knew as soon as he started speaking that I was hearing truth on how to live. So, I continued going on Wednesday evening to hear him.

Then I moved to Charlotte, North Carolina and started studying horticulture. Around 1981, I had gotten to a point in life where I felt something was lacking. Things were not coming together. I was not getting anywhere.

What do I do at times like this? I go to Black Mountain. I always know something good will come from being here. I stayed a few weeks at the house and then, after getting a job in Charlotte, I came up on weekends.

By this time, I wanted to know my mission so badly. It was not appropriate for me to waste time anymore. I felt this so strongly. So, I went up to Jim and told him, "Jim, I really want to know my mission." Jim said to me, "When Jesus wanted to find some answers, he prayed all night long. Maybe that's what you should do." I thought, "Dang!

That was Jesus. This sounds like a lot of work. I was hoping somebody would just tell me what my mission is! But, to keep credibility, I'd better do it." I decided I would pray all night long.

Around nine or ten o'clock, I was all ready to get answers. Jim said I would. I went through all the contortions – all the different prayer and meditation techniques I knew. I did the Seven Steps. I'm a recovering Baptist, so I did all the good 'ol Baptist prayers. I meditated: I got into a lotus position and said, "Om." I tried to get my mind still. I had friends who were Catholic, so I tried to remember what they had told me about their prayers, and I said the Hail Mary. I went through everything I could imagine.

I did these techniques all night long and managed to stay awake. I could tell it was just getting ready to be dawn, and I still hadn't gotten my mission. I thought, "Well, I guess it just doesn't work for me." I started up the hill from the Light Center and ended up sitting on a rock on top of the hill. The sun was just coming up.

At that moment, I was totally empty. I was so tired from having prayed all night long that I was empty. Then, this voice boomed out of the air, "GO TO FINDHORN!" I thought somebody, maybe Floyd, had snuck up on me and was fooling with me. When I saw that no one was around me, I realized I'd heard something.

I had never heard of Findhorn. I was looking for an easy answer. I had expected something like, "Go move to this town." This was not what I had imagined.

Then I said out loud, "If I go to Findhorn, then what?" And there was this booming voice again, "GO TO FINDHORN AND YOU'LL KNOW WHAT TO DO NEXT." At that moment I made a commitment. I said out loud, "If I've got to sell everything I own to get to Findhorn, I'll do it."

I went back to Charlotte and spent the next three weeks asking people if they knew what Findhorn was. Finally, I was checking out at the food coop when I asked the cashier if he knew what Findhorn was. He didn't, but a girl in the line behind me said, "Oh, I was just there." She mentioned that Findhorn had gardens and, well, I was a horticulturist, so it all started to make sense. The girl told me, "I think they have a garden school. If you'll give me your phone number, after I get home I'll call you with information about how you can contact them."

She called with the information and I wrote Findhorn. They sent me a packet of information. Their garden school had 12 people from around the world each term. I filled out the form for that garden school with the greatest care. I really wanted to be accepted.

The garden school cost around $1,500 for the three month term. It had a June 10th start date. I didn't have the money. I had no savings. The only things I owned were a pickup truck and a TV. But, I had a new roommate. We shared a house in the country. I figured it would cost me $3,000 – by the time I paid tuition for the garden school and bought a roundtrip air ticket and had a little bit for spending money. I told my roommate about my predicament and he said, "How much stuff do you have? If you write on a napkin what you own, I'll give you $3,000 for it." So, I literally sold everything I owned – just as I had promised on the hill above the Light Center.

I allowed seven days after arrival in England for hitchhiking to Scotland, where Findhorn was. I have a good sense of direction, so all I need is a general sense of where I need to go and I can get there. After the plane arrived in London, I went up to a bobby [policeman] and said, "I got disoriented from all of the flying. Could you just point me the way to Scotland?" He looked at me like I was crazy. When you travel, you wrap yourself in things that make you feel safe. So, I had on my L. L. Bean boots, a pair of jeans, my dad's sports coat, a backpack, and a Daniel Boone coonskin cap! Even though the bobby thought I was crazy, he did point me in the direction of Scotland, and off I went.

I hitchhiked up to Scotland and met many interesting people who gave me rides. I was dropped off by my last ride at 10 a.m. on Saturday morning, June 10th – exactly the date and time I had been told to be at Findhorn for the start of the garden class.

There was a manor house that was a part of Findhorn, and I had imagined an incredible, wonderful summer in the manor house with people from around the world. But Findhorn is a caravan park, a trailer park. Living in a trailer park was not my idea of a wonderful summer. On top of that, the Findhorn people put me in the furthest trailer with a guy from New Jersey! I had expected to room with people from Japan or New Zealand or some other foreign country – not from New Jersey!

I guessed it was the Divine's plan. It turned out to be the best place to stay and he was the greatest person to room with.

We gardened, but it wasn't at all about gardening. It was about spiritual growth. They used what they were teaching about gardening as metaphors for spiritual truths. For the past 25 years, I have continued to use those truths.

The people at Findhorn asked me to stay and teach. But, while I was at Findhorn, I kept having vivid dreams about the Light Center and how it could be developed. There could be gardening, sacred dance, and healing activities on the land and the land could be way more a part of activities at the Light Center. The Light Center could become another growing, healing center. I felt strongly that I should come back to North Carolina.

So, I came back and moved into the Goure house. I had made a drawing from the visions I'd had at Findhorn and started to put the plans into action. I talked with Jim about the dreams I'd had at Findhorn. He wasn't enthusiastic enough for me. He basically said, "That's cool. Now, you go do it." I drew a color pencil drawing, a rendition of the Light Center property with trails and gardens and hung it on a wall at the Light Center. Jim's idea was that if we hung it in the Light Center, it would manifest the people and the money to make it happen. He connected me with people who might be willing to contribute money to the project. We got a few hundreds of dollars – enough for landscaping around the Light Center and planting daffodils along the driveway and painting the wooden fence along the drive up to the house. Then, the money died out.

I thought Jim could have made it happen. The ego part of me was disappointed. But, I learned that this was not Jim's thing. It was my thing. His thing was effective prayer.

His birthday and mine are about two days apart. We both have strong Gemini natures. We're troublemakers. We stir things up, try to make things happen – maybe we try to make too much happen!

I moved back to Charlotte after about half a year of living in the house and trying to make a reality out of the visions I'd had. I started teaching horticulture in a high school. The way I got the job was in the way I answered a questioned put to me by the principal. He told me my students would be big football players who couldn't pass any other science classes. He asked me, "How are you going to get these *big* people who can't pass other science courses to be interested in your class?" I said, "Remember the Tom Sawyer story [of how Tom got others to whitewash the fence]? I'm going to have so much fun, they will *want* to know what I'm doing." He said, "You've got the job."

Since then I've gone on to teaching at a community college. I teach lessons in life as much as I teach horticulture. I help people turn onto themselves. Empower themselves. Grow spiritually. I funnel what I teach through what I learned at Findhorn and at the Light Center. The Effective Prayer has affected me every day since I first heard it. It's been a dynamic force in my life. Just three days ago, I had taken an Effective Prayer card out of my pocket and put it on my desk at the college. A work-study student who's been having some personal problems picked up the card and asked me, "Do you think this really works?" I said, "Oh, yeh, I *know* it works." She then said, "But, I don't know that I believe it." I said, "You don't have to believe it, just practice it."

I'm so grateful to Jim, for the prayer, for the Light Center. I've always turned to the Light Center. I always find answers when I come here. If I can get out of my ego, boy it works.

REMEMBRANCES:
FINDING GOD IN THE A&P

I had been coming up here for what I could receive from Jim, and I am finally ready to give. In my way, I hope I am doing it.

All my life I've been a loner. I've never really had a family. When all my children left home, I was alone and I knew there was more to life than this.

It took me two years before I could believe what Jim was saying. It was too far out for me. I wasn't ready for it. It was only when I began to use the prayer that I knew I was on to something.

I have my family now. I'm no longer alone. You're all my family.

Jim taught us we could change people or change things using prayer. It was fine when I saw it in myself, but then I became very dissatisfied at work. You all know the A&P is closing down, going out of business and what not in places. I thought, "How can I continue to work here, in such an environment?" Jim gave us a prayer technique for changing things. Well, alright, so why not change the A&P? So, on my way to work, I'd do the Seven Steps for the A&P, and while all around me there was discontent and griping, I was able to sing.

I would go to work and people would say, "How are you?" And I'd say, "Great! You are, too! You just don't know it!" Finally, two or three of them, you'd ask them how they were and they'd say, "Great." And I'd say, "Fine. You're getting the message!"

When things got real bad there and they laid off all the help, a girl who worked there said, "Do you think that your prayer really worked?" And I said, "Well, I don't know if it changed A&P, but it changed me."

I was up here one weekend and Jim promised us we would be changed. And when I left, I knew that something had happened. I knew this was a holy place. I didn't want to speak going home – there were three of us in the car. Hardly a word was said.

I went to work the next day at the A&P and I was putting candy up on the shelves and all of a sudden, this Beauty, this warmth came over me, and I knew I was in a holy place and I just wept for joy for about thirty minutes.

And that's really all. If it changed me so that I accept whatever, well, that's fantastic. And I owe Jim my life. And, I'm so thankful for you, my family.

Jim's reaction: One moment like that is worth all the money in the world.

© United Research, Inc.

REMEMBRANCES:
SAYING, "I LOVE YOU"

I have changed tremendously since I first met Jim and started doing the Light prayer. At first I was a very negative person. I hated *everyone* – mostly because I was afraid. It was just fear showing through. If I stood next to them, I was sure they were going to fall on the floor dead because they would feel my hatred.

When my husband first got involved with the Light, I saw him change, and I thought, "If he can do it, by golly, I can." So, we began to pray together many times a day.

Eventually, it did work tremendously for me. I now know my husband as a Divine being, which was something I didn't know before. I thought I loved him, but it was a possessive type of love. By knowing the Divine in him, it let me know that others are Divine also. I can see the Divine in him and love him – something I just couldn't do before. Our love has grown. It has grown through our daughter. It just keeps growing.

For the first time, this weekend, I have found a family, something that I never had before, something I always wanted tremendously.

I just want you all to know that I love you. Because of Jim and the Light, I am able to love you as you deserve being loved.

Jim's reaction: That's fantastic. That's worth a fortune right there. Your message probably touched me most of all [several others had spoken at the same Advance]. To come from pure hate of people to sitting up here and saying, 'I love you' – that's fantastic. That's something that will endure in me. If we can do this [learn to love each other] in a very few years, look what this country is going to be – because this love is spreading and it's going out and it's causing change. It's a beginning of a whole new type of people, a whole new type of country, a whole new type of planet. When we first came here in 1970, I did not realize that by 1980 we'd be right here in this building hearing people say, "I love you." It's fantastic!

© United Research, Inc.

REMEMBRANCES:
A NEW LOVE

"God is easy! God means, 'I love you one hundred percent right now and I'll do anything to help…and make it simple for you!' That's God!" Jim was really talking to me. We were sitting across from each other in his office at the Light Center and I had touched one of his sore spots (someone told me later) in asking about gurus who laid out ancient paths with prescriptions – proscriptions – Sanskrit prayers, postures, long rituals – for disciples to follow.

I was brand-new to the Light Center - floundering and hurting and in the process of making the painful decision to end a twelve-year-old relationship with one of these teachers. I had for the past fifteen years been on my own intense search for God, having thrown out all of my training about the way life should be, about what it meant to be a success.

Peer groups, church doctrine, college, being married, having children, having a career and belonging to many groups were supposed to be fulfilling. They were not. I observed that people got sick and died from these things. I myself was also on the way out because I worked too hard at being successful.

A dear friend had been healing some of this defeat and hurt with her patience and had gently coaxed me for an eight month period to the

Light Center. This was over my LOUD protests that I did not want to go to another place with a teacher – and maybe I wasn't finished with that last one after all.

And so it was on that sunny August morning, I was Jim's 10:00 a.m. appointment and was asking one more time all the questions that had been bothering me so deeply about life and about finding God.

"There's no long pathway," he continued. "You are the sun! You are the Light! You are the Creator! If you could see yourself, you'd say, 'Thank you, God! I made it!' You are made! You are Light! Every time you see a person, you are seeing Light, you are seeing God."

I liked this man. Almost old enough to be my father, he had an unassuming dignity and an authority of knowing what he was saying. He literally glowed when he spoke this passionately about God. I had never considered myself to be psychic, but I could see this Light and wanted to see my own.

Here I was being cajoled, persuaded, and charmed into trying once more. God! What a cheering section he made!

How could I not try? It sounded easy. Everything was in simple English. People here dressed sanely – like me. No rituals, no Arabic or Sanskrit tongue twisters. Yea! What would be lost except a little extra time in feeling sorry for myself. And if it didn't work, I could always just go back and become a business success. (Not true, actually. A few months before, I had taken a vow – my second in this life – to do everything to find God before I ever worked again, and that did quite literally include a willingness to die while trying hard.)

Jim also invited me to an Intensive, promising great things. "Fantastic," he said. All right, I'd try. And so I began.

You must understand that I don't just listen to something if I'm interested in it. I take it to heart, study it, think about it, chew it up, and really try it if I'm persuaded. I take copious notes. I ask copious numbers of questions. And I did this with everything, e-v-e-r-y-t-h-i-n-g, Jim handed out. I wanted God and was going to give it all I had, because, by God, this was my last effort. Besides, I trusted something in Jim's saying, "Your eyes lie; don't believe them. Don't judge yourself or anybody. Base 10 isn't real (if you remember high school algebra). Base 2 is. Get on the train going to Base 2 and stay on it." Over and over he'd patiently repeat. (I've only been here three months, but understand he's been patiently repeating this for YEARS!). And I went deeper and deeper into practicing.

My mind was wild at first. I couldn't rein it in to pray. It wanted to fantasize, to be somewhere else. There were "real" things to think about! Besides, how was I to know there was even a Base 2, let alone anyone at the station to meet me when I "arrived," whatever that meant. And it was hard to sit very long. Many times I felt the minutes in prayer were wasted. Many times during the day I'd forget to be Light, to see Light. Many times at night I'd fall asleep and never finish the routine. But I kept at it anyway, as if it were all true and being successfully done.

What I didn't bank on, had never experienced, and was completely surprised by was the fact that these things – subtly at first, and then more strongly – began doing things back to me. They were alive! I began to let go of doing the prayers and began just loving them because that was the change. I literally began loving them. It came naturally. I began to love saying them over and over. I began to love the sitting. I began to love the Light Center itself. The more I loved, the more I could do, the longer I could do, and the more I understood what Jim was telling us. I had no way to explain to others what was happening. They would ask and all I could say was, "I don't know why. I'm just impelled to try, to do it, because I'm in love with what I'm doing."

My sleep patterns changed; me eating patterns changed; my relationships changed; my daily thoughts and activities changed. And none of it was scary or hard or impossible or too weird. It just happened. I let it happen because I loved what I was doing.

As a Montessori teacher, I know it's possible to teach a child every subject from the one point of his particular interest, whatever it may be; and I brought my knowing of this from the classroom to the doing of what I was learning. There were no gaps in the teaching. I did not read other teachers' material or books or listen to tapes for understanding. I had no desire. They were "trips" to me and confused the issue of wanting only God. I never questioned anything Jim said, because I could ask – and was reminded several times by him to ask – the Creator within, to perform my own experiments, to verify it for myself.

He asked me to do some things which seemed beyond me, and *that* has been harder. But I have finally learned to change my emotional response from "I can't d-o-o-o that, Jim" to "I must do it. The Creator in me does it." And the doing has always come when the time "to do" has come. And it's not hard, because the prayers given are not affirmations; they're declarations. Your authority with them grows with your doing of them, with your trying them out, and with your learning to love doing them, rather than all the old tapes which have never worked anyway.

But the important point is yet to be made. This is the hardest part to tell you, because this – and here I must get very serious – is the part where words fail entirely. You must read between the lines to get a feel for what I'm saying. There has begun to develop a new feeling, a new love – not that of a mother, a friend, a passion or an emotion. It is not human love at all. It is...God. Sometimes the power of it overwhelms me and I can hardly sit up; or the expansiveness of it overwhelms me and I can hardly contain it; or the beauty of it overwhelms me and I weep; or the gentleness of it overwhelms me and I surrender to it like a flower bud opening to the sun.

In this feeling, my practicing ceases, because I have arrived at a station along the way. This Love is still so new, it's not consistent yet. It is fragile and easily hurt, so that I lose it for periods of time. So I don't talk about it to anyone. I mostly protect it by continuing to practice hard. It's growing stronger now and is with me more frequently and for longer periods of time.

It is so wonderful that in the very beginning I just sat and felt it. Then I began giving it away to whatever was at hand – you, the family, the galaxy. Because, after all, that's the training – to give it away.

I want you to feel it. And if you could, you would do anything, a-n-y-t-h-i-n-g, to have it all the time. That includes doing four hours of prayer a day. If you do four, you'll do twenty-four. Then you'll come to know who you are, if that's what you want.

My journey continues. My practices continue because I'm not "done" yet. My priorities in day-to-day living continue to change. Divine Love does that. It changes you. It changes your life. And it's wonderful. It's fantastic. Just like the man says.

"It is not important what you've been," Jim said. "You can run to a zillion things forever. God right now is all that's important. We cannot be just an island with nothing around. You know you must love everyone and everything because it's in your soul. We can't give our personal love because that will hurt others. The Creator uses Light and Love, which is a step beyond individuality and which hurts no one. So, if we can love the Creator in each other from inside ourselves using Light and Love, then we're making it. We're becoming better for it. It's the beginning of life. Then we move from there into the Divine where we exist inside of everyone and everything, where we can truly love – to help the Creator even more to love…just to love, just to love. That's all. It's wonderful."

And so, I tell you that even at the very beginning of this Love, from deep within, I know it is true. And it *is* wonderful.

REMEMBRANCES:
THE PRAYER MISSION TO INDIA

For me, India was very special. I have wanted to go to India all of my life. When I heard about the prayer tour, I knew I had to go.

I ignored that for awhile. It was very impractical and sort of an irresponsible decision, I thought. When I finally released that and made the commitment to go, everything fell into place.

For me, the trip was very easy. I didn't get sick, and I didn't get sleepy [during the prayer sessions]. I slept like a log when I could sleep and woke up well rested.

I thought that if you carried the planet within you, any increase in Light that you did for yourself, any releasing was done for the planet, too. So, that's the way I pray.

Everyone has their own way of praying and I wouldn't suggest [how you should pray]. The only thing I'd suggest is that you forget about yourself. You pray for others, you pray for the country, you pray for the planet, you can merge with the universe, you can pray for all that, but forget about yourself.

Some people when they pray have great visions. They have beautiful visions, they see great beings, they see angels, they see beautiful symbols, they see other dimensions, and they get messages from those beings and those dimensions. And then some people are feeling very inadequate because they don't do that.

Well, I don't do that, either. I, in the past, have had some words come through and I've had some feelings. But, on this trip I began to see some things and I began to feel a great deal. What I felt from the beginning of the trip was this fantastic love. I felt it all the time.

One of the first messages I got was, "You are the Creator. Therefore, what you see with limitation will be created with limitation." So, I tried very hard in the things we saw – some were very beautiful and some were not – to not limit what I was seeing by judgment. That was pretty hard to do sometimes. At one point in prayer, I went back over my whole day and I re-walked the streets and saw everything again and looked at it with the eyes of the Christ, saw the Divinity in everything.

Pretty soon, I was not on the Earth anymore. I was above the Earth. And then clouds covered the Earth and there was a great deal of Light. It was very, very beautiful. And I heard a voice say, "Ascend unto me." And I felt this wonderful love. It was just pouring. It was the most intense love I've ever felt. It was pouring into me and it was also pouring from me. It occurred to me that maybe this was the true meaning of the words "born again" because I felt I had no past and that the only reality there was was this love and to live in this love and to be this love.

Later on in prayer I saw the outline of India, like an outline map and it started to become a woman's face. Then I merged with India and became India. And these are the words that came through: "I am India. Help me to restore my place among nations. Send me Light and heal my past and my people. The Light is here within. I will restore myself. I will heal myself. The Light sends new blood through my veins, new energy to my cells. Rejoice in the Light. Thanks be to God who restores my soul. Thanks be to God for making me whole."

About this time, Jim mentioned in our prayer group that the wheel of karma had been lifted. I took it into prayer for what it meant for me because I never believed in karma anyway. I remembered a dream I'd had some years ago. In the dream, life was a spiral. You kept going up the spiral, but you kept meeting the same problems as you went up the spiral. The message of that dream was that as long as I believed in the limitations of space and time and the concepts of life and death, I would have to stay on the spiral. The real message was that the Christ in me would continue to be crucified over and over again as long as I believed in the limitations of space and time.

So, I started affirming, "The limitations of space and time have been lifted." Nothing happened. Until I decided I better do it for the planet and not for me. So, I took the planet within and affirmed again, "The limitations of space and time have been lifted." And I saw the planet. It had a gold band around it, like the rings around Saturn. The planet left its orbit and flew off into the universe. Later, I was still thinking about this and decided that since I was the Creator I could be more creative with what the planet was doing.

The Earth, within the universe, is a very tiny speck. But it was a speck of Light. And it appeared here and there. It didn't travel. It just manifested, all over the universe. And everywhere it manifested, it left Light. And the Light remained. And I saw all the people on Earth jumping up and down and saying, "We did it! We did it!"

Then, finally, I was in prayer and I was just sitting there imaging Light. All of a sudden this body dropped down in front of my eyes. It was hanging by a hook screwed to the top of its head. It had been sliced down the back and all of the organs and muscles and bones exposed. It was pretty gruesome. And it was more so because I knew it was me. I didn't know where it had come from, but I figured I needed to release something more in my past. I remembered a couple of episodes that happened on this tour where I was off by myself and alone and frightened. Separated. And I realized that I had probably created those episodes to bring this to my attention. So, I started releasing and sending Light to the body. I saw it start to heal. And then I was the body. I was inside the body. I felt the healing take place. It started at the base of my spine – somehow it was gold – it went up my spine. It touched each chakra and filled it with Light.

I opened my eyes and there was Jim smiling and nodding at me. You don't have any privacy. He said, "You are totally free. Totally free." It's a wonderful feeling. It's what we all can do because it's what God wants for us. Thank you.

© United Research, Inc.

REMEMBRANCES:
BRINGING THE EFFECTIVE PRAYER TO THE CHURCHES[8]

It was the summer of 1977 as Effie Gay and I (Libby) drove from Kentucky to Pennsylvania to hear again the teachings of Jim Goure whose seven-step effective prayer technique had changed our lives. Etched within our souls is the remembrance of the private talk with Jim when he asked, "Will you take the Seven Steps of Effective Prayer to the women's groups of the churches in a two hundred fifty mile radius of where you live?"

Our first reaction was, "Why us, Lord? Someone, anyone else, but not us!" Yet, in our souls, we were already committed.

Living over two hundred miles apart, how would we have the time? Would we have the money for extensive travel? How would our husbands react to the news? What would our friends think?

Through the years our husbands had tolerated our searching. Their first reaction to this new "trip" was, "Well, what are you going to do,

---

[8] The following has been excerpted from *You – The Living Truth!* by Libby Steinmetz and Effie Gay Given and is reprinted by permission of Libby Steinmetz.

stand on street corners and hand out pamphlets?" Now we would be in the public eye and might be a source of embarrassment to these men of responsible positions.

We discovered our friends' reactions were similar. Many of them had labeled us as slightly kooky, but this new step was a real shocker to them and their responses were a downer for us. One man asked, "What are you going to do, try to save the world?" And we lightly answered, "Yes, we're going to try to!"

It became a busy time for us as we brought together thoughts and ideas for a program that would be acceptable to the women of all churches. All of our work sessions began with the prayer that the ideas for the program would go perfectly in the Divine creative flow. Spending hours listening over and over to the Seven Step tapes, re-writing, re-wording, adding personal experiences that would help others in their understanding.... We cried a lot and we laughed a lot.

Finally, with a sigh of relief, we completed and mailed the tape of our presentation that Jim had requested. Then came days of nervously waiting for his reaction, which was, "It's all right, but not the way I would have done it." We had hoped it was all right, so we didn't ask how he would have done it!

It was time to start contacting the church women's groups. We were scared! Neither of us had ever spoken in public before.

Kentucky, the ancient and bloody Indian hunting ground, the "dark state," was our territory.

November of 1977 was filled with our inner urgency to "be about the Father's works." In putting first things first, we found the free time for hundreds of miles of travel. There were good days – and some discouraging times. We learned a lot in the first two months of travel, driving over 700 miles and contacting 18 churches. From all of this, we were accepted to give two programs the following year.

We would stop outside each town for prayer contact with the angel of the town, asking it to prepare the way for us and to use and intensify our Light for the good of that area.

Our first "baby" came in Frankfort, the state capital, on November 3, 1977. We had planned to take the first freeway exit into the capital, missed the turn and every other turn. Suddenly we were placed in front of a church with its door ajar. It was the South Frankfort Presbyterian Church, an old and prestigious church where the governor worshipped.

As we walked down the church hallway, the minister's study door was open. He waved and invited us in. Reverend John Hunt, a sincere, warm and aware man read the Seven Step prayer card and questioned us on each step. He inquired how we happened to come to that church and laughed with us at our "getting lost." He said, "Yes, I know. I have experienced this, too!" Forty-five minutes later he asked, "How soon can you come here to give the program?" Calling the ladies' group chairwoman, he set March 20, 1978 – the first day of spring – for our program.

March finally came. After the program, the chairwoman, a former Nazi war prisoner, came to us and said, "You gave my soul three things that I had been searching for." This comment alone made all our efforts worthwhile.

We were beginning to get a picture of the inner church structure and guidelines of various denominations. In some, the minister is all-powerful. In others, women's groups have more freedom of program choice. But all are responsible to the minister.

This required that we be interviewed by each minister. Usually, the opening question was, "What type of program is this?" Followed by, "Do you speak in tongues?" Our reply was that it was a simple sharing and explanation of the Effective Prayer and that we hadn't had the experience of speaking in tongues. We could almost hear their sighs of relief.

We discovered that there is a great need and hunger in ministers to share their concerns and problems. This touched us deeply.

The program was set up mainly for women's groups. We could sense when we entered a home what the attitude would be. Some of the chairwomen were courteous and enthusiastic. Others said, "I don't think this is for *my* ladies." Often the Divine softened that attitude. Other times the barrier wasn't penetrated, and we left with heavy hearts.

Nineteen seventy-eight was a good year. Contacts were easier. Ministers were showing a growing interest in world events and were talking about the need for prayer in all situations.

We felt ready to go into Lexington, Kentucky's second largest city. We got "lost" again! We saw an elderly lady raking leaves in her yard and stopped to ask directions. Would you believe that she was the chairwoman of a large Christian Church ladies' group? Only the Divine could arrange something like that! This dear little lady set it up for us to give the Seven Step program at the annual combined church ladies' group meeting at the new, large Tates Creek Christian Church. As Daniel Boone said, "I've never been lost, only confused a few times!" We were learning that you are never really lost. There is Divine direction in all things if you just relax and stay in the flow and attune to the little signs along the way.

Reverend Walden opened our part of the program by having the group sing, "Alleluia." How magnificent those one hundred voices sounded...and how our hearts sang! After the program concluded, several ladies remarked, "We could have listened to you all night." Isn't it wonderful how people love to hear Truth?

We remember one lady standing quietly aside, waiting so that she could share a private moment with us. Taking our hands, she said, "My daughter died two weeks ago. You have helped me."

We left with the words of the "leaf lady" ringing in our ears, "I'm glad I was in the yard raking leaves that day!"

In Ohio, an invitation came from the large Shawnee United Methodist Church in Lima. A friend who had heard the program talked with the minister about the program. It being the middle of winter, she was concerned whether many people would come. We assured her that those who were supposed to be there, would be.

One of those who drove in the snow from Toledo, one hundred miles away, was a friend who came to share her experience with the Effective Prayer. Her daughter, a young nurse, was being treated for a malignant thyroid condition. She hadn't been told that others were praying for her, but sensed it anyway, telling her mother, "Your friends must be praying for me because their thoughts of love and warmth are filling me." The daughter surprised the doctors with her rapid improvement and the speed with which she was able to return to work. This personal sharing touched everyone and wove all together in love.

The summer of 1979 found us back in Kentucky. We had yet to visit the state's largest city, Louisville, and now was the time. The closer we drove into the city, the harder it rained. We finally pulled out of heavy traffic to get our bearings. A few blocks away, we spotted church spires – a welcome sight that looked mighty inviting as the rain slacked off and the sky finally cleared. Our stop at the church proved fruitful. The assistant minister, Reverend Summerall, said that they had been planning to start a prayer group. He was impressed with our appearing at that time as an answer to their prayers for how to begin an active prayer group. The Christian education director hadn't planned to be in her office that day, "but something brought me in." She called the women's group chairwoman who came directly to the office. The four of us met with Reverend Summerall to discuss how they would go about starting a prayer group. We were invited to give the program for those ladies in two months.

Tapes were made of the talk, and we were delighted that they would be shared with others. Afterwards, many of the group said they would be using the Seven Steps in various problem areas. One planned to share them with her whole apartment complex of elderly people, and others were going to use them in family and health situations.

The women's group president wrote to "thank you for starting the whole series off for us." Five months later, she wrote that the group had grown and had a warm and loving feeling, and "You will be in our prayers."

Social contacts and word-of-mouth were instrumental in getting some of the programs. The circle on the map was extended, and our last program was the longest distance away.

A thoughtful friend opened her home to us, arranging for the program to be given to her Episcopal church friends in Glasgow, Kentucky, near the Tennessee border. Theirs was a close, friendly, and enthusiastic group. After the talk, the group asked to be led in prayer for members who were ill.

A few days later, one of the ladies wrote that she had experienced a healing after the program. She had a neck injury which the doctors said would cause pain for at least several weeks. The night we gave the Seven Steps program, the pain was gone and never recurred.

Nineteen eighty-one found our contacting women's church groups coming to a close. We thank you, God, for the blessing of being a part of the New Age of Love, for our families who stood with us, for all those who helped in this small beginning step of Thy way coming into being. May this help and encourage each of you in becoming the Living Church.

REMEMBRANCES:
HEALING CANCER

I'd like to start three years ago. I lost my husband. He was forty years old. To me it was a tragedy. In that first year I was without him, I was so low, so devastated, I just wanted to die. My children were all grown and on their own. And many times I had said, no one can feel this low without getting sick. I'm bound to develop cancer or some other kind of disease.

Six months later I did just that. I developed a rare skin cancer, malignant melanoma. The doctors told me there wasn't anything they could do for me. There were three operations. And there's no cure for it. You can't have radiation or chemotherapy. So, they gave me one to ten years to live and sent me home.

I saw them six months ago. In between, I started on these Seven Steps to Effective Prayer. Marvelous things started to happen. It was just fantastic. My cancer is gone. My doctor said, "Whatever you're doing, just keep doing it." And I'm thrilled by it. It's all such a miracle. And I thank God.

REMEMBRANCES:
HEALING A FRIEND

This is a story about a real good friend of mine – John, a young black man who has been a student of mine for quite a few years now. John comes from a broken home. He has a lot of grief and this type of thing. I didn't realize this for years. I had taught the man how to kick and punch, but I didn't teach him about his spiritual side.

John came to me one day and said, "I'm dying. What am I going to do?" This had a real impact on me. This is when Debby, who sang the song earlier tonight, told me about the Light Center – this is around a year-and-a-half or two years ago. I got John and we came up here to see Jim. Jim spent some time with us. Now, I do appreciate this. He spent some time with us on an afternoon when he didn't know us. We called and said, "Here we come."

He told John what to do. The doctors had given John six months to live. He had sickle cell anemia. At the time period we came up here, he had four months to go. We started doing the Light prayer. Jim told him to release this energy from his body, to search back in and release all of this negative energy from childhood and to radiate the Light daily. There were about six of us there that day. We started praying for him morning and night.

In two months, what Jim said would happen happened. He went

back to the doctor and they said, "We must have made a mistake. You don't have sickle cell anemia any more." It works. And I thank you.

REMEMBRANCES:
BREAKTHROUGH

Several weeks before I went to North Carolina for the first time, I had a dream about a man who lived in the mountains, worked with colored lights, and had the same energy as Jesus. His energy was really holy.

Then, my friend called at 10:30 one night and I thought, "Who is calling me at this hour of the night?" She was calling to tell me that Jim had said we could come and visit. On May 18, 1972 – a Thursday – we arrived at 10:30 p.m. Jim was waiting for us.

Jim did a workshop in October of 1972. Bill Asher and I arranged it. It was in Norfolk, Virginia. Jim was shaking in his shoes. There were 25 people. Jim was nervous speaking in front of others. It was at an Episcopal retreat center.

I lived in the house from the summer of 1981 to the fall of 1982. I processed a lot of inner stuff. There were a lot of ups and downs. I did a lot of crying. I thought I was the worst person around.

I had a crisis from January to February of 1982. I didn't feel I belonged on the planet. I wanted to cease to exist. Jim called me into his office one day. He asked me, "What are you going to do?" I said I didn't know. I went up into the dome and thought about suicide. When I came downstairs, Jim said to me, "Committing suicide in the dome is not the way to go."

The next morning, a friend of mine called Jim to say I was really in trouble. Jim agreed. Jim walked up to the dome and came over to me and said, "You are really beautiful" and walked out.

I guess I broke through. On February 3, 1982, I had a knowing that, "I'm all that is." It had been raining continuously for two days. I said to myself, "I don't like this rain." And it stopped right like this [snaps her fingers].

Jim was in Asheville at that moment and realized that someone had broken through because the sun had suddenly shone through when it wasn't supposed to.

When I got the call from Betty Robertson that Jim had passed away, I felt no sense of loss. I could see his face in the mirror.

Everybody at the memorial service was asking, "Why did you go?" But, he was right there.

Several months later he came to me and held me and held me and held me.

REMEMBRANCES:
LIVING AN ENLIGHTENED LIFE IN THE WORLD

I was living in Virginia Beach around 1971 or 1972 when a friend told me, "You've got to meet Jim Goure." Four of us got into a VW and went to Black Mountain.

Jim and a woman did psychic surgery on me on my twenty-fourth birthday. While they worked on me, I had to recall the karmic patterns that had caused my physical condition and then release those patterns. Jim took energies out of my feet and transmuted them. My spine, which had been crooked, was no longer crooked. X-rays have confirmed that the curvature is no longer there.

On another occasion, I became quiet and, as Jim had suggested to us, listened for my mission. My inner self said, "Politics." I said, "No. It's dirty stuff." The answer that came back was, "That's why. More people of Light are needed in politics."

I used the Effective Prayer to guide me through other steps I took in life. I left Black Mountain and finished my undergraduate degree and then went on to get my PhD.

Jim offered people a prayer technique that gave people a way to be in the world and achieve enlightenment in their own time and way. My feeling was that Jim said, "Here's a way. Go use it."

It's easy to be enlightened when you're around other like-minded people and you get affirmation. It's harder to attain enlightenment if you're living in the world.

When I heard that he had passed away, I had a feeling that he was done with his mission. Dying would have been a choice he would have been aware of. I was sad at the loss but felt fortunate to know him as well as I did. I never feel separated from him. Jim is always there. I still hear his laughter, his comments on things.

One to five words to describe Jim? Enlightened. God-conscious. Way-shower. Jim was a very loving person. Loving in a very personal way – warm, loving, caring.

So many enlightened people estrange themselves from personal relationships in order to maintain their enlightenment. Jim didn't do that. He had needs and vulnerabilities and he cared for people.

He showed us how to live an enlightened life in the world.

This individual is a political science professor at Montana State University and former chair of the university's political science department. In 2005, she was appointed by Montana's governor as head of the Montana Human Rights Commission.

REMEMBRANCES:
GENEROSITY AND SPONTANEITY

He was a tremendous catalyst. He changed my life. I became a composer, recorded seven albums, and traveled all over the country performing my music. I don't know if this would have happened without Jim telling me, "You are Divine and everything you need is within."

The first recording I did was hard – singing the same number again and again and working with the musicians. It was frustrating. But he came in one night for a recording, and that was soothing.

He was always full of surprises. He always appeared when you least expected it. I was traveling with Jim and Diana on one of his speaking engagements when we pulled off at a restaurant. I wondered why we had done this when he brought out champagne and cake to celebrate my birthday. I hadn't told him it was my birthday, but somehow he knew.

He was very generous and spontaneous. When my son was fifteen years old, I took him to Columbia-Presbyterian Hospital in New York to have his scoliosis treated. While we were there, Jim came to New York just for the day. We prayed together for my son. Afterwards, he took me to the Rainbow Room in Rockefeller Center for dinner. That was such a generous gesture. My son, who is now forty-one years old, is fine.

I left Jim at one point because I felt too dependent on him. That exit sign in the Light Center was glowing, "It's time." I told him, "I need to go," and he said, "You're right."

I tried describing Jim and what he had to say to a priest, who told me, "It sounds like John the Baptist, crying to the church and the people to wake up." I always liked that analogy.

REMEMBRANCES:
MY MISSION IS TO HELP PEOPLE

I had been praying for help. I wouldn't have gone to a church. I was turned off to that.

It was 1977 and I was living in New Orleans with a woman who, on a trip to North Carolina, had met Liza and lu at a place where she was performing. They took her to the Light Center and she had a reading with Jim. She called me in the middle of the night to tell me, "He says it's a matter of life and death that you come up here." I thought she was crazy. Besides which, I didn't have the money to go up there.

But, I was working at a bar at the time and a patron gave me a $100 tip. I took that as a sign and bought a plane ticket to fly from New Orleans to Asheville.

I ended up living at the house for a couple of months. It was a magical time. It was like Jim was a magnet, drawing people. We used to have these wonderful Christmases and Thanksgivings at the house. People felt they had found family.

But, there were 13 of us in the house. It was too much. People were tuning into each other psychically, which added to the intensity.
Jim pushed himself. He would not eat or sleep. One day I heard

cursing outside the window. Jim was chewing out Diana for something that was not her fault. Whatever it was had occurred because Jim himself had not taken care of it. It was winter and it was icy around the house. Jim was taking bags to the car. He was on his way to the airport for a speaking event.

The lasting message that I received from Jim is that God is everywhere. It's not just in one person. I don't know whether I feel as omnipotent as we all felt at the time. But, I wouldn't be working at the Cancer Society and doing what I'm doing if it were not for Jim. My mission is to help people.

REMEMBRANCES:
RUNNING A DAY CARE CENTER WITH LIGHT

The same summer I took a Jim Goure workshop at Elizabethtown College, another workshop leader told me I was to start a day care center. I certainly was not interested in doing that! I knew *nothing* about preschool centers and I *enjoyed* my job teaching accounting. The Divine was not about to accept my "forget it" attitude.

The Wee Love Childcare Center opened on March 6th, 1978 with two part-time students. We now [1998] have between 110 to 120 students and a staff of between 33 to 38. As we became aware of needs, we expanded our programs. To the original preschool program we have added an after-school program, summer camp, a kindergarten, infants (as young as six weeks), toddlers, dance classes, and an additional music program.

On Monday mornings at 9:30, a few of the staff meet for meditation and prayer for the Center and any other concerns brought to our attention. All board of directors meetings, staff meetings, and other meetings start with a time of silence.

We have had many extremely difficult challenges, but we learned quickly. We learned to put situations in the Light and never doubt that the Divine was in charge. We learned it was the only way to survive.

Mary Jane, a teacher, asked her kindergarten class to describe the Center, using the letters in Wee Love's name. The youngsters immediately came up with L for light and C for centering!

I believe that because most of the staff and board have accepted the mission I was given, we are making a difference in the lives of the center's children and parents.

© United Research, Inc.

REMEMBRANCES:
SCRYING

Once, long ago, I had a vast vision. I really did. So, I rushed to the Sage on the Hill who was, as usual, playing a spiritual game of solitaire. And I announced breathlessly with all the modest holiness one must muster when revealing personal Vast Visions, "Lo," I said lowly, "I come to you because I am the receiver of holy information revealed to me – lu – only by God. Hark, He sent His angel Harold to tell me I must scry." (As you can tell, I tried to keep this conversation as close to holyspeak as I could.) (Also, "scrying" is the oldest known word – a Greek word – for crystal gazing.) Anyway, I then fell to my knees in reverential awe, awaiting my Leader's amazed, astonished, overwhelmed approval and blessing.

He didn't look up. He just put a black jack on a red queen and said, "Great – go scry."

I did. I didn't speak to him for a week. But I did.

REMEMBRANCES:
HE LIVED WHAT
HE BELIEVED

I met Jim in May of 1972. I was part of an A.R.E. study group in the Chesapeake/Portsmouth, Virginia area. My husband was a minister at a nearby Methodist church.

We wrote Jim, asking if we could visit him. He sent a note welcoming us and telling us to put ourselves in a bubble of Light. It probably was a good thing that we had that extra protection because we arrived in the evening having driven on a road with no median stripes and such dense fog that you couldn't see anything.

I saw him as the most God-like being I had ever met. He lived what he believed.

I could not believe he would not take money, that there was no charge.

I look back on that time of life as the most wonderful thing that ever happened to me. I am so much better a person because of him.

REMEMBRANCES:
HE HAD THE FULL PACKAGE

I was living in Berkeley, California, when I first met Jim. There was a flyer saying that he would be speaking in Sacramento. Four of us went to see him. The talk was held in the classroom of an elementary school.

Everything he said clicked. Prior to hearing Jim I had studied raja yoga. Where that left off, Jim started.

Jim did a mini-reading for each one of us attending his talk. He told each person what was holding them back. After he told me what was holding me back, he apologized if he had embarrassed me. But, I told him, no, I wasn't embarrassed.

After the talk, I started to use the Seven Steps. Jim came back to California two years later with Diana. During that second visit, he told me, "I don't know what you're doing, but you have so much more Light than the first time I saw you."

Some time later, my life went out of control and I wrote or called Jim. He called back at 7:45 one morning, just before I was to leave for work, and said, "Why don't you come to the Light Center and work for me?" I told him I would get back to him.

I had a dream soon afterwards in which I was working for Jim on a submarine that was going into very deep waters. Jim wore a backpack with a smiling baby on it. I interpreted the dream as a sign that I should go to the Light Center as Jim had suggested.

Jim picked me up at the airport in Asheville. My luggage had been temporarily lost by the airline, so I had nothing but the clothes on my back. On the way from the airport to the Light Center, there alternately was sunshine, rain, sleet, and snow. In the car, he asked about my abilities and after I answered, he said, "You should do prayer readings," which I later did.

He told me Lavida would take care of me – and then he and Diana left on a trip, probably one of the international prayer missions.

Nobody said anything to me about what I was supposed to do. I had no idea what the function of the place was. When I asked Jim what I should do, he simply told me, "Come from the Creator."

The only thing he required of me was that I attend the prayer sessions at 9 a.m., 12 noon, 5 p.m., and 9 p.m. He also asked me to attend meetings of the Expansion Committee.

At one point, Jim asked me, "How does it feel to live without having the expectations of others? How does it feel to just be?"

Those times at the Light Center were my happiest moments. Jim provided an environment in which I could flourish. I learned about prayer and meditation and how they can totally transform you. I went from being totally un-centered and shut down – I had been hurt – to having a mission of helping others. I totally changed.

I had so much fun there. I liked his open-door approach and the fact that anyone could share their experiences or talents at Light Center events. He loved creativity. If you were a musician, you could perform at the Light Center. There were no committees to decide who could play. Jim said that whatever your gift was, it would be amplified at the Light Center.

Sometimes he lost his temper with us because we were not getting it. We were kind of silly. We didn't know that what we were getting was so valuable.

If you walked past the open door of his office, sometimes he would say, "Come in." Then, he would either give you hell or give you help. On one of these visits, he confirmed that, yes, "It's time for you to be the Christ."

He told me to read everything in the Bible that was a quote of Jesus. He got me in touch with Christian mystic spirituality.

Later, at an event he was leading, he handed me the microphone and said, "Here's the start of your public speaking career." I was taken aback, but did it. And I have been speaking publicly ever since.

I was a challenge for Jim. Everything he said I challenged. I would say, "I'm going to put it to the test."

One time some of us bought him a gallon of moonshine from Tennessee. He was mowing the lawn on his birthday when we presented it to him, and he said, "Bless you." That evening, when several of us were drinking the moonshine, I remembered that Jim had said you could change food and drink by praying over it, just like Jesus did. This moonshine was strong. It was 100 proof. I said a prayer over my glass of it. I did not get drunk. It was like water. Steve, who was part of our group, got drunk after not even two glasses. He couldn't believe it wasn't affecting me. Jim simply nodded at me. From this experience, I realized the power of Jim's teaching.

He told us, "I'm training you guys as teams of people who will go from Light Center to Light Center. It's no longer one person who will be doing this."

He handed me an atlas and told me to identify all the cities in the U.S. with a population of at least 200,000. He wanted a van of us to go and pray for each of these cities.

When Jim was away from the Light Center and people would ask for someone who did what Jim did, they were sent to me and I did prayer readings for them, just as he had told me I would on that first day when he picked me up from the airport.

He wanted me to head the Light Center in California. For eleven years, I was attached to having my own Light Center. Then my life fell apart. When this happens, I go back to the Seven Steps.

Once at the breakfast table there were only three of us – Jim, Gail, and me. Jim started talking about Machu Picchu. He broke down crying when he talked of the dedication of the Daughters of God. They had committed to staying on Earth until they had blessed everyone.

The night Jim died, I started seeing thigles and crystals. At the time, I didn't know what the thigles were. Other friends of mine in Berkeley who had met Jim only once had dreams the night he died of him downloading teachings. He has also come to me in my dreams and given me teachings.

If there is a gauge for spiritual teachers, Jim is it. He was the best. He gave us the nuts and bolts, showed you could lead a normal life and still be spiritual, showed you could still have a personality, and showed us how to lead a life of service. He had the full package.

We weren't ready for half the stuff he gave us. He emphasized the Oneness. He told us that we were complete and whole within ourselves and that we did not need to go outside of self for wholeness. He wanted people to evolve beyond what he taught.

He totally changed my life. He gave me a keen awareness and world-view. He helped me to trust my intuition more. He catapulted my growth. Everything he taught me I've integrated into my life.

REMEMBRANCES:
HIS LOVE SHONE ON ALL

J im could slam a door in apparent anger that would rattle windows in a two-mile radius. He could *appear* to be the meanest man in half a dozen states, sending even grown men away in tears. There were times he manifested cold indifference towards a person.

But he *was* the kindest, gentlest, most loving person one ever met. Jim made himself available at all times to perfect strangers as well as to those he had known for years.

Jim knew what each soul needed for unfoldment and growth and he used many techniques to help a person let go of the teacher's hand and look to the Divine within. He appeared in many guises, trying always to direct attention to the Creator within.

There was no ego motivation in anything he did. Jim drew as little attention to himself as possible while accomplishing his mission. Heaven help anyone foolhardy enough to suggest that Jim was a guru, a master, or someone special. He would take that person's head off at the ankles and remind him that "the guru is within."

The sun of his love shone on the unlovable as well as the lovable. Through it all – the door slamming, the warm conversations by the fireplace, the animated discussions, and the stony silences - Jim was the epitome of Divine Love.

REMEMBRANCES:
HONESTY AND SACRIFICE

I was living in Boston, but I was impelled to come down here. I kept having dreams that were telling me, "Got to go to North Carolina." A book on North Carolina would jump off the shelf.

I had visited the Goure house previously, and the woman who was recording Jim's lectures got my name out of a register at the house and she sent me tapes out of the blue. One of the tapes talked about something I was very interested in – hydrogen energy.

I attended a lecture of Jim's at Sanibel Island, Florida. Jim looked over at me as I walked by and stuck out his hand; he said, "It's been a long time." He was referring to our lifetime together when Jesus was alive.

Jim was zealously honest. Almost painfully so.

The New Age mantra is, "Heal me. Heal me." But Jim told us, "Heal all."

Jim once said there would be twelve Light Centers – a couple in the U.S. and the rest on other continents. Then, the prayer trips became a substitute for that, although Jim did not say this.

Jim said that a geodesic dome was life enhancing.

He thought he was it. He had a pretty big ego. Jim said to me once, "The world won't know what I did until people can go back in time, to the akashic records."

What do I want the biography of Jim to say? Show how much Jim truly loved the planet and the people on it. It was like Jim sacrificed his family for that. The nuclear family is very important during the developmental time for children and the Goure children did not get this. The Light Center was built so we would not have to sacrifice family again.

REMEMBRANCES:
THE MAGIC OF IT ALL

I met Jim when I was in my thirties or early forties when he came to Cincinnati to speak. He talked about the simple Light prayer. I remember his friendliness and his wonderful wife, Diana.

I have mother issues. I wanted to heal my past with my mother. Jim gave me the Light prayer and told me to call my mother by her first name when I prayed for her. It took me almost two years. I was quite estranged. Then I went back to see my mother. So much had changed. I was so much more in a loving presence.

My husband, Bob, also spent time with Jim. Bob remembers Jim as amusing and fun. Bob, like Jim, was also a Navy man. Bob is not always comfortable with spiritual stuff. But Jim was relaxed with himself and with spiritual subjects and made it easy for Bob. Jim was just a regular guy.

Jim certainly had a lot of patience with me. Thanks to him, I went from believing something to knowing something.

I get the Light prayer out in my books and classes. It's a simple, profound way to work.

When I think of Jim, I think of clarity and depth. I think of the truth that he carried. The stillness. From stillness wisdom arises. His wisdom and his energy always felt fresh.

Words that come to mind when I think about Jim: Simplicity. Loving. No extra frills. (I have been around plenty of teachers who have frills. And many of them also have power, sex, and money issues.) Clear breath of fresh air with a big smile attached. Clear eyes. Enthusiasm to keep on going. The magic of all of it all.

PART III: TEACHINGS

TEACHINGS

Over the sixteen years that he taught, Jim Goure gave hundreds of lectures. Many of those lectures were recorded. In preparing this biography of Jim, recordings or transcripts of over one hundred fifty of Jim's lectures were reviewed.

By the early 1980s, Jim had developed a core message around which he organized most of his lectures. What follows is a synthesized version of those teachings that has been organized thematically. Everything in this section that is not in italics is a quote from Jim. In some instances, the quotes have been lightly edited to enhance readability.

The order in which these teachings are presented is:

You
Mission
Joy
Love
Healing
The Christ
Superconsciousness
The Creative Force
Staying Grounded
Practice
Problems
Why? Why? Why?

More Questions
The Old Ways
The Mind
Insights
Identity
Male and Female
Family
Creating Peace
Terrorism
The Military
Worlds To Pray For
Be Divine
Code of Life
The Creator in Daily Life
Citizens of Light
The Cosmic Dilemma and the Cosmic Answer
A New World
Prayers

YOU

Everything is Divine. There is no place that God is not. In the deepest part of the ocean, "I Am there," sayeth the Lord.

So, you can never, ever move out of the heart of God. You can never, ever move out of that which God is, one hundred percent Divine Love.

You were made in the image and likeness of the Divine. That image and likeness of the Divine is the Light within us or the God-self within us or the Christ-self within us.

Being made in the image and likeness of the Divine means that you are Divine. You are It. All that is is within You. All that is is You. There is nothing else that exists in the whole universe except You. You are the Divine. Accepting this is all that is required.

It is said in Revelation that people will see God face to face. What that really means is that we see each other as Divine. It will be our joy to see each person as Divine.

Looking into your face, I see the Divine. It is magnificent to look into your eyes and see the Divine. In seeing the uniqueness of you, I feel total awe for the Divine. This particular planet is *so* beautiful. It has you on it. When I see people, I want to cry…it is God that I see.

As Jesus said in the Sermon on the Mount, you are the Light of the world. You are the Creator in action. You are God. You are not limited. You are totally free. Your capabilities are unlimited.

Because you are Divine, wherever you are is holy ground. Don't make any one thing or place greater than anything else. There is only God. Accept reality.

You don't need a guru. You don't need a master. You are a master as soon as you make up your mind that Light is the way for you. The greatest master, the Creator, is within you. You are the Creator-in-action. You are the one who gives Divine Love. You are fantastic.
Let go of your desires. The Divine is Life itself. Be Divine and create Life in everyone and everything. Create more Love. Create more Light. So that everyone becomes more Love and more Light.

Become pure Light. Be Divine. Every moment of your existence, declare Divinity throughout your beingness. Declare your reality.

A PRAYER OF ONENESS WITH THE DIVINE

I am One. And this One is all that exists. I am in all things. I am in all that is. I create more Love in everyone. I speak deep within, "I love you." I create Life, abundant Life, in everyone and everything. Thank you. Amen.

MISSION

In each one of us, there is an inner urge that says, "There is more." There is a knowing that we are here for more than just food, water, and shelter, that we're not on Earth just to have fun and games, that we're here for much more than satisfying our personalities.

The ultimate goal of each one of us is to know our Divine mission and do it. And to merge into the Creator. To become totally one with the Creator.

And yet, we do not strive for this. We do not make this a goal at all. Our goals are two cars in the garage. Two houses. Two boats. Two trips around the world. Two affairs. Four children.

Once we attain these things, we say, "What else is there? I've had two affairs, two marriages, four kids. What else is there?"

And the what else is there is to find this Divine mission and get on with accomplishing it.

"You Are the Light of the World"

Jesus gave all of us a mission when he said, in the Sermon on the Mount, "Ye are the Light of the world." This means *we have a Divine mission to love this planet.* To fill it full of Divine Love. That means filling everyone and everything full of Divine Love, so much Love that everyone and everything will change.

We're here to transform Earth into a new type of planet where everyone is aware that God is amongst us. That God is in each and every person. A planet where we see God in one another. Where we see God in planet Earth. Where we see God in all things. This begins the process of bringing Revelation into reality: Jesus said in the Book of Revelation that we *will* have a new Heaven and a new Earth.

In this process of transforming Earth, you have something special, something unique to do on planet Earth. You have your own, special Divine mission.

The Joy of Fulfilling Your Mission

How would you feel if you actually knew your Divine mission and began to accomplish it? You would feel complete joy because you would know without any question that you had made contact with God and that God was with you. This feeling that God is with us is the ultimate joy for all of us. There is no greater joy than to know your own Divine mission - and do it. The joy of accomplishing that mission is absolutely fantastic.

When you are aware of your particular mission and you do it, nothing can hold you back. You become unflappable, unshakable, unstoppable. You know it is a *Divine* mission and *nothing* can alter that Divine mission. No matter what people do against you, nothing can alter that Divine mission. *You will accomplish it because it is from the Divine.*

The joy of accomplishing your mission is absolutely fantastic because you know God is with you. And if God is with you, nothing can interfere. That gives you a sense of tremendous joy.

Oneness with the Creator

Without any question in my mind, Jesus was the most joyful man who ever existed because he was one with the Creator. He said, "The Creator and I are one." His name for the Creator was "the Father," and he said of his relationship with the Creator or Father, "The Father and I are one, yet the Father doeth the works."

And then he said, "The things I do, you can do and greater." Simply meaning: each one of us can attain to that oneness. Each one of us can have that Divine mission and not only have it clearly defined but accomplish it. There is nothing limited in the Creator. The Creator can accomplish anything.

So, you, too, can say, "I and the Creator are one, yet the Creator doeth the works." You, too, can say, "I and the Creator are one. The Creator in me loves. I program this Creator in me to love you and you and you." It's not you, not the personality, not the human identity doing the works. The Creator and *only* the Creator doeth the works.

Getting Started

How can you accomplish this mission of being the Light of the world? Change your concept of yourself and your concept of your world. Your concept of your world is that it consists of your house and a little area around it. You may be afraid to make this world big because you may have a fear that the world will get you if you make it big. But, if you truly love yourself, there can be no fear. There is *nothing* to fear. There is only that that is Divine Love.

When you get your Divine mission, do not be afraid to step out and begin. It has nothing to do with age – how young or how old you are - or with your physical condition – how perfect or imperfect it is. Look at Scott Hamilton, the Olympic medalist: he was in a hospital for years and yet he was still able to win a gold medal. The same ability to overcome obstacles and achieve missions is true of all of us. There is no end to our capability once we get into the idea that we *can* do this.

Techniques

We have been given, "Pray without ceasing." We haven't known how to. But there is This which is constantly awake within us. If Jesus said, "The kingdom of heaven is within" and "The Father is within," then the Creator is there. The Creator doesn't sleep. The Creator can give Love from within ourselves while we are asleep – if we learn how to program the Creator within ourselves.

Program that this Love from the Creator, deep within ourselves, flows in and around the whole planet, so that everyone is touched by this fulfilling Love. If all of us do this, then there will be a tremendous flow, an unlimited supply of Love for everyone. And we will feel fulfilled because we will be fulfilling our Divine mission.

Excuses

We tend to let go of this responsibility of being the Light of the world because we think, "Who, me? Me, do that?! I'm just little ol' me. I'm nothing." But, in thinking that, you are putting yourself down. You are not "little ol' me." You are the Christ. And how big is the Christ? It is as big as you dare to be.

Everyone has gotten into something other than being the Light of the world. "My bailiwick is little old me. I can't handle this Light of the world business. I have marriage problems. I have children problems. I don't have enough money. Let me clean up my own act and then maybe I'll take on being the Light of the world."

Or you may be thinking, "I have so many things to do. I don't have time for being the Light of the world." You *do* have time. You have ample time. God never said, "You've got to close your eyes to pray." So, while you're driving or walking from one classroom to another or sweeping the floor or any other activity that can be controlled by a very small part of your brain, the rest of you can be into the act of giving Love and fulfilling the need of every person.

You must accept responsibility for planet Earth. When you do so, your own particular world will straighten out.

Dedication

The example of Olympic athletes is relevant for each one of us. Olympic athletes attain their gold medals through dedication. They achieve their medals through total effort: eight hours a day of practice and the rest of their time spent on mental and emotional efforts towards accomplishing their goal. How many of you spend a minimum of eight hours a day towards attaining your Divine mission?

How many of you really have that dedication - the dedication of your life - eight hours a day, or ten, or the total desire within you for the life of God?

Healing the Nations

In the Book of Revelation, it says that the leaves of the Tree of Life are for the healing of the nations. This Tree of Life is you. You *can* take on nations and heal them as a part of your own Divine mission. That means loving everyone and everything. The power of Love is not limited by space.

In doing your mission of being the Light of the world, you will be altered: you will *know* rather than merely *believe*. Everyone who practices loving the planet begins to know things intuitively about the universe. Your joy will be to know things about other people, about the planet, and about the creation that come directly from the Divine. You will know that there is more than just the extra-senses, you will know that there is something that goes beyond the beyond.

You can know everything. You can do anything. There is nothing to limit you. The power of love cannot be stopped.

Accept Your Mission

Accept the fact that planet Earth is your mission. Everyone has planet Earth as their mission. The more we practice being the Light of the world and praying for planet Earth, the more we'll have freedom for planet Earth and the people on it.

Every person – every one of the billions on Earth – is calling out to be loved. Our whole purpose is to create more Love than there was in the beginning. Our whole purpose is to make this a planet of Light.

You are significant. You have a significant job. That's the way it is. Let's get on with it.

TECHNIQUES FOR GETTING YOUR DIVINE MISSION

How do we find out what our Divine mission is? The Divine reveals all. The how-to is, every day say, "The Divine in me reveals my mission" or "The Creator within reveals my Divine mission to me." It will be revealed. It will come to you. It has to! The Creator does not reject anyone.

Don't prejudge your Divine mission. Let it come loud and clear to you from deep within yourself. Earth is just one of your missions.

And don't be surprised at your Divine mission. Learning how to love a cockroach may be the first thing that comes to you as a Divine mission, because once you learn how to love, truly love, Divinely love *anything*, then you can move on to some fantastic things.

If you don't get an answer right away, don't give up. Don't say, "God doesn't love me or I would have gotten my answer by now." Don't have a guilt trip.

Declare with your whole being, "I *do* accomplish my Divine mission. I *am* accomplishing my Divine mission throughout this day and every day." Whether you consciously know what your Divine mission is or not, recognize that the Creator is within you and in having this Creator within you, you are affecting everything.

JOY

A lot of us experience happiness. But happiness is of a short-term duration. It's like a sine wave or like riding a roller coaster: we reach a high, we go to a low, reach another high, go to a low. We are always seeking things that will stimulate us and make us happy. We seek a mate to love us, and that is where most of the hurts occur. When we are capable of letting go of the need for love from another and find that love within ourselves, then we have joy.

So, what are you going for? Happiness? That's nothing. Happiness is not enduring. On a scale of one to ten, happiness is right close to a one. Joy, on the other hand, is out to the zillion mark.

What brings joy? What is joy? The only way we can experience joy is to be aware that we have a distinct Divine mission and that we must be about doing that Divine mission. How would you feel if you actually knew your Divine mission and began to accomplish it? You would feel complete joy because you would know, without any doubt, that you had made contact with God and that God was with you. This is the ultimate joy for all of us.

When you are aware of your particular mission and are doing it, then nothing can shake you. You know it is a Divine mission and nothing can alter that Divine mission. No matter what people do against you, nothing can alter that Divine mission. That gives you tremendous joy.

LOVE

Two thousand years ago, Jesus gave us the commandment to love our neighbors, to love ourselves, and to love God. In the interim, the killing rate has gone up.

Because of this, when I first started lecturing, I didn't feel we really understood what love was all about, and for me to say anything about it after the millions and millions of words about love that had been produced since those commandments came out, and still there's no love, I just didn't think it was appropriate for me to talk about love.

So, I've talked mostly about Light. And Light is easy to understand. It's either light or it's dark. We'd all rather have light. And using Light works. It's been easily demonstrated.

But Jesus came to me and said, "You've got to talk about love." I didn't like that. But, when he speaks, I salute. So, here's my attempt at it.

Learning To Love Ourselves

Jesus gave us the commandments of love: the first was to love God with your whole being. The second was to love your neighbor. And the third was to love yourself.

In looking into the souls of some eighteen thousand people who have come to our house and to the Light Center, all of their problems narrow down to wanting to be loved, wanting to love someone, and knowing there is a God - but not knowing how to love.

In discussions with people and seeing their souls and hearing of their problems, I see that hardly anyone has loved themselves. We focus on our mistakes - and everyone makes mistakes. We focus on those mistakes and declare, "I'm not as good as I ought to be." Everyone can say that. We say it all the time. We negate the idea that we should love ourselves by pointing out negatives about ourselves to ourselves. In doing so, we create chemicals in our bodies that are detrimental. Ulcers, cancer, and the like come from depreciation of self and from a belief that, "There's nothing here to love."

We keep plowing into our consciousness, "I don't love me. I'm really terrible." And the unconscious says, "You're terrible." Everybody picks up on it and subconsciously starts thinking, "Gee, you're a lousy person. I don't want to have anything to do with you."

But, if you can go around saying, "I see Divine Love in you and *I* am full of Divine Love," you will be loved by everyone, because the whole world loves a lover. People automatically pick up on this kind of energy. It's something they sense.

If we analyze the words of Jesus – "the Kingdom of Heaven is within" – we come to understand that if the Kingdom of Heaven is within, then God is within. If the Kingdom of Heaven is within, the Divine must be present within you. Therefore, if you are thinking a negative thought about yourself, if you are condemning yourself, you are literally condemning the Divine. You are condemning this Light that God has put within us, this Love that God has put within us.

So, this is the biggie: to learn to love ourselves. We must first learn to love ourselves, because in loving ourselves we automatically love everyone. No one is separate from us.

Once we begin to love ourselves, the frequencies, the vibrations coming from us change in a fantastic way. Our physical body responds instantly to these new vibrations. Our mental body instantly responds. Our energy body instantly responds.

Human Love

We tend to seek love from another. But, in seeking love from another, we automatically make them a god, and God has said, "I will have no other gods before me."

We strive with all our might to be acceptable to others. But the easiest way to be accepted is to love yourself. However, we don't do this. What we really do is look for one person – a soul mate – someone who can really love us. If we can find someone who really loves us, then we feel like we have it made. We go out of our way to find that particular one. But, human love will fail and we will always be disappointed in seeking love outside of self.

And so, we continue to be hurt. Our heart is hurt. "He doesn't love me anymore." Or, "My children don't love me. I've given them everything and look at them. They're doing this and that." Or, "The world's all wrong. *I'm* alright, but the world's all wrong."

Why would you look to any person for any kind of love? Why? When you do so, you are asking that person to be a god, to give you a little bit of love, to touch you. That is not where it's at.

After running into the wall a few times, we remember that Jesus said to love God, to love our neighbor, and to love ourselves. Not asking for love from anyone or anything. Just giving love to everyone and everything.

Misunderstanding Love

We have a misunderstanding of love. Love is so misunderstood I don't think it even should be called love. We have all types of love: "brotherly love," "mating love," "motherly love," "fatherly love." I don't know that any of that is true love. Our love – mother love, father love, mating love – is one of, "I'll give you love if you give more than I give you." It's an exchange – "I need love and damn it why don't you give it to me." We are asking for an exchange from one person to another. We have been calling it love, but I don't think it's love at all. It's more a case of, "You rub my back and I'll rub your back." That is not necessarily love.

What happens when we fall in love? We are near the same vibration level and we relate to that vibration level. Rather than calling it "love," it might be better to call it an "exchange of energy" from one to another. The energy exchange program that we've got going on between people is more of a demand – "Give me more than I give you." "Give me energy" is really what we're asking for, rather than love. It's a strange thing.

Since there is a hang-up about wanting to get love from someone, I would like to state, you can know that I love you. So, you don't have to go looking anymore. You're free now. Totally free. You can get on with loving yourself, get on with being who you want to be. For this is the urge within you. This is really what you want.

The present things we call love just aren't. What we are truly seeking is a different type of love. It's not mating love. It's not mother love. It's not brotherly love. It is more than all of these.

You don't need to look outside of self for a lover. You have the greatest lover within you: the Divine. The Divine within you gives one hundred percent – and never asks for love, just gives and gives and gives.

With Divine Love, there is a feeling of not being alone anymore. We begin to love everyone. This Divine Love is not a personal love. It is not mother love or father love or mating love or human love. This is the Divine Love from within us. That type of love has no strings attached to it. That type of love gives constantly, no matter how seemingly evil other people can be. That type of love gives even to the criminals. What are the criminals really seeking? They are seeking love. That type of love gives to the nations. That type of love gives to the continents.

A New Understanding of God and of Love

It may be that we need to understand what love is. In understanding what love is, maybe we can get into loving.

I'd like to point our attention to a new love that needs to be in our consciousness, and that is the love of God and the love from God.

Our problem is that we don't know God. We don't know where God is or who God is. The Bible tells us that God is love. But when I watch most people praying, I see them praying to a mythological image of God: a father-like image with a long white beard who sits on a throne and has a scepter in one hand (to bless you if you've been good) and a sword in the other (to punish you if you've been bad). This is our concept of God.

But, the Divine is not that which is individualized. The Bible says that God is Light, and Light is everywhere equally present. God is Love, and Love is everywhere equally present. God is Spirit. And God is Truth. Spirit is everywhere equally present. And Truth, evidently, must be everywhere equally present. So, how can you individualize Divine Love? How can you individualize Divine Light or Truth or Spirit?

Jesus said, "The kingdom of heaven is within." Therefore, Light, Love, Spirit, and Truth are within each of us. So, it's not an image outside of ourselves that we need to pray to. It is the image of Light, the image of Love that we need to get into.

Jesus also said, "Worship in Spirit and in Truth." Meaning: we must *become* Spirit, Truth, Light, and Love. We must become one with the Creator's Spirit, Truth, Light, and Love in order to really worship God. The only place that Spirit, Truth, Light, and Love are is in the Creator. And that Creator is within you.

Since Spirit, Truth, Light, and Love are within – not outside of self, in the sense of an individualized being – then these aspects of the Divine are universally present. Once we come in contact with Spirit and Truth, we begin to see Spirit and Truth in everyone and everything in the universe.

Becoming one with this Spirit and Truth, as Jesus did, you begin to recognize Spirit and Truth in everyone else. That is the beginning of worshipping God.

Physicists see the universe as energy. They see people as being energy. As energy, nothing is separate from anything else. That means you are not separate from anything else. Nor is anyone separate from you.

Now, then, the idea that God is Light, universally present, begins to make sense. Since we are not separate, this Light that is within us is within everyone. We are equally present with everyone and they with us.

If all of creation is inseparable energy, then by loving yourself, you love all of creation.

<u>Changing Our Consciousness</u>

Most of us when we look at someone are caught up with trying to find something wrong with them. We are past masters at judging. We look to find something wrong that we have overcome. Then we feel we're pretty hot stuff.

But if you are sending out a vibration of negative thoughts and emotions to someone, they are picking up on it and sending it back to you. A hundredfold of negative comes back to you.

On the other hand, if you give out love – because you love yourself – and if Divine Love is radiating, is pouring out of you, then everyone picks up on it because they are not separate from you. And in picking up on the fact that you love yourself, they return love to you because everyone loves a lover. When you love yourself, everyone else is giving to you a hundredfold more than you are to yourself. You begin to feel great.

Therefore, let us seek this Divine Love that is within us. That kind of love doesn't see the negative aspects of other people. You are no longer into judging when you're full of Love. It's impossible to judge then. Divine Love holds steadily to the consciousness of, "You *are* Divine Love and that Divine Love means you are super-fantastic."

So, the objective is to Divinely love, to Divinely love one hundred percent, rather than seeking love.

Once the search for love outside of self is altered to the search for Divine Love within, then the hurts from others begin to cease. We let them be. Jesus, in the Book of Revelation, said, "Let the unjust be unjust. Let the filthy be filthy. Let the righteous be righteous. And let the holy be holy." Simply meaning: let people be. Don't try to change them. Don't alter the way they want to exist. Let them be.

If someone does something mean to you, just let them be. You don't have to correct them. You don't have to feel hurt. Just say silently, "I know the Love is in you. I know the Divine Love is in you." Don't get caught at the level of the unjust or the filthy. Rise above that.

In letting them be, there is an instant flow of love towards them. A higher type of love. A type of love that says, "I give my love and I don't expect anything in return. I give one hundred percent, and I expect nothing in return for it."

If we can get into that consciousness, then obviously we have not made anyone a god. Obviously we cannot get hurt because we are not asking for ought from anyone. We are free, in the sense of not asking.

Once we come in contact with this Divine Love that is available to us from within, we automatically change. It is super-fantastic what happens to everyone who gets in touch with this consciousness, with this Love. The people who tune into this Love - before they attained Divine Love - were just average, normal people. Some of them were real bounders, negative types. But once the consciousness changed, every one of them went out into the world to see what they could do to help their fellow man. They instantly began to love. They instantly began to help fulfill their fellow man's need. And the greatest need in everyone is this feeling, "You are loved, truly loved." Once you know you are truly loved, then you are free. Totally free.

Loving All

Jesus said to his disciples – and to everyone - "Love one another as I have loved you." Love one another with a high type of love. A type of love that gives and doesn't ask anything in return.

Jesus also said, "I and my Father are one, yet *the Father* doeth the works." We, too, can say, "I and my Father are one." In our merging or oneness with the Father, there is total love. Unlimited love. It's a high type of love that asks naught from anyone. There is only giving. In the oneness with the Father, we are into merging this Love into everyone. Once we become one with this Father or Love, once we become one with That, we constantly and consistently give love one hundred percent of the time to everyone and everything.

You are not limited then. You are totally free.

Being the Light of the World

In addition to saying that the Kingdom of Heaven is within, Jesus said, "Ye are gods" and "Ye are the Light of the world." Being the Light of the world, you are the source of love for everything on planet Earth. Since there is no place that God is not, it is our requirement to give love to everything, because in doing so we are giving it to God.

You know deep within that the greatest need in everyone and everything is to hear, silently, "I love you." And once *you* begin loving, the love comes back a hundredfold, more than you can imagine.

Having this Divine Love energy sent to others heals them. If you look into the inner causes of illness, you will find that all of them are related to a lack of love and a misunderstanding of who we really are. When people learn to love themselves, they're healthy.

To fulfill the commandment of loving God, see and know the Spirit of God in everyone and everything. Divine Light, Love, Truth, and Spirit are equally present everywhere. There is no place that this Light, Love, Spirit, and Truth are not. Declare it so.

The stars in the sky tell us how. They have been there for eons of time. They have been there for one reason: to tell you how to give Divine Love. Every star is like our sun – giving and giving and giving forevermore. A star does not hold back, ever. Give Love yourself until you *become* Divine Love, nothing but Divine Love. The whole idea is to give one hundred percent of the time. Then we will never need love from another person ever again.

There is a tendency to give love from the front only. But we should give Love like our Sun gives light – in all directions, on all dimensions, at all times. You want the living water of Life, Divine Love. You need Divine Love. But, the need is to *give*. So, start giving, giving, giving.

Altering our concepts of self and starting to give of this Love will alter man, the planet, and the universe. The ability to change anyone and everything without having to speak is within you. You have enough Love to fill everything on planet Earth. The power of Love is not limited by space or time. In Love there is no space and time.

It is not enough to bring the living waters of Life to our country or to give it to our families and allies. *All* need this living water. Every nation and all people need to know that Divine Love is there and that they are being filled with Divine Love. Once they feel fulfilled, they, too, begin to accomplish the greater works.

All of creation is crying out for what you have to give. All of creation is crying out for this Divine Love that you are. Everyone on Earth is calling out to be loved. Everyone is calling out for you to give of this Love that you are. The greatest need in everyone is the feeling, "I am loved. Truly loved."

Divine Love

Divine Love just is something that is not describable at the present time. But, to give you a feel for it...[there was a long pause; then, with an exhalation, filled with emotion, Jim continued], well, I don't know that I can. But a little feel for it is an absolute, overpowering urge to meet the need of the creation. Total creation. That's a beginning. And only a beginning. To fill the need throughout the creation. And that's in everything and everyone. And the creation has some needs. You will know you have attained when you have fulfilled. Until then, you cry out to do that. Maybe that will give you a feel for Divine Love.

When one begins to fulfill the need of the people on the planet and the things in the planet and on the planet, we have just touched the hem of Divine Love. That is the first awakening in us of Love. Everything else is an exchange of energy.

Becoming one with the Divine Love within, you begin to recognize it in everyone else. That is the beginning of worship.

In loving Divinely, you will be altered. Your consciousness will be altered to that of the Divine. Once you become one with Divine Love, you consistently give Love to others one hundred percent of the time. And when you do this, you are not limited in any way. You are totally free. By radiating out Divine Love, the flow of Love in you will increase and increase – so much so that your problems will be dissolved. In loving, you will be fulfilled. You will feel that you are accomplishing your Divine mission.

How much power do you have? You have an infinite supply. You can surround every person, every thing, the whole planet in Light and Love – so much so that everyone *has* to change.

Do this and there will be awakenings all over the planet. The flow of Light and Love is the greatest magnet there is. And that's the way it is. It's fantastic.

If every person is so surrounded by the Light and Love you give that they have to eat, sleep, and drink Light and Love, they obviously will change.

Become so dedicated that the Divine in you takes over and you can truly say, "The Creator and I are One, but it is the Creator within that doeth everything."

God is Love. You are God. You are Divine Love. This Divine Love that you are is the greatest love there is. It is God in action.
You are loved Divinely and you are loved perfectly. Cease asking for love. Seek the only true, enduring love – the Love from the Creator within you. Be the giver of Divine Love.

TECHNIQUES FOR DIVINELY LOVING

One of the techniques for loving ourselves that helps so many is to begin saying, "Thank you, God, for me." By saying that, you give honor to God for this *tremendous* being that you truly are. "Thank you, God, for me. Thank you, God, for being in me. Thank you, God, for Thee."

Love yourself. Every day, look in the mirror and say, "I'm a really great person!" It may take you a month or two to believe it. But one day you might be able to say, "I am the Light of the world" – because you *know* it. Your impact then is fantastic. And you don't have to tell a soul about it. You just *do it*.

How do you get into the Divine love? Practice. How did you learn to walk? Practice. Simply practice saying silently to yourself, every time you see or think of another person, "I know the Love is in you."

By practicing, you begin to alter yourself. You begin to feel loved. You begin to feel fulfilled. You begin to *know* that you are truly loved. You know that life is perfect and that it is getting better. The effect on the planet is instantaneous.

"I see Divine Love in you. I *know* Divine Love is in you." If you maintain that consciousness throughout your day, you are worshipping God on a continuous basis. Because God is constantly present, we must worship consistently and constantly. Not just for an hour on Sunday.

Through prayer you can touch everyone and everything with the love that you are.
Silently say to another, "I love you." Say this over and over and over again. Keep saying it day after day. From all of this Divine Love that is available to us, people automatically will change. If you hold to the Divine Love in your loved ones – saying silently, "I know the Divine Love is in you" – they will change.

"I love you." Deep within, you know that the greatest need is for everyone and everything to be hearing that, silently. Every soul should be hearing, "I love you." They should be feeling that love coming from the Divine. The more troubled the person, the more they need your love.

As you walk through a crowd of people, say, "I see Divine love in you and you and you. I *know* Divine love is in you and you and you." When you see an automobile or a political candidate or an entertainer or a member of your family, say, "I see Divine Love in you."

Another how-to: "Divine Love flows from me to everyone and everything."

In doing this, everyone will be changed. Everyone will be awakened to the Divine Love that is within them. They will begin to be satisfied.

By carrying this consciousness throughout your day, you are worshipping God on a continuous basis.

Before you go to sleep, declare that the Creator in you creates Divine Love and Light throughout our country, throughout all the nations, and for all the peoples of the world, so that they are filled with Divine Love and Light.

PRAYERS FOR DIVINELY LOVING

Thank you, God, for Thy Love, for Thy Divine Love flowing forth from Thy center in me to everyone and everything. Thank you, God, for Thy Divine Love being present in everyone and everything. Thank you, God, for the flow of Thy Divine Love from everyone and everything to everyone and everything. Thank you, God, for making it so. Amen.

I am One. And this Oneness is all that exists. I am in all things. I am in all that is. I create more Love in everyone. I speak, deep within, "I love you." I create Life. Abundant Life. In everyone and everything.

I create Divine Love throughout my being. The Creator in me creates Divine Love in everyone around me, filling their beings with Divine Love. The Creator within me creates Divine Love throughout this area that I am in, so that everyone and everything is changed by

Divine Love. The Creator within me creates Divine Love throughout our country, so that everyone and everything is changed into following Divine Love. The Creator in me creates Divine Love throughout this planet – in, through, and around the planet – so that everything and everyone is blessed by Divine Love. The Creator in me creates a radiance of Divine Love and Light, flowing out, to everyone, to everything, to our sun and all the other planets, so that the planets and the sun are touched and blessed by this Divine Love. This radiance of Divine Love and Divine Light continues to flow out into the universe, touching all the other stars and all the other planets and all that is. This radiance of Divine Love and Light, from all the stars and all the planets, flows back into Earth and into our world and into everyone's heart and mind and soul, so that everyone's hearts and minds and souls are touched by this universal Love and Light. And now, in the stillness, we declare Divine Love and Light flowing throughout our whole beings and changing us. And as we go forth into the world, this Divine Love and Light is in us, around us, and through us so we are always in the right place at the right time, doing and saying the right thing for the good of all. Thank you, God, for making it so. Amen.

HEALING

The absolute, paramount need is to heal our fellow man. When we heal our fellow man, he changes from creating negativity to creating Light. Once he begins to create Light, things start changing all over the planet.

The term *healing* most often brings to mind the idea of curing a person of some condition. Your mother has arthritis, your child has a cold or the flu, your friend has a broken arm, and so forth. These are all effects. We believe we should heal the effect when what is really needed is to heal the cause. And the primary cause of every illness, every discomfort, every physical and mental disability, is a lack of loving self, a misunderstanding of love, or a misunderstanding of who we are. It's that simple.

Every one of you should be healers. But first we must understand how to heal ourselves.

Perfection

The reason we do not love ourselves is that we think in terms of imperfection. We know we are imperfect physically: our eyes, ears, feet, back, muscles, and bones bring that to our attention. In addition, we have hurts in our hearts and hurts in our minds. Because our minds, bodies, and hearts have all been hurt, we have little respect for ourselves. We believe that if we were perfect, we would not have these hurts. We feel there must be something wrong or we would not have these problems.

Jesus gave us the key to the perfection we seek. He said, "Be ye perfect..." – and we end his sentence there, not recognizing that the full statement is, "Be ye perfect *as your Father in heaven is perfect*." Where is the Father in Heaven? Jesus said the Father in Heaven is within. If the Father in Heaven is within you, then obviously that which is the Father in you is perfect.

Well, where has the perfection been? Why hasn't He been doing his job? Why isn't He here, functioning through me? Why isn't He filling me full of love? What have I done to Him that He is not expressing through me? Or, maybe you are at the stage of, What have I done to Her? Either way, we are putting down God. We are saying, "It is even worse than I thought. God does not love me. I am not worthy." And we become ill.

Death

Another problem is that all mankind has been programmed to see death as inevitable. If the body is going to die anyway, we may as well let it have its aches and pains. The idea that sickness and death are not only possible but probable is in our cells. This programming must be changed.

The Body

Some of us reject our bodies because of what religions have taught us. Both Eastern and Western religions seem to teach that the body is not important, that the Divinity is located outside of our physical selves. We reject our bodies. We think they are mere shells surrounding the Kingdom of Heaven within. We say we acknowledge our Divinity, but we tend to think of it as a nonphysical part of ourselves.

This is totally false. Every cell of your body is Divine. Every bone and muscle and organ and gene is Divine. Every molecule in your body is Divine, and you are not separate in any way from that Divinity.

Yet, we still say, "I have a pain," or "I have a problem," and we feel that these things cannot be Divine. You think that if all of your being were Divine you could not experience pain. But the reason there is pain is because you have rejected your body. How can you change this rejection when for millions of years humans have declared that their bodies must be cast aside?

Loving Yourself

The first thing to do is to declare, many times every day, "I love me. I love the total me." If you had done this every day of your life from the moment you were born, you would be a different being. But, start now. Say, "I love me. I love the total me" one hundred times a day. Then, declare, over and over, "I am fantastic. I am a really great person." You can say that to yourself, but if anyone asks you how you feel, just reply, "Fantastic!" – no matter how sick you are. The body complies with whatever you declare. All these years you've been rejecting your body. Now you need to work hard to change both your conscious and subconscious thoughts.

The next step is to love every part of your body: "I love my eyes. I love my brain. I love my feet. I love my stomach. I love my liver." Do this every day and you will be renewed and revitalized. You are loving yourself Divinely and the power of this can change every part of you.

Because other people judge you and see you as being imperfect, you need to protect yourself. Do this by naming every part of your body and putting it in a bubble of Light. Don't ever get caught in anyone else's concept of you. Be proud of your particular body. There is no other body like it in the whole world! You are Divine, and so you can easily say, "I am loving me because I am loving the Divine. I love the Divine in every part of me."

When Jesus said, "The things I do you can do and greater," he meant that you are the Christ. Did he mean just a part of you, separate from all other parts of you? That is impossible.

But, if we manage to say, "I am the Christ," we immediately feel sheepish and mumble, "Well, the Christ is in everyone, so it must be in me – somewhere." We limit ourselves so much by doing this.

Therefore, the next step in healing is to name every organ the Christ: "My heart is Christ. My kidneys are Christ. My lungs are Christ." It is essential that you put each organ in a bubble of Light and name it "Christ."

"I am Light in operation. I am fantastic." This way of healing oneself is most important.
Whatever we think of ourselves – "I am dying day by day" or "I am Light. I am Divine" - radiates out and affects everyone. So, by healing yourself, you heal others.

<u>Healing Others</u>

To consciously heal others, the techniques are the same. Suppose your brother's name is Tom. You declare, "Tom's heart is Divine. Tom's eyes are Divine. Tom's circulation is Divine." Name every part of Tom's body. Place it in a bubble of Light and call it Divine or Christ. Healing another person in this way demands total respect for that person – and absolutely no judgments. You *must* change the way you see things, knowing that God and only God is present in everyone and everything.

All of us tend to see incorrectly. When we look at ourselves or anyone else, we instantly think male or female. That is false. You are not male or female. You are Divine. Other people you see are Divine.

Every time you see a person, say, "I see the Divine." The Book of Revelation describes this as seeing God face to face. You may think you don't have time to do this, but it takes just a second to say, "I see Light." There are three thousand six hundred seconds in an hour, so you certainly have ample time. If you follow this practice, you will realize that if other people are Light, you must be Light, too.

Don't judge other people – for any reason – especially other people of Light. Make no judgments about another person under any circumstances, for any reason. Do not make a judgment that they are sick. Do not make a judgment that there is something wrong with them mentally or emotionally. See the Creator in action in every way and love the Creator in everyone.

Jesus healed people by increasing the Creator in each person. And where there was the Creator, there was no ill health. It is time for us to increase the Creator in the people of planet Earth. How do we increase the Creator? We declare with the *authority* within us, "The Creator in you fills you with Love. The Creator in you fills you with Light." Do this not just for individuals but for cities, nations, continents, and the entire world."

Healing means loving the Creator in everyone and everything. Start with something you dislike most or something giving you a big problem. State, "The Creator is present." Hold to it. Do not let anything interfere with this. Then move on: heal and love everything and everyone.

We have finally come to this: there is only One. When you love the Creator in all, you have begun to love God.

Healing Anonymously

Every one of us should be a healer. But we need to be healers of a different type. The objective of this new type of healer is never to be recognized as a healer. There is a tendency to in all of us to want to lay on hands and cause the healing to take place. That is no longer valid. That is saying, "Look at me."

What *is* valid is to recognize the Creator. Let us suppose someone you know named Mary has greater capabilities than she is exhibiting and you want to help. Just hold to the Creator in Mary: "The Creator in Mary fills her with Light and Love. The Creator in Mary directs her life. The Creator in Mary fulfills the capabilities in her." Declare and hold to this. In doing so, you're not holding to what *you* think the fulfillment of Mary's capabilities should be. You're holding to the fact that the *Creator* will manifest Mary's capabilities in a way that is perfect for Mary.

This approach, where we pray anonymously and silently, eliminates the possibility that anyone might be aware that we've done anything.

The ultimate healing we can perform for others is to anonymously pray, "The Divine in you heals you." If we try to take credit for the healing, that has ego attached to it. But if you come from the Divine within yourself, it doesn't matter how you heal.

Healing the Planet

Don't stop at healing people. Heal the planet. Wherever you step, change it. Where you stand is holy ground. Heal the stones. The earth itself is Christ.

You are the Light of the world. Therefore, it is your mission to heal the planet. The negatives that mankind have created go deeply into Earth. Wherever you go, wherever you step, you need to change the earth itself. Know that where you stand is holy ground, all the way through the planet. The Earth is a living being. It is Christ. Because you are creating from the Divine, you will recognize Earth's Divinity and see how this living being has been hurt. By being filled with Light, Earth will become so vibrant, so full of life, that it will be a joy to all. By having Earth filled with Light, there will be joy everywhere. Our planet will be so fantastic that it will automatically heal everyone.

Loving God

Living from the Christ consciousness means seeing the Christ in everyone and everything. The Bible tells us that the way to the Father is through the Son. In other words, the way to the Creator is through the Christ.

Jesus gave us three commandments: love God, love your neighbor, and love yourself. These commandments have yet to be followed. We need to understand them, and as a result of this understanding, we can begin the process of healing – not only of self but of all people.

There is actually only one commandment: love God. There is nothing else – there is only God.

Love God. Love God in self. Love God in others. Then, you're just beginning to worship God. See the Creator in others. Don't see others in terms of their personalities or even their names. Just see them as the Creator: "The Creator in you creates Light and Love."

As citizens of Light, you have a tremendous responsibility to begin this loving of the Creator. It is easy to love the Creator because that is not you. As you continue to love the Creator, there is an expansion until you *are* loving you. That is the secret.

Now that you're loving God in yourself, you begin to look at other people and you no longer see people – you see the Creator, you see God. At that very moment, you have begun to learn to love God. You've begun to worship God when you see and declare the Creator in others.

Speak to the Creator in them: "The Creator is in you. There is only the Creator present in you." By doing this, the Creator in you begins to expand and all aspects of you change because you love the Creator.

Then you realize that if it's true for people, it's true for the cockroach, it's true for your car, it's true for the gasoline you put in your car.

If you are judging, "This is no good; this other thing is really good; the Christ dimension is hot stuff," then you're creating problems. Change your perspective. See only the Creator. How many truly love the Creator in the prisons? How many truly love the Creator in the economy of the world? As long as we're seeing plus/minus, our eyes are out of focus. But, when we see the Creator in all things, we are seeing reality.

Healing All

The Divine is you. You are the doer. You are the Creator.

The Divine is conscious of everyone on planet Earth. So, being conscious of everyone, you don't stop at healing yourself and those you love. You heal all things by creating Light. Healing is not a matter of changing negatives to positives – that involves judging.

Healing is creating Light – by being Light, by seeing Light, by expanding Light.

The Divine is unlimited. The Divine in you is unlimited. See only the Divine in yourself, in your loved ones, in every other person, in everything and throughout the planet. This is the greatest healing that anyone can do.

Scientific Research into the Causes of Healing

One of the things I wish the scientific community would get involved with is the investigation of healing. How does it really take place? In my opinion healing is strictly a scientific thing. It is not a miracle. It is an energy flow that scientists could research.

The way healing occurs is that we are One. There is no separation. There is an energy flow that is Oneness. There is an energy flow from your mind to your liver or your kidney or your knee.

That type of energy flow can awaken energy in another person. That is the healing that takes place. As you experiment with healing others, you will find that it is like healing yourself.

So, I think there is a matter of an energy flow that can be investigated. The energy flow is what awakens the energy in the other person. That is the healing that takes place.

A lot of scientific research should be done in this area so we can wipe out the idea that healing is a miracle. It's a way of life for all of us to get into.

Once we become aware that healing is purely scientific, that it is an energy exchange that is causing the healing, it is a matter of making energy devices that have this energy in the home.

After 2,000 years, I don't think anyone should be sick on planet Earth. Jesus said, "The things I do you can do and greater." We should have long ago done a lot of research into healing and come up with an electronic device that can create a healing energy and have it available everywhere – in everyone's home, office, automobile, in the mall, everywhere. Can you imagine walking through a mall and getting healed? I know it sounds far out, but to me it's as natural as breathing – that we should have this energy available to us. I know it can be done.

It can and should be done. It would allow us to evolve, to get on with greater things, and not be stuck at the level of having to heal anymore. So that we, man, can get on with Life, with Joy, with creativity – with finding creative ways of helping man elevate himself.

TECHNIQUES FOR HEALING

Set aside a week for saying a million times a day, "The Creator in me fills me with Light and Love." If it becomes rote, so what? See what happens in a week.

"That which is real in me is the Creator. That which is perfect in me is the Creator. I and the Creator are one." Declare this fact a million times a day until it becomes a reality. "The Creator in me fills my body, my mind, my heart and my soul with Light and Love." Try it. It's that simple. You do not have to say long prayers. You do not have to have any prayer. Just say it over and over again. So what if it becomes rote? The Creator likes rote.

THE CHRIST

In several ways, Jesus told us that the Christ is in everyone, that the Christ principle is within each one of us. He said, "Ye are gods" and "The things I do you can do and greater." He also said to his disciples at the Last Supper, "This is my meat, eat me. This is my blood, drink me." When he said that, he was telling them in every way possible, "*You* are the Christ. Don't look to me. If you have eaten me and you have drunk me, obviously you are the Christ."

Perhaps the term "Christ-being" troubles you. If so, use "superconscious-being." It's a new day of superconscious beings doing superconscious, super-being types of work. So, use the word "superconscious" if the word "Christ" bothers you - and it does bother some people. But working with and being superconscious literally is the Christ in action.

Scientists say we have three states of consciousness: the conscious, the unconscious, and the super-conscious. We tend to say the super-conscious is way beyond our capability, our ken. So, we put it off. But it is a part of us. It is not separate.

We think, someday, maybe, the super-conscious will take over. But, we *can* be superconscious. Anyone can do it because it has happened to ones who are dummies, in a sense. If it can happen to one of them, it can happen to you, through practice.

There is no end to the greater works that can be done, once we let go of our ego, *totally,* and think like a Christed being. The Christ consciousness or superconsciousness can change the possibility of war or alter the likelihood of an economic depression.

Every moment of one's existence, one should think, "How would a Christ do this? How would a Christ think about this? How would a Christ handle this situation? How would a Christ bring about this new heaven and new Earth?"

Begin to image the real you. Put it in writing. There is no end to the capability of the Christ Light within you. Dare to be big.

What we are aiming for is the awakening and strengthening of this Christ principle through activity and thought, through thinking like a Christed being and acting like a Christed being, so that all will be changed, so that all will be awakened to their own Christed self, without having to rely on a particular being or master who does the works.

The world is becoming unified in its thought, and unified thought, particularly unified Christ-principle thought, is stronger than guns and tanks. If we surround everyone with so much Light and Love that they have to be changed, we can do this with nations. Where there is Light, where there are unified Christ-principle thoughts, the darkness *has* to change direction.

So now, after two thousand years of hearing what Jesus said, "The things I do you can do and greater," we should be doing these greater things.

The thing to do is start. If you wait until you are perfect or until you think you are perfect, you will never start.

Can you work toward a goal without knowing everything about it? Yes. You worked toward the goal of knowing algebra when you learned 2+2=4. Eventually, you got algebra. It comes. And the Christ consciousness will come as you practice. You will know your algebra. You will know your Christ. And that's the way it is.

Just as when you went to school and learned that 2+2=4, become the Christ through practice. The Christ consciousness and the way of the

Christ will become a part of your world. It will be a natural way. Do it constantly, twenty-four hours a day, through programming your Christ self to consistently manifest in you more and more.

Once we come to know the Christ consciousness and once we learn to overcome some of our own difficulties and to heal others, we begin to think we're pretty high in the pecking order of God's world. But there is no pecking order in the universe. There is no one being greater than another. If you are one with the Christ, then you are one with the Father, and in the Father no one is better than another. No person is better than another: if you are the Christ then everyone is the Christ. Everyone.

So you slip. That's OK. Don't get caught in a guilt trip. Keep on with this beingness that you are.

Once we say, "The Father doeth the works," we can never take credit. We can never, ever, take credit for anything that has been done. Because we know it is the Divine principle, the Father principle, the Creative Principle within us that accomplishes everything.

The main mission of each person, as I read what Jesus said in Revelation, is to bring about the new heaven and the new earth, combined as one. Imagine Heaven and Earth joined together. What is heaven really like? What is Earth really like? It is your inheritance, your right, to know everything in the whole universe. It is your right to know the Divine plan for planet Earth. It is your right to know the Divine plan for the sun and the solar system.

In knowing, then we have the responsibility and capability of altering things it and increasing the amount of Good. As co-creators with the Divine, we can increase the amount of Good. And that's the way it is. We're here to do just that. We're here to do the greater works.

SUPERCONSCIOUSNESS

W hen you read all the bibles of the various religions, you find that great beings have done significant things. Moses, Jesus, Krishna, Mohammed, and Buddha did some tremendous things. The things these great beings have realized and done are available to us when we finally let the Divine or the superconscious take over. These great gurus who have walked this planet have said, "The things I do you can do and greater." Well, let's get on with these greater things.

Some Basics

When you study saints and masters, you find that a housewife became God-conscious and you find that a real bounder like St. Augustine did some really fantastic things as result of the Light. It doesn't make any difference what you have done in the past. It's what you do now that counts. What you have done has been forgiven by the Divine because the Divine is one hundred percent love. So release everything of the past right now.

Little miracles mean a lot. It's the little bitty things that say to you, "Boy, you've got it! You're one with It." When you see a little bitty thing, you think, "Maybe God loves me after all."

People who attain superconsciousness – people who have attained the state of truly loving themselves, of knowing who they are, and of knowing they have this infinite supply of Love and Light to give to everyone - are completely dedicated to the Divinity and are completely balanced male and female. Everyone who has gotten into this state has altered great numbers of people.

In the superconscious state, you no longer have to die to find heaven. It's right here. You can enjoy heaven right here. There is no place you are not.

Letting Go of Preconceptions

Break out of any preconditioning and get into the superconscious state.

You don't need a guru. You don't need a master. The great guru is within you. The greatest master, the Creator, is within you. You can know anything. You can do anything. *You* learn to be the master. *You* do not let something outside of you control you. You become One. You become that which gives G-O-O-D.

Let go of the idea that you need to be initiated into certain states of consciousness. All of that is for nothing. There are no initiations. There are no masters. There are no disciples. Those are man-created things. God is individualized in everyone. Not one better than another. Everyone is indeed Divine.

Your concept of God and your concept of God consciousness may be one of the big blocks to your attaining superconsciousness. You think God consciousness may be a bolt of lightning and "I see stars," that kind of thing. That may not be God consciousness at all. Let go of what you think God consciousness is. Let go of gurus. Let go of following. Let go. If you make God consciousness a god, you will lose it.

Practice and Knowing

Each of us should get into the superconscious state. You do that by learning how to love. In Divinely loving, you will be altered, and in being altered, you will know, rather than believe.

Your joy will be to know Divinely and to become a different person in your knowing. You will know that there is more, that there is more than just the extra senses, that there is something that goes beyond, something that goes beyond the beyond. You can know everything. It is your right, your inheritance, to know everything. It is your right to know the Divine plan for planet Earth, for the Sun, for our solar system. In knowing, then, you have the capability and the responsibility of altering it and of increasing the amount of Good. As co-creators with the Divine, we can increase the amount of Good there was originally. We are here to do just that.

We do that through practice, practice, practice. Practice in a different way than you have before: ask yourself, "How would the Divine do this?" Get into the Divinity consciousness. Practice by saying, "I create," knowing that that I is the Creator, not your ego or personality.

It is fantastic! The things you begin to affect from this superconscious state put you in an entirely different ball game. You get involved with people, places, planets. You definitely are involved with what is going on. You cannot be limited. There is nothing to limit you. You are changing things. You are altering the conditions of Earth, of people, of the whole universe. You have to realize that everything you do, every movement of your hand, affects the whole universe.

Once you become universally conscious, you allow the Creator to do everything because you don't want your ego or personality to cause a disturbance or create more burden.

Beyond Superconsciousness

Let us look into what is beyond God consciousness. There is something far beyond the consciousness of God. One of the things that is beyond is Being. Can you imagine what it would mean to say, "The Creator and I are one, but the Creator in me does the works"? That Oneness is so great that nothing else matters. Being one with the Creator is indescribable. Go for that ultimate joy, that feeling of Life itself.

It is time for new man to begin. It is time for God-man to begin. So, let us dedicate our lives to going beyond, to going for "The Creator and I are one," with the total knowing of its truth. Repeating "The Creator and I are one" will bring this knowing into reality. Practice, practice, practice is the way.

THE CREATIVE FORCE

Anyone can paint – artist-type painting - because everyone has this creative force within themselves. And it is time that we lock in to that creative force.

How do we do it? Begin to do creative things in your spare time. You have great amounts of spare time. Everyone does. There are special creative things you can do. You can create an energy vibration throughout your home. That is creativity in action. You can create a feeling of well-being in the people around you. It's like this man who played the sitar last night. I have never experienced such a healing power in music as there was last night. He said he had played in the greatest places on the planet, but he said, "Never have I played in a place like this [the Light Center]. It is the most powerful place on the planet."

This is just a building. You could plant it anywhere and it wouldn't be the same. What makes the difference? The difference is the use of this creative force. This creative energy. And this creative energy is constantly being enhanced because there are more prayers said here than anywhere else.

Prayer is an energy. It's a force. The first thing people say when they come here is, "There is a force. It feels good to be here." It's creative energy. It's power.

Well, why limit it to this place? The Creator is not limited to here.

The Creator is not limited anywhere.

So, you, with your creative energy, wherever you put your foot, can make this same creative energy present. Wherever you put your foot, the Creator is present.

You say, "I have too many problems. I want to clean up my own act before going out there and wherever I put my foot, saying, 'This is holy.'" The heck with your problems. Learn to be creative and your problems will dissolve. Because the Creator pervades your being. The Christ pervades your being.

STAYING GROUNDED

There is a tendency in us, as we become more creative, to believe that we are better than others. It is a very difficult trap that people get locked into: "Boy, I know the Truth and they don't. I have less of a responsibility of doing the small things of the world. I being such a great Light creator should not have to cook breakfast, lunch or dinner. I should not have to vacuum. That is far below what I think I can do." That is the biggest trap because that is an instant block. Instant. It is like putting a wall over you and it is like solid steel.

That's why Jesus washed the feet of the disciples. To let everyone know. That was considered the very lowest of jobs in those days. Only the very lowest servant had to wash the feet, and he put himself into that category to show that The Christ is in every job. And to do that job correctly you must know the Christ is there and you must become the servant. You must do these things as part of your existence. You are not better than.

No one is better than. Never has there been a being better than because everyone has the Creator within them.

We have a tendency to think, "I have only this mission to do, so I don't have to drive a car and I must have a chauffeur." Having a Divine mission doesn't mean that.

The carpet has to be vacuumed. If we do it with the Creator in operation, "The Creator is cleaning the carpet. The Creator is filling the carpet with Light and Love" – eventually, if we do it right, the carpet will be radiant and it will feel great to be in the presence of the carpet.

Think of the Divine mission Jesus had of bringing eternal life and going to the cross and yet washing the disciples' feet. This was one of the greatest lessons for all of man. He was saying to his disciples, "Don't think you're so damn hot. Obviously you're not, you're not even hearing what I'm saying." He was getting them into the consciousness of serving.

Obviously we must serve all of man. Obviously we must serve this planet with our whole being because Jesus gave us the mission of being the Light of the world.

PRACTICE

J ohn Denver was hired by ABC to be present at the Olympics – to interview the athletes and others – and to write a song about the Olympics. I like very much what he came up with. It was absolutely fantastic: "Go for the gold...and beyond." With his sensitivity, he had picked up on the true meaning of the Olympics. Just going for the gold is not enough. We have to go beyond.

An athlete attains the ultimate of nine years of dedicated effort, the gold medal. The next thing he knows there is nothing. These athletes have made getting a gold medal their mission and suddenly their mission is over. That seems to me to be a catastrophic situation, to have trained and to have dedicated so much of your time and effort and then end up with just a gold medal and a brief, shining moment in the media spotlight and then there is nothing else.

But John Denver gave these athletes something else – the gold *and beyond*. I like the idea of giving these champions a hope, a desire to find out what is beyond the gold medal.

The "beyond" is to find what you really want in life.

What applies to us is that these athletes attained their gold medal through dedication. They attained it through total effort – eight hours a day of practice and the rest of the time involved with emotional and mental conditioning towards achieving their goal.

How many of you spend a minimum of eight hours a day towards attaining your Divine mission? How many of you are dedicated to knowing your Divine mission and doing it? How many of you are dedicated to becoming totally one with the Creator?

We are the limitation. We have not set our goal as knowing and doing our Divine mission. We have not dedicated our lives to this that is the ultimate.

But, look at the Olympic athletes, these young people who have dedicated their lives to going to the Olympics and getting a gold medal. They *do* it, with all of their energy, sometimes under great duress. One man who won a gold medal had spent nine years in a hospital with a rare disease. It was his greatness that drove him on.

In every case of the Olympic champion, there is the desire to become number one. Desire, then, is one way: desire God and say the heck with everything else. Nothing else matters but That.

Consciousness of God, of the Creator, is attained though practice. Practice saying, "I create Love and Light. I am one with you. I am one with everything that is."

When you study the lives of great masters, you see that all of them went into a period of total prayer, of oneness with God. They all worked at it. Buddha sat underneath a tree until he reached enlightenment. Jesus went off for forty days until he had total oneness.

If we dedicate our lives – not to having two of everything, because this does not bring happiness – but to oneness with the Divine, it will happen. If we can dedicate our lives to that which is real, we shall know great joy.

This does not mean that you *can't* have two of everything. Jesus was a wealthy man, according to the Bible, and he traveled and did lots of things. He was so wealthy he had a treasurer and had to pay taxes in gold.

What all of this *does* mean is an internal dedication to finding our Divine missions and accomplishing those missions. It's worth everything to do this. It is life itself.

Let us dedicate our lives just as the athletes have dedicated their youth to winning a gold medal. Let's go beyond the gold medal. Let's go for, "The Creator and I are one." Repeating, "The Creator and I are one" will bring a total knowing of this reality. Practice, practice, practice this reality of Life.

Practice Oneness one hundred percent of the time. Not just eight hours. Can you practice God for eight hours and for the next sixteen practice being human? You need to practice Divinity one hundred percent of the time.

Practice, practice, practice. It's a matter of practice. That's how you be Divine.

PROBLEMS

We tend to get caught up in our personal problems. We tend to get caught up in the money problem. We tend to get caught up in the human relationship problem. We tend to get caught up in problems with our bodies. These are major problems we face. They are heavy upon us and we keep these problems in front of us.

You tend to let your problems control you. If you clean up one of your problems, immediately you're going to have another one. You may end up with five or six at the same time. Getting caught up in them, they get bigger and there are more of them - just to control you. Because once you lock into being a Light being, these problems and this personality know they're dead. They're gone. And they want to exist, to control you, so that you will keep them alive. The second you lock into who you really are, those problems die. Personality is gone. There is only the Christ manifesting.

Most people say they aren't ready for the mission of being the Light of the world. They've been sick. They've had operations. They say, "I'll take on that job when…." But, then, all we are accomplishing is focusing on our problems, and this keeps us from accomplishing our particular Divine missions.

If you analyze the money problem and the human relationship problem, it is simply a part of your past. In the now, you don't have a money problem. You are here in Light. And the Light is infinite. It has all capabilities.

If you look at everything you do in life, you see that its function is to please somebody. You try to do things perfectly to get a little bit of love or praise from someone. What we need to do is to work for and to satisfy the Creator within and only the Creator within.

If we can get into working for the Chairman of the Board, the Divine, then our lives will straighten out and we will affect those around us for the better.

Getting on with It

Once you begin to take on this mission of being the Light of the world – really take it on as one of your own missions – these little problems that seem so big will begin to dissolve. They will begin to fade away. Not only fade away, they will have been solved without your having done anything about them.

When you do these greater works that Jesus asked us to do, the Divine finds that you have become valuable. In becoming valuable, your time can't be wasted on little things. So, the little things are solved for you. They are moved out of the way so that you will have more time to do this greater work.

In giving out Divine Love, the flow of Love in you will increase and increase – so much that your problems will be dissolved.

The more you work at this, the more things around you begin to alter so that you're not occupied in the plus/minus world. If you get involved with this being the Light of the world, it will be fantastic for you.

You have a responsibility to clean up your act. Not just to wait until you are well in every way and then to accept responsibility for planet Earth. Do both simultaneously. Really work on cleaning up yourself. Because when you get yourself straightened out, the energy and vibration you put into planet Earth become more beautiful. It's super-fantastic: the whole of Earth is affected in a really great way.

TECHNIQUES FOR RELEASING PROBLEMS

The easiest way to address your problems is to say, "I release all of this to the Light right now. I turn these problems over to the Light. There is only Light here and there is only Light within me. I *know* where the Light is, and the Light takes care of all things. This Light within me has all capabilities."

See the Light in all of your problems. "I see Light in my financial situation. I see Light in my human relationships. I *know* there is Light in my loved ones who are giving me such a hard time. I know there is only Light in them. I know that Light is the way out of my problems. So, I'm going to turn over this problem to the Light. The Light is in my work. I am not involved with making money. I am not involved with this job. I am involved with the Creator accomplishing this mission. I am involved with Light."

Say a million times a day, "I am Light and only Light can be here. And that Light that is in me is in money, is in my relationships, is in my body."

You're not shirking your problem by turning it over to the Light. You are accepting responsibility in the correct way. Rather than personality fighting and trying to overcome the problem, you are letting that which is the ultimate – the Light that is within you - accomplish it for you. That Light will solve the problem for you. It will make it nothing but Light.

Practice, practice, practice a million times a day, "I am Light and only Light can be here."

WHY? WHY? WHY?

The most frequent question I get is, "Why?"

- "I've been praying and yet I got sick. Why?"
- "I've been coming here for years and I haven't changed. Why?"
- "I have listened to the great gurus. I've read all the books. I'm still the same. Why?"
- "Why would the Creator take someone's life? Why?"
- "Why am I on planet Earth? It seems hopeless. Everything is wrong. The world is all wrong. *I'm* all right – it's the world that's wrong. Why?"

The greatest answer to questions such as these was given by Jesus when he said, "Everything that happens is for the glory of God." *Everything* is for the glory of God.

When Jesus was confronted with the blind man – the man born blind – they asked him, "Why? Whose fault was it? Was it his parents' fault? Was it karma?" Jesus said, "None of the above. This – and everything that happens – is for the glory of God."

But we don't accept that. We believe, "I've been good and yet I got sick. Why?" The answer is: for the glory of God – although we don't see much glory in it at all.

So, when you think of the glory of God, think of the glory of yourself, of the glory of your beingness, of the glory of your becoming a new type of being. And give thanks to God for that happening. Give thanks to the God within, to that which You Are. Give thanks that you are indeed changing and that it indeed is a glory.

It may take years before the changes take place. During those years, there is travail, there are tears. But every experience is a glory – if we can see that.

You might get a flat tire and react, "If I were really spiritual, this would not have happened." But it may have saved your life. You see only a little bit of the time-space continuum. God sees the whole picture. He may have seen a big truck coming where you would have been that might have eliminated you from planet Earth.

We cannot make a judgment. Everything is for the glory of God. If we can get into that consciousness, then a knowing comes that God *is* in the universe, in everyone and everything. There is no place that God is not.

So, accept whatever happens as the glory of God, as the glory of yourself, as the enhancement of yourself. The glory of God is not limited. The more we become aware that happenings are for the glory of God, the more that we have Energy, the more that we have Life, the more that we have the ability to accomplish the things that Jesus did or greater.

World Tragedies

"Everything is for the glory of God" applies not only to things that happen in our lives but to events that occur on the world stage. People such as you who have been praying for the planet are affected by events such as the downing of the Korean airplane.[9] You have been trying to do something for the planet as a whole, whether through

---

[9] On September 1, 1983, Soviet fighter jets shot down Korean Airlines Flight 007, killing all 269 passengers and crew members, including a U.S. Congressman, Lawrence McDonald.

prayer or through another approach. Whatever it is that you have been involved with, there has been a desire to help man become better. And then something like this happens.

When something like the downing of the Korean jet happens, we have a tendency to want to withdraw and, in some cases, to say, "It's hopeless." We tend to go into a negative phase because the world is in a negative phase. The mass thought of the whole planet is impinging on each of us, and the mass thought is pretty negative at this point.

We need to look in a different way at the downing of the Korean airplane and the anger and the hurts and despair about the world condition and "What's the use?" consciousness. Let us replace that with: Out of this will be the glory of God. Not that the blindness of man is the glory of God. But out of this, man's eyes will open and there will be God. We must get into the consciousness that this is for the glory of God. Not that killing is for the glory of God. But, the wholeness of this thing is for the advancement of man.

Everything that happens is for the glory of God. It is hard for us to see that when so many people lose their lives. We can't say, "Is this God's will that all these people lost their lives?" God did not cause this incident. *Man* caused it.

The key is for us – not to add to the negative, the judging, or the hate – but to get into the consciousness that out of this is glory for God. It is an advancement for all of man. It is an awakening for man. Out of this, man will be increased in Light.

There are many good things that come out of something like this. The whole international situation is changed [snaps his fingers] just like this. All of it for the better. Because the world is saying, "We *must* become civilized. We *must* advance. We *must* stop killing. This is senseless."

Our holding to the Light – and not judging why or calling Russia whatever - is so important. We need to change our consciousness to: "Let's help all of man at this point in time." All of man is hurting over this incident. So, let us help him. What does he need? What does all of man need when he despairs, when he cries? He needs Light. He needs Love. Out of Light and Love comes Peace. When an understanding of Light and Love comes in, Peace is right there. There is a feeling of, "It wasn't lost and hopeless after all."

Every time something happens to you that seems to be negative, if you allow an understanding of Light and Love to enter, Peace is right there. There is a feeling that, "It wasn't hopeless after all. There is something good that has come out of it."

Out of everything, we can find something that is good. This incident obviously is the blindness of man. Man is not looking at the Light when he does something like this. At this point in the blindness of man, let us hold to: "This is for the glory of God."

Do not get caught in the negative aspects of incidents like this. Stay focused on the Light. Raise the consciousness of everyone to a knowing that this is for the glory of God and that Light is for the glory of God. Out of this Light, Peace will come to all of man. Killing will stop.

Everywhere on Earth there is an urge in man: "We *must* stop killing." It isn't stopping weapons. It's stopping killing. The consciousness of killing. And what causes people to kill? Lack of love. And you have an infinite supply of Love to give.

Just have complete, one hundred percent love – not only for the people who passed on but for Russia and for our country and for Korea and for all people on the planet.

Coming from the Creator consciousness and knowing that the Creator is in each person, all of man is raised up.

From that state of love and of being loved, man will do away with nuclear weapons, will do away with guns and knives and anything else that could be used to kill another. With people so filled with love, there would be no need for weapons.

It is paramount that we break out of our personalities and our desires and take on the mission of this planet, filling it with so much Love that killing begins to come down to nothing.

If everyone in this country were that way, I guarantee there would be peace. Simply because, when we wear blue jeans, the rest of the world wears blue jeans. When we get into this Creator consciousness, the rest of the world will also. If we just start, it will spread. That's the way it is.

It is time that we take up this challenge that was given to us two thousand years ago by Jesus: "You are the Light of the world." It is time that we take up this mission – each one of us – and not hold back any longer. Be the Light of the world. We have this responsibility. There are enough people right here to change the course of events on planet Earth by being the Light of the world. If all of us are working with, by, and for the Creator, consciously – not only individually but collectively – then the whole will be helped. All will be advanced. Be so much Love that every person is altered, that every thing is altered, that the whole world is altered.

TECHNIQUES FOR REALIZING THE GLORY OF GOD

Simply say, "Thank you, God" a million times a day. No matter what happens.

Every time you look into a mirror, declare to that image: "You are the living Christ." Your declaration of it makes it a reality. When Jesus said, "The things I do you can do and greater," he effectively declared, "You are the living Christ." It is time to accept that so we never again ask the question, "Why?"

Declare that the Creator is in all people, filling them with Love, healing them, and directing their lives to Light. They, too, are the Christ, and need to know it and feel it. "The Creator in me fills me with Light and Love. The Creator fills all those involved in this incident with Light and Love. The Creator changes the consciousness of man so that he becomes aware of the Good coming from this incident. The Creator changes the negative thoughts and negative emotions of this incident to Light and Love. The Creator changes the consciousness of aggression to Light and Love and Peace. The Creator changes the consciousness of killing to Light and Love. The Creator creates Light and Love in, through, and around Earth. The world is filled with Light and Love. Man's consciousness is changed to Light and Love. And that's the way it is."

By saying prayers like this, eventually you'll lock into oneness with the Creator. You will say, as Jesus did, "The Creator and I are one, yet the Creator does all the things I've ever done."

MORE QUESTIONS

Some of the mysteries that need to be answered....

Who am I? You keep saying, "Who am I? Who was I in my last life?" You want to know and I will tell you. Your name has always been "The Christ." There has never been a time that you have not been the Christ. When you go back into your own history of the Christ, you will experience every other Christed being. So, you can let go of the question, Who am I?

The next question is: *Why am I on planet Earth?* You are on planet Earth because wherever you are is holy. Wherever you put your foot is holy. And you are here to make it holy.

What am I doing on planet Earth? You are doing your Divine mission. Even though you may not know what it is, declare each day, "I accomplish my Divine mission."

Where am I going? You are not going anywhere. You Are. You have arrived. You are the Christ and there is no place to go. You are That that was in the beginning, is now, and ever shall be. There is never a time that You will not exist. There is never a time You haven't existed.

What can I do in my spare time, besides looking for my soul mate? You are the Creator in operation and you can create. Every one of you should begin creating something. Write. Paint. Become a musician.

Do something creative.

And in your workaday world, do not separate the Creator from your work, that which you make money at. *Know* the Creator is present, that You are present, that You are creating Good for all of man, wherever you are.

Being who you are, you are the giver, the giver of Divine Love, and you do not need a mate because you are the soul mate to everyone. Because you give Divine Love, you are the soul mate to everyone. That's the way it is.

When will I find my soul mate? Your desire to be loved is your desire to be loved by the Creator within yourself. There is nothing else you desire. There is *nothing* else you desire. You think that will come from someone out here. That's not the way it is. It will come from the Creator deep within yourself. And then you have an unlimited source of love.

On planet Earth there are billions of soul mates because you are the soul mate for all of them. Everybody wants to get married, but you are married to billions of people. Who else do you want to get married to? You are married to Jesus. You are married to Buddha.

And you are helping them to accomplish their mission. *You* are helping *them* to accomplish *their* mission. That's the way it is. You are helping this sun to accomplish its mission. You are helping this galaxy to accomplish its mission.

Cease looking outside of self for love.

When we accept ourselves completely, do negatives fall away? Little by little. No one on Earth could experience the totality of God quickly or instantaneously because you would dissolve into nothingness right away. So, the experience of God, of that oneness, is one of the great joys of your beingness. The only reason you exist is to experience God moment by moment, until you become the Totality.

Why is there conflict on the planet? The only conflict we have on planet Earth is not finding God. We've been looking for God out there. God in heaven. We've been told to seek God out there. And we've been told, "The only place you can find Him is in these temples." That's less than a child's mentality. That's incomprehensible. So, therefore, conflict arises within each of us.

So, as you declare who you really are and speak with authority and increase the amount of love on planet Earth, conflict within people will dissolve. You are inside of everyone. You are doing it inside of everyone.

Why do we fluctuate between knowing and unknowing? So we will find God. The knowing is so great and so sweet and wonderful that, once we have experienced it, when we fall back into the unknowing state, we know with everything in us that we must have the knowing state again. You want to return to this knowing state more than you want life, what you consider "life."

It's getting easier all the time, because you exist. We are sufficient in number, right now, to change every person on planet Earth, to raise all people up to where you are right now. We are sufficient in number to accomplish that. Because you are the Creator, and the Creator is not limited, except by your own consciousness, your own concept.

Why do value judgments seem helpful on one plane and untrue on another? Let us straighten out one thing right now. *Stop separating, for any reason.* There are no planes. There are no dimensions. You have been trained falsely. You are all that is. *Stop creating problems by separating. You are all that is.*

The idea - and I have spoken of the soul plane, the astral plane, the Christ plane, the Creator plane - all of those are false. All is God. All is You. As soon as we separate, we create problems. We demand death then. That's the way it is.

What is there to do if we judge no longer? I think we pray. Oh, God! There are many things to do, many things for us as Creators to do.

Four negatives that I have spoken of - judging, death, negative thoughts, and asking for love - when you realize that is all nonsense, each of you will create in a unique way. Each of you will create Love and Life through all dimensions. You will eliminate separation on all dimensions. And it is promised, you will see God face-to-face on all dimensions. No dimensions will exist then. That's the way it is.

As Creators you will enjoy life, more than you have ever enjoyed it.

THE OLD WAYS

It is time for us to break out of the old methods. As the Bible says, we must put away the old earth and the old heaven. That means putting away every book and everything that has been taught – and becoming that which Is – God with us. In each one of us. Speaking to one another as God-people.

All that has been is now gone forever. What is, is You. You being Divine. And carrying out the greatest mission – that of giving Divine Love to Total Man so that he can rise up and carry out the Divine mission for the universe, for the creation. That's You. And that's each one of us. And we are going to do it.

We are going to do it quickly. In the twinkling of an eye. God Is. And that's the way it is. It's going to be a joy for us.

The Past

If you really apply the Seven Steps of Effective Prayer, there is only one requirement in step number one and that is to release all of your past. If you truly release all of your past, then the other problems are already gone. There is no fear. There are no negatives. There are no problems with your loved ones. You have no problems about the future. You have no problems about anything. Because all of your problems are the result of your past. And if you truly release your past, then you are free of any hang-ups.

What is important is to live right now, to the maximum of your ability, with Life itself. To be aware of Life. To become Life.

Throw out all of your concepts from the past and from gurus. Throw out all the laws of man. Let go! The Creator is new, right now! And that Creator is one hundred percent Love. And there are no laws in one hundred percent Love. It is fantastic.

Sin and Karma

All the religions have taught sin and karma. We have been taught this again and again. It's a control mechanism. But, God-man says, "Yuck! That's not it! Tilt! Tilt! Tilt! There is no time! No space! No karma! No none of that! There is only Divinity!"

Man declares sin and karma. But, God-man is free of karma and sin. In the consciousness of *God*, it is impossible to see anything but perfection, anything but the Divine. In that which is Divine, there can be no karma, there can be no sin. God-man sees Divinity all the time. He may not be able to stay in that consciousness all the time, but his goal is to hold to that consciousness at all times and in all places.

As a human, if you want sin and karma, you can have millions of years of it. And you can say, "I've got to experience this in this lifetime and the next lifetime." Everyone lays down the law of karma for themselves until they say, "I've had enough!" There is no law from God that says there is karma. There is no such law. It's a law from man.

If at any instant along that time frame - of which there is not - you can say, "I am Divine" and get into that consciousness, from that second on, there is no past, there is no karma, and there is no sin. There is only NOW! GOD! That's the way it is!

And it's not difficult. God is simple and easy. Sin and karma are tough. It's hard to live according to the world of sin and karma. You have to work at it. You really have to work hard at it to make it in that world of sin and karma.

When you break out of the consciousness of sin and karma – and you can break out of that and be in total Light – that instant, that very instant, everything changes. You live entirely differently. You are not subject to any laws that you have laid down for yourself.

Once you see the Divinity, there can be no yuck. There is nothing but the Divine. There is no time. There is no space. No anyone. No Earth, no stars. There is only the Divinity.

You have had two thousand years of practicing sin and karma. And we're all fed up with it. Now let's have two thousand years of being Divine and see what happens. Let's start right here. All of us. Today.

Fear of Death

One of the big hang-ups on Earth is death. Well, there is no death. We appear to die physically. But, we have so many examples of the opposite, like Jesus proving that you can't die physically. There is no way you can die.

There is also the evidence of those who are able to communicate with people who have passed on. Through that, too, there is a realization that there is no death.

There are also examples of people who have been clinically dead who have come back to life. Some have been dead for several hours – eight or nine hours in one case. The people who come back from being clinically dead say that there is no death. There is only life. Physicians have written books about this.

What has been revealed to me is that when we lay down this physical body, we are, in a sense, rejecting God. We are saying that this body is not worthy. That's wrong. Every thing that has been created – *everything* - every cell in you, every bone, even that on which you sit in the bathroom, is sacred, is Divine.

We are breaking through the concept we have had heretofore. We are breaking into the concept of reality. God is real, everywhere.

We appear to die physically. And yet, we have so many examples of the opposite, like Jesus proving that you can't die physically. There is no way you can die. Some people are able to communicate with those who have passed on. This brings a realization that there is no death.

There are also examples of people who have been clinically dead who have come back to life. Some have been dead for several hours – eight or nine hours in one case. The people who come back from being clinically dead say that there is no death. There is only life. Physicians have written books about this.

We limit God. We reject God. If you look into your own life, are you rejecting God? Of course. Because we are caught up with declaring, "You must die." We declare it every day. We declare, "There must be death."

Do not let the scientific community or the media control your life. The scientific community and the media are constantly saying, "You must die. You must die. You must die." It is not so!

Death must be eliminated from our consciousness.

Imagine a whole planet of creators into the consciousness of creating Life. Could there be any death at all - of trees, plants, anything?

Killing

Obviously, the original amount of Life, Love, Spirit, and Truth given to man was not sufficient, because lo these many millions and billions of years that man has been in existence, we are still killing. All over the universe, man is killing. Earth may be the number one killing planet in this universe. We kill fifty thousand people a year on our highways alone.

We accept killing, even though we have a commandment: "Thou shalt not kill." Having a commandment from God, "Thou shalt not kill" hasn't changed anybody. To think, we have a commandment from God, "Thou shalt not kill," and yet we do all kinds of things to keep right on killing. No one seems to take this commandment seriously.

We kill even though we have a commandment to love our neighbor. Some people get medals for killing. Deep within, we know this is not the way.

Rather than going out and saying, "Dummies, God said, 'Thou shalt not kill,'" let us go at it a different way. Since you and I have the power of the Divine, we are required to increase Divine Love and Divine Light over the original amount, so much so that everyone eats, sleeps, and drinks Divine Love and Divine Light. In doing that, the killing will stop. If we have more Love, more Life, more Light, then man will change throughout the universe. You are the Creator in action. You are God. Do it.

Money Fears

The two major fears of man are the fear of dying and the fear of not having enough money. We make money a god. We are caught up with the idea that the only way we can get abundant life is through money and the only way we can live longer is through money. We believe that we must worship this god, money.

But in God's world, the words are "abundant life." There is an infinite supply for everyone. It's all available now. It's just a matter of people and governments getting into the idea that there is an abundance.

Money is energy in action. Food is energy in a different type of action. Once we get into the consciousness that we can direct this energy, things change. When Jesus walked the planet, he made food – fish, loaves, and so forth – right out of the energy in the air.

We are beginning to learn that maybe it's the consciousness that we're after. The power of each one of us is magnificent, but we are limited in our consciousness. We limit our consciousness by thinking that we can't do these things, simply because we haven't seen anyone else do it. Well, dare to be first.

Now is the time for us to begin a new type of living where we serve as an example of this abundance in every aspect of life. We need to bring this energy into everything we do. Every drop of water that we drink, every bite of food that we eat, every breath that we take, every consciousness we have should be one of God-in-action. Declare it: "This is God in action. Everything I do is God in action. Everything I think is God in action. Everything I be is God in action." Declare it so that every moment of your existence is a new way of being.

Judging

We tend to want to judge. We need to let go of this. We need to let go of our judging - of ourselves and of other people. We create problems when we judge. We have *no* permission, *ever*, to judge.

Most of us, when we look at another person, are caught up with finding something wrong with that person. We look to find something wrong that we know we have overcome. If we can find something wrong in another person that we've overcome, then we feel that we're pretty hot stuff.

We are past masters at judging. We judge our spouses because we want them to be better. We judge the weather, our cars, our work-mates - we judge everything!

No one is permitted to judge. A god cannot judge anyone. Just as Jesus could not judge the woman caught in the act of adultery. He could not judge her in any way. He could give her advice. But he made no judgment. If you hear a judgment, hold to the Light, to the Divine within.

We need to see the Christ in each person. From the moment we begin to see the Christ or the Creator in each other, there can be no judging. "I see and *know* the Creator is in you." By saying that we are elevating each other. In doing so, we have replaced judging with a positive way of being. The moment we get into this consciousness is the moment we truly begin to love – our mates, our children, the world.

"I *know* the Creator is in you." Do that for everyone: the minister at your church, the congregation, the used car salesman, the real estate agent, the politician. If all Americans saw our president as the

Creator, what would our representative be like? If we can know our politicians are the Creator, this will change the course of events. It is a fantastic event when we see that we no longer need to judge.

Fear of Being Divine

Our consciousness today is highly limited. We have been programmed in a negative way by all of the religions and we do not pay attention to these words of Jesus – and of every great master - "Ye are gods." I don't see anyone acting like gods.

Most people are afraid to be a god because the rest of the world is not in that state of consciousness. We are afraid that we would be different and unacceptable - if we were in the consciousness of a god.

Being Human vs. Being Divine

Being human is the toughest thing in the whole universe. You really have to work hard at it. But, it's easy being Divine. It is simplicity itself. God is simple.

Love, Light, Truth, Spirit, Life, Mind, Wisdom. These are the attributes of the Divine. You have all of them. Everyone has them. No one is better than another.

Now is the time for all of man to express a new consciousness of God. It is time for us to go beyond how we have been programmed. Let go of the past. This moment is the only one that counts. You are Divine. All that is is within You. All that is is You. You are the Light of the world.

The Divine in Daily Life

Instead of saying, "I have to go home, take a shower, go to work, etc.," put the Divine into it first: "The Divine is at work. The Divine is in the car, the shower, etc. The Divine is in operation." This frees one from the tensions of having to do anything.

I applied this when I was in the Navy and found that the more I worked with the Divine, things were done by people easily and correctly. When I got into the concept that I had to do it myself, that's when things got messed up.

This requires just a little switch in consciousness. Switch to thinking, "All that is is Divine."

You have to break out of the boxes to that which creates Good. Break out of concepts of being a male or a female. Don't let sex, personality, or money control you.

The Creator does not control. The Creator only *gives*. The Creator only gives Light, Love, Truth, Spirit.

Thank you, God, for this Divinity, this of Thee in each of us, in everything, in all that is, in all dimensions. Amen.

DEATH

W hat has been revealed to me is that when we lay down this physical body, we are, in a sense, rejecting God. We are saying that this body is not worthy. That every cell in it is yucky stuff.

That's wrong. Every thing that has been created – *everything* - every cell in you, every bone, even that on which you sit in the bathroom, is sacred, is Divine.

We are breaking through the concept we have had heretofore. We are breaking into the concept of reality. God is real, everywhere.

We appear to die physically. And yet, we have so many examples of the opposite, like Jesus proving that you can't die physically. There is no way you can die. Some people are able to communicate with those who have passed on. This brings a realization that there is no death.

There are also examples of people who have been clinically dead who have come back to life. Some have been dead for several hours – eight or nine hours in one case. The people who come back from being clinically dead say that there is no death. There is only life. Physicians have written books about this.

THE MIND

We all have an inner urge to be one with the Creator within. It's there in everyone and it's there in everything that is. Even though that urge is there, there seem to be interference patterns. That is what I want to go into – the inner world of the mind.

We have been trained to think. We have been trained, through our schooling, to be logical. We have been trained, through the media saying to us, "Use your mind." And the men tell their wives, "Why aren't you like me? Why don't you think like men? Why aren't you logical?"

We find this thinking process going on all the time. We try to force ourselves to think. Logically, one, two. We are all involved with thinking, with our relationships with people; we're involved with thinking in our problems.

Our world comes from the mind. We honor the mind. We honor the person who comes up with the PhD degree. We honor the person that comes up with being able to be a genius. We honor these people because we think this is the ultimate. We think this is where we will find God.

But, when we attempt to find God by becoming still, the brain, the mind races. It thinks. It has patterns of thought that come through and they interfere. We have thought patterns going on and they're going on and going on. They interfere with what you're really trying to do.

We have been taught in the Eastern religions that the ultimate is the crown chakra. There is no part of you that is not Divine. There is no part of you that is better than another part.

Therefore, break free of the brain, of the mind. Break free of the consciousness that we must think, that we must be a genius, that we must get 67 degrees.

Every time we strive we find that the brain is what we are really striving against. It is not providing Truth. It is not providing Spirit. It is not providing Love. It is providing logic, cold. It's providing communications that hurt.

Almost all of the communications that we're hearing that come from the mind, no one listens to anymore, because we've been hurt by it, because it seems to be not true. And we're in a constant state of turmoil because our mind is always interfering.

When Jesus walked this planet, Peter, speaking from the mind, spoke to Jesus and Jesus said, "Get thee behind me, Satan." When we are trying to become one with this creative source, literally the Satan within us is this brain, this mind, this man's mind.

And we want to break free of this inner world of interference. And the question is: How to? The yogis teach a system that takes thirty-five years of one-pointedness, actually mastering the mind. It is a good technique. And there are many techniques out about mastering the mind. It means literally, when you get to trying mastering the mind, most people cannot master it, and the maximum may be one tenth of a second, of mastership. Some people can do it for one second, and that is tremendous. That's an accomplishment, to be able to master the mind.

There are all kinds of books out on it. There are even people who go to hypnotists to hypnotize away interference patterns. And there is rebirthing going on through regression of hypnotic effects. To go through things that can free us so we *can* finally get there. All of these techniques are wonderful and helpful. This rebirthing thing that is being practiced throughout our country is tremendous.

But after rebirthing, we still have the brain, the mind, and interference patterns. We want to get through this.

There have been all kinds of techniques. I have given several myself. One is to move your consciousness from your brain to another part of your body. As soon as you have moved your consciousness away from your brain area, you have moved away from ego. You have moved away from personality. You have moved away from Satan. You have moved into oneness with the Creator.

Another technique is practicing the Creator prayer: "The Creator in me controls my mind so that only Divine actions and thoughts can be." You bring your own creative prayer into existence. You will find that when you attempt to become One it will be easier.

It's a lot like learning how to walk. Practicing the Creator prayer is the same way. Just because it doesn't happen instantly – we all know this is Instant America: we have instant coffee, instant everything - just because it doesn't happen instantly, don't give up. You didn't learn how to walk instantly. You fell. You hit your head. You cried. But you maintained this desire to walk. If you have this same desire that you had for walking, you will attain Oneness with the Creator within.

INSIGHTS

We're just in the embryonic stages of understanding that God Is, that Light Is, and that we are not restrained in any way from attaining That. The only thing that restrains us is our own concept of who we are.

But the scientific world has said it, the Bible has said it, and all the great gurus of the world likewise have said it – exactly the same thing – that we indeed are not separate. We find it hard to accept this, but there is an urge to try to prove it. So, we try to find a mate. The reason we look so diligently to find a mate is that we want to become One.

That does not mean you have to hug, kiss, mate, or anything like that. The merging is not with personality. When you merge with the Light in everyone, personality falls away. You cannot be hurt by anyone then. There tend to be many hurts to the personality, but you cannot be hurt. You cannot hurt God. There is no way that can happen.

Living in the World

Though you may have been told you are very special – a child of God, Divine – it is a different thing to know this and to act accordingly.

We declare we do not have enough money, that we need more supply. But, once you begin loving the Creator, all these things will be added unto you.

The Body

Some of us reject our bodies because of what religions have taught us. Both Eastern and Western religions seem to teach that the body is not important, that the Divinity is located outside of your physical self. We reject our bodies. We think they are mere shells surrounding the kingdom of heaven within. We say we acknowledge our Divinity, but we tend to think of it as a non-physical part of ourselves.

This is totally false. Every cell of our bodies is Divine. Every bone and muscle and organ and gene is Divine. Every molecule is your body is Divine and you are not separate in any way from that Divinity.

Yet, we still say, "I have a pain," or "I have a problem," and we feel that these things cannot be Divine. You think that if all of your being were Divine you could not experience pain. But the reason there is pain is because you have rejected your body. How can you change this rejection when for millions of years humans have declared that their bodies must be cast aside?

Jesus gave us the key to the perfection we seek. He said, "Be ye perfect…" – and we end his sentence there, not recognizing that the full statement is, "Be ye perfect *as your Father in heaven is perfect.*" Where is the Father in Heaven? Jesus said the Father in Heaven is within. If the Father in Heaven is within you, then obviously that which is the Father in you is perfect.

Now you have the technique of loving self – the Creator within you.

You can live forever in your physical body. It's just a matter of how long you want to do it.

Seeing Correctly

All of us tend to see incorrectly. When we look at ourselves or anyone else, we instantly think male or female. That is false. You are not male or female. You are Divine. Other people you see are Divine. Every time you see a person, say, "I see the Divine."

Rising from the Dead

We are like dead people. Jesus said, "Let the dead bury the dead." What he meant was that the people walking on planet Earth are dead until that moment when they dedicate their lives to the ultimate source of all that is.

Everything Is from the Divine

It is good for us to realize that everything is from the Divine. Everything we experience is from the Divine. And when we become one with That, we create experiences. Divine experiences. In all that is. And that's the way it is.

Praying for the World

Have fun! Try it! It is just a matter of trying it. Get a picture of your city. Put it in a bubble of Light. Merge the Light into yourself and stay with that until you can feel what is going on in the people. I have yet to feel one thing in all people – enough love. All people have a great need for Love, a great need for true, Divine Love. When you merge with the creation, you begin to satisfy that need.

It is not enough to bring the living waters of Life to our country, to give it to our families and allies. *All* need this living water. Every nation and all people need to know that Divine Love is there and they are being filled with Divine Love. Once they feel fulfilled, they begin to accomplish the greater works.

It is not necessary to go through a difficult period. It is only necessary for each one of us to realize that we indeed are God. We only need to accept this and work with this reality moment by moment.
You are the Light of the world. Therefore, it is your mission to heal the planet. The negatives that mankind has created go deeply into Earth. Wherever you go, wherever you step, you need to change the earth itself. Know that where you stand is holy ground, all the way through the planet. The Earth is a living being. It is Christ. Because you are creating from the Divine, you will recognize Earth's Divinity and see how this living being has been hurt. By being filled with

Light, Earth will become so vibrant, so full of life, that it will be a joy to all. Filled with Light, there will be joy everywhere. Our planet will be so fantastic that it will automatically heal everyone on the planet.

The world is in you. There is no place that you are not. Sooner or later you must get into the consciousness that, "I and the cosmos are one. I and the creation are one." Don't limit yourself to the creation. Merge with the All.

All That Counts

All that counts in the feeling of Divine Love pervading the Earth. There is nothing else. It is you.

Future Generations

Can you imagine what it would be like if all children were taught this all the way through school? What would Earth be like?

Bliss and Doing

You have an inner world that is entirely different from any you have spoken of or been aware of.

The first aspect of this inner world is bliss. Because all that you have been – all of your past, all of your personality, all of your ego – dissolves. The dissolving of all that becomes bliss. Freedom.

But you can stay in a state of bliss only so long. You know you must become a doer, a Creator, an actor upon the stage of life, that you must carry on from the Creator aspect.

Immediately, you become aware of the needs you can fulfill from that state of bliss, filling everyone and everything full of Divine Love and Light. And your great urge is to do just that. And not just for people but for the whole planet. *You are the Light of the world.* You *are* the Light of the world. Declare it so. Declare the Creator creating the Light of the world in you, through you, and around you. Declare Oneness with the Creator and Oneness with the Creator of the world so that the world of planet Earth moves into you. And when it moves into you, you are no longer this physical being. You have moved into a height of two hundred thousand miles at least. And the world is there within you. And you know it is your responsibility at that point. And the great need of the peoples, plants, animals, and minerals on planet Earth is love. Divine Love. You know you must fill Earth and everything on it full of Divine Love. So that it is totally full and so that everyone will totally change.

Once you do this, immediately you are one with everyone and you know it. You can actually know everything there is within another. You can increase the Creator within them. The Creator in everyone wants to be free to express total creativeness. That is true of everyone. And Jesus gave us the commandment to love everyone. And if you truly love everyone, you want that Creator in them to expand throughout their being so they are creators creating that which is Good. And no longer can anyone be called Satan. No longer will one be thinking negative thoughts or doing negative things. That's true free will. That's true Love.

TECHNIQUES

Name every organ in your body male and female merged together, man and woman merged together, Father and Mother merged together, and Messiah and Goddess merged together. This will offset the unbalanced condition in everyone.

Use the same techniques you use on yourself to heal others. For example, "So-and-so is a really great being. So-and-so is Divine. Every organ in so-and-so's body is in a bubble of Light."

If you're praying for one person who has a specific disease, expand your prayer to include *everyone* who has the same disease.

To consciously heal others, the techniques are the same as those for healing self. Suppose your brother's name is Tom. You declare, "Tom's heart is Divine. Tom's eyes are Divine. Tom's circulation is Divine." Name every part of Tom's body. Place it in a bubble of

Light and call it Christ. Healing another person in this way demands total respect for that person – and absolutely no judgments. You *must* change the way you see things, knowing that God and only God is present in everyone and everything.

IDENTITY

W hat is deep within us is the urge to live the life of God, and in order to do that the obvious thing is to transform our consciousness into God-consciousness. And yet, we have difficulty doing so. We've heard what Jesus said, "The things I do you can do and greater," but we reject what Jesus and all spiritual masters have been communicating to us for thousands of years, that every person is God.

What is holding us back from accepting the reality that we indeed are God – *the* God, the one and only? What is keeping us from accepting this? It is our identity and the belief that without it we are nothing. This is the biggest holdup in our evolutionary jump from human consciousness to God consciousness.

There is a great desire for this identity to exist. We are fearful that something will happen to it. This fear overrides almost everything. We'll do anything to protect our identity. We'll do anything to keep it alive.

So, our identity becomes our master. It controls us. It says to us, "Take care of me. Feed me. Clothe me. Provide shelter for me. Make me acceptable to others." And we do it. We do all kinds of things to make it presentable and acceptable so it will have an easier existence on planet Earth. We dress it up. We add to it through education and through religion, making it more acceptable and therefore more protected. We put boxes around it to further protect it.

We lock our homes and cars to keep it safe.

At some point, we go to a guru. We hear words that begin to expand the box we have put around ourselves for protection. We awaken to the fact that the identity continues to exist after the physical form ceases. We learn to lose the fear of death. But, we should be asking, "If I'm going to be around again and again and again, why? Is that all there is?"

We should begin to think in a new way: maybe this identity is something we *should* lose. Then we would take on a new identity, the identity of the living Christ. Not the dead Christ who was crucified 2,000 years ago. But the living Christ, the living Christ spirit that lives and breathes inside of you. Once we exist as the living Christ, we lose this identity with great joy.

This living Christ is not concerned about the physical, is not concerned with the personality, is not concerned with judgments by anyone for any reason. This living Christ is unflappable and unshakeable. There are no barriers, there is no being boxed in with the living Christ. You can do anything. You can go anywhere. The new way is beingness everywhere.

This new identity, the identity of the living Christ, is concerned with increasing the amount of Light over the original amount, so that everyone eats, sleeps, and drinks Light. This living Christ is concerned with increasing the amount of Love over the original amount, so that everyone becomes Divine Love.

The original amount of Light and Love – after these millions of years of existence on Earth – obviously wasn't enough: man hasn't changed. The identity of man hasn't changed. There is still killing.

So, we're changing this identity to a true, Divine identity that has no human identity. Going forward, one only identifies with Love – Divine Love everywhere – and Light – Divine Light everywhere. We lose our human identity with great joy as we take on the identity of the living Christ.

By changing this human identity to that of Christ identity, we help elevate the material world. This material world is Divine. It is not, as some maintain, maya or yucky. It is Divine.

Experiment with this living Christ. Through prayer, command that this living Christ accomplish fantastic things for all of mankind. Command the giving of only Divine Love, the giving of only Divine Light, so that beings throughout the universe will change. Increase Divine Light. Increase Divine Love. Don't hold back, ever again.

The history of your personality is nothing. It dissolves away and becomes the history of the Christ you are. Let go of your little world. Let go of your ego. Become a Christed being. Do the greater works.

It is time that we get into who we really are. Not Jane, Joe, Mary, or Bob or whatever our human name is. But, get into our God-identity.

TECHNIQUES FOR TRANSFORMING IDENTITY

Jesus gave us the technique for transforming our human identity into a Divine identity: Pray without ceasing. It's a wonderful technique. As you pray without ceasing, your identity simply drops away.

The way to break free is to say a million times a day, "I am Divine. I am Light. I am Life." A million times. Every day.

You have the time. You have so much spare time. To say, "I am Light. I am Divine," is a prayer. You can say it while you're walking. You can say it while you're driving. You can say it while you're working.

We tend to place our identity in our brain. But the brain is like a computer. It is there for you to master. The brain is not there to be the focus of our identity. It is not the most important part of our being. When we die, the brain goes away. That which is Divine Love, Light, Truth, and Spirit is the most important part of our being. We need to identify or become one with That – with the Love, Light, Truth, and Spirit.

One way to get beyond your human identity is to move your consciousness from your brain to another part of your being.

Scientists are saying that you are not separate from anything else. With that in mind, you can move your consciousness anywhere. Move it into anything – your big toe, a piano, anything. By doing this, you overcome ego, identity, or personality desires and can then become totally one with the Divine aspects within yourself.

Once you move your consciousness into something other than your brain, you will think from another part of your being. You do not need to think from your brain, amazingly enough. Once you think from another part of your being, you are into Divine thinking.

In thinking Divinely and in becoming one with all aspects of the universe, you are fulfilling your Divine mission.

MALE AND FEMALE

For a billion years, we have been caught at the level of believing that we are either male or female. This male-female world that we live in is unbalanced. It is a world that is into separation, into judging, into seeing things as plus-minus. It is a world in which we allow our animal nature and our desire to control others in order to have the upper hand. It is a world that has not brought great happiness – much less joy.

Our search for happiness includes seeking a mate or seeking someone to love us. That is where most of the hurts take place. When we find someone we think will love us, for a time we have a close relationship and then we see we are beginning to get hurt and we say, "This is not the answer."

When we let go of the need for love from a particular person and find Divine Love within ourselves, we have joy. We then are able to unconditionally love our mate – and every other person.

The male and the female are in each of us. Every individual on the planet is a combination of male-female within themselves. The average male is seventy percent male and thirty percent female. The average female is seventy percent female and thirty percent male.

The true objective for each one of us is to be totally balanced, male and female. Not fifty-fifty, but one hundred percent of each: one hundred percent female and one hundred percent male.

This balancing of the male-female – within self and within the world – is the beginning of the salvation of the world.

As we think about balancing the male-female, it might be helpful to recognize that there is a continuum of consciousness regarding the masculine and feminine aspects of our being. At the lowest level, the male-female level, we are totally involved with the material world, seek only temporal happiness, and search outside of ourselves for that happiness. At the next level, the man-woman level, we begin to emerge from our animal nature. We have a feeling that there must be more. We awaken to the fact that there is the Divine and we begin our spiritual search. We also begin to look beyond ourselves and we develop a desire to help our fellow human beings. At the third level, the Father-Mother level, we are no longer into mating. We are totally one with the Divine Father-Mother. We are whole and complete within ourselves. But, there can still be a separateness, so we go beyond the Father-Mother to the Creator. The Creator is the Father-Mother joined as one. At this level we begin saying, "I and the Creator are one. The Creator within me creates. I create Life in everyone on planet Earth. I create more Life than there was in the beginning." What follows is a brief description of each of these four levels.

Male-Female

The male-female level is our most basic, primal level. The male-female is involved with the material world, with that which is outside of ourselves.

The male concept has been the dominating one and it has hurt females. Men have rejected the female aspect because, they believe, it's not manlike. The male level is very low. It is into sex and temporal happiness.

The female concept has viewed itself as being less than. The whole biorhythmic experience reminds women that they are less than. There is no need for this biorhythmic thing. It's childlike. There is no law from God saying this must go on. The very sex act puts women down below. There is a tremendous fear in all females of being a woman.

At the male-female level, we try to fill in our missing male or female pieces through marriage or relationships. We try and try and try to gratify the mating instinct. But it doesn't work. We think, "Marriage is the answer." But the divorce rate for first-time marriages is about fifty percent.

And yet, we keep looking outside of self for the answers. What we have been involved with is separation – male here, female there. As a male, we look outside of self for a female, for happiness. As a female, we look to the male for happiness. We search for a soul mate. This search for the perfect mate is the search to balance the male-female within ourselves.

The true soul mate is the opposite of yourself within yourself. It is not something outside of self. No matter how perfect a potential soul mate might appear to be, if you were to marry them, you would find something wrong. They would snore or they would put curlers in their hair or lipstick would be on all night. I don't know all of the problems, but we've got a few million – each one of us does. After finding problems with our mate, we say, "Gee, this is my perfect mate? I'd better look somewhere else."

In all of the stories of Cinderella finding the prince or of the prince finding Cinderella, it's the male-female within self finding self. When *that* is married, you live happily ever after. *Ever* after.

As soon as you say, "I see a male," you are judging. As soon as you see a female, you are judging. It's a limitation. It puts that person in a box. It limits their ability to be Divine. Stop judging. Stop limiting. See the Divine in everyone. Let them be free to be the Divine they know is within themselves.

Don't see male or female. There is only Light. You are the Light of the world. I see you as the Light of the world. I know you as the Light of the world. I hold to you as the Light of the world.

Man-Woman

At the next level, the man-woman level, we begin to look outside of self. We begin to search for God in our lives and we begin to seek ways of helping others.

The woman aspect within us – that which is intuitive - awakens to the fact that there is the Divine and begins the spiritual search. We have a feeling that there must be more. We read mystical books and join peer groups that have similar interests.

But, we begin to feel we must get beyond studying and joining groups. We want to help our fellow human beings. We develop a knowing that, "I am made in the image and likeness of the Divine. I am *whole* man. I am *whole* woman. Being whole, I know I can create. I can create life." Jesus was such a whole man, whole woman.

When you are merged as whole man and whole woman, you feel, "I want to go out and help man. I know I can do it. I know I have the power of Life. But I know it's not me doing it. It is the Creator within me that does these greater works."

It is at this level of the continuum that people become nurses, doctors, and other types of professionals who help people.

But deep within, we want something that endures. We want joy. As we advance and as our quest becomes more spiritual, we realize there is more: total man and total woman merged as one. In this balanced state, there is no need for gratification of either the male or the female within. Balanced and merged together they give off joy within our physical being. Once the male-female and man-woman within us have been balanced and merged,
then we can help others awaken the whole man-whole woman within themselves. We can do that through the greatest power there is: prayer that touches deeply.

<u>Father-Mother</u>

There is more to this balancing and merging. There is that which Jesus talked about when he said, "I and my Father are one, yet it is the Father within that doeth the works." (Jesus had to say "Father" because it was a male-dominant world in those days.) Jesus gave constant credit to the Father. His experience was one of, "I do nothing; the Father within does everything. I don't think - He thinks. I don't walk or move an elbow – He does it."

What a tremendous freedom from the turmoil of being male-female! You are free to be one with the Father! You are free to be one with the Mother! At this Father-Mother level you no longer are into mating. At this stage, you are totally one with the Divine Father-Mother. You are whole and complete within yourself. Such a marriage cannot be separated.

Living in this consciousness, Jesus had broken through to the level of the Father-Mother, the level of Light. It was in this consciousness that he said, "You are the Light of the world." When the Father-Mother in you is balanced, you are Light. That's when you know, "I am the Light of the world. You are the Light of the world. Everyone is the Light of the world." In the consciousness of Light, we see that all are Light. We see that the Father-Mother exists in everyone.

From this consciousness, we have a knowing that, "The Father-Mother in me is balanced and floods my whole being with Light." In this consciousness, there is no sense of being male or female. There is only a consciousness of the Father-Mother principle, of total Light flowing in, through, and around us. Changing us. Increasing the Light in us and in everyone and everything.

In this consciousness, we no longer look at others as being male or female. We don't see personality. We no longer see separateness. We see Light and only Light. Our thoughts are, "I *know* the Light is in you. I see *only* the Light in you. I hold *only* to that Light. You are the Light of the world. I see you as the Light of the world. I know you as the Light of the world. I hold to you as the Light of the world."

In the consciousness of the Father-Mother, everyone is our child. Everyone is a part of us. As such, the responsibility is tremendous. It no longer is appropriate to say, "God will take care of it" or "Let God do it." We know that we have a responsibility for everyone and everything.

At the Father-Mother level, we heal, raise the dead, walk upon water. The rules of man and nature, such as gravity, no longer apply.

We are afraid to move into this level because of peer group reactions. We are afraid of losing our friends. But, the Father-Mother is merged with everyone, so there can't be any separation. At the Father-Mother level you are no longer concerned about having friends. You are concerned about increasing the amount of Good that exists.

If you increase the Good in yourself, you automatically increase the Good in everyone else. You have a responsibility for increasing the Good until everyone attains the awareness of the Good, of God, within themselves.

You have to go beyond the male-female, beyond the man-woman, beyond the Father-Mother. You have to break out of the boxes that hold you back. Don't let sex, personality, or the economy control you. Break into that which is Good. You have to hold to the greater Good in everyone: "I see the Divine in you." With this perspective, the Good automatically increases.

<u>The Creator</u>

When we say, "Father-Mother," there still is a separateness. Beyond the Father-Mother, we keep hearing, deep within, the Creator. The Creator is the Father-Mother joined as one. In the Creator, nothing is impossible. So, rather than talking about the Father-Mother, we begin saying, "I and the Creator are one. The Creator within me creates. I create Life in everyone on planet Earth. I create more Life than there was in the beginning."

Once you say, "I create," your whole being responds, throughout every cell. That word "I" is oneness with the Creator, and in that oneness is the joy you seek.

Don't let the laws of man limit you. In the Creator consciousness, you're totally free.

You don't have to evolve through the male-female, man-woman,

Father-Mother consciousness. You can simply take the gigantic step of being the Creator. Say, "I create" a million times a day. Think how the Creator would think. Act how the Creator would act. Get involved with this consciousness on a continuous basis. It is not a matter of waiting for a lightning bolt to strike you. It is a matter of doing it.

Going into the Creator aspect, the cells take on a different structure. The laws of man, of the medical world, of nature no longer apply.

The Creator does not control. The Creator gives only Light, Love, Truth, and Spirit to everyone and everything – and increases it in everyone and everything. This is the Creator's only urge.

Have no fear. Don't be afraid to declare, "I am the Creator in operation." Command it! Command the Creator in operation through you! Command it so!

In this new world, we will dress differently. Instead of dressing to attract the animal nature, we will dress to radiate the Light, and Light beings will quickly recognize each other. There will be a unity, a oneness. It won't be mating. It will be oneness.

The Sun is an example of the Creator in operation. Balanced male-female, man-woman, Father-Mother, the unified Creator in operation.

The world of the Creator is a world of beauty and joy, enduring forever. How great is oneness? How great is Joy? Would you ever slip back into measly happiness?

TECHNIQUES FOR BALANCING THE MALE-FEMALE

Saying one or more of the following prayers, over and over, will help balance the male-female within you:

- "I am whole and complete, male and female."
- "I balance the male-female within me."
- "I seek only the oneness of the male-female within myself."

■ "I live a balanced male-female relationship within myself."

The right hand of every person – whether you're right-handed or left-handed – is the male aspect. The left hand is the female aspect. Bringing these male and female aspects together – by bringing your hands together in prayer or by holding your hands up to the palms of your partner - is another way of balancing the male-female aspects within yourself.

If you are married, praying together with your spouse is a quick way to achieve this balanced state. If you're not married to another person, then marry the male and female within yourself by putting your hands together and praying for balance.

If you have a partner, you can stand or sit facing each other and place the palm of your right hand against the palm of your partner's left hand. And place the palm of your left hand against the palm of your partner's right hand. Holding your hands in this position will balance the male-female aspects within both of you.

Don't stop at balancing the male-female within yourself. Earth itself is male-female and it's unbalanced. There must not be a male and female world. It must be a Christ world. We must declare the Christ-world and break out of this male-female death knell. Pray for the balancing of the male and the female in the planet. The planet is a living entity and it, too, is imbalanced in its male-female nature. Your prayers – filling the male-female of the planet with Light and merging the two together – will bring balance and wholeness to planet Earth. By changing the planet the way you change yourself, you will speed up development of the planet and speed up development of the people of Earth.

We must create a new world, a paradise. Here's a prayer for creating this new world: "The Creator changes the male world to Light. The Creator changes the female world to Light. The Creator merges the male world and the female world into the Christ. The world is Christ."

FAMILY

The most important group in the world – and the one with the biggest problems – is the family.

I have lectured to several thousand people and have found that everyone has a problem with a parent. Everyone. I have yet to see anyone free from family problems. Everyone has been hurt simply because parents have not known how to love. Everyone has problems with parents because no one on the planet has been trained to be a parent.

The present system of being dads, mothers, brothers, or sisters is causing trauma. Many parents feel they have to be the boss, that they must dictate, and this has created many hurts. The divorce rate in our country is close to fifty percent and the children involved in this tremendous turnover of parents are having problems. We need to re-evaluate everything – parenthood, our educational system, our whole existence.

The primary requirement in the high schools of our country should be a four-year course on the family. It should be mandatory for every student. How great it would be if adults were taught how to raise a child. If parents were into Light and recognized that their role as parents was to help their children accomplish their Divine missions, then the children would grow up beautifully.

What we are really here for is to help every person find and complete their own particular Divine mission. Everything that we say, do, see, or touch relating to any person should be to confirm that they indeed are accomplishing their Divine mission. In doing so, we would know that the living waters of Life coming forth from every person are Divine Love – not human love. And allowing these living waters of Life to flow forth would bring about an inward recognition that God is our Father, God is our Mother, and God is the doer in each person. There is a tremendous freedom that accompanies this recognition. People would no longer be hurt by their earthly mother or father. They would not be hurt by their siblings, by their peer group, by anyone – because they would know that they have the ultimate – Divine Love – within them.

Imagine everyone doing that for everyone else on this planet – what a joy! What a great happening!

True Marriage

The Bible says that God is Light; God is Love; God is Spirit; and God is Truth. It also says that there is no place that God is not. That means God is everywhere present – in me, in you, in everyone and everything – inseparable. The scientific world has arrived at the same conclusion: we are not separate from anything or anyone.

All of us think we are separate and distinct from everyone else. All of us think we are different. But the scientific world has said it, the Bible has said it, and all the great gurus of the world likewise have said it – exactly the same thing – that we indeed are *not* separate.

We find it hard to accept this, but there is an urge to try to achieve oneness with another. So, we try to find a mate. The reason we get married is to try merging as one. The mating process we use now is a very poor attempt to reach that oneness. The problem is that we think we are male or female. The truth of the matter is that we are Light.

I would like to present a different idea about marriage, that it is total merging into Oneness. In this state, we are mentally one, emotionally one, magnetically one, electrically one, and telepathically one.

Separation and Oneness

The family is a proving ground for learning how to become One – not separate from others. All the efforts of married life should be directed toward Oneness. The sole objective in having children is to become totally One. The sole objective of the family is to learn total Oneness. That's the ideal. It's not being taught anywhere.

We do not understand Oneness. We understand separation. We continue, in married life, to force the idea of separation rather than unity, rather than total oneness mentally, emotionally, and in every other way. This consciousness of separateness is holding us back.

When we merge with everyone, we cannot be separate. Once you merge as a family, you can't stop there. The Love is overflowing. You can establish a group with another family and merge with them. And then keep on merging with others.

People who stay married a long time begin to look alike. After you stare at a person for ninety years, you are going to look like them! Thinking alike also happens. The man will be driving home from work and he will feel as though he should stop at the store and get eggs, butter, and a couple of other things. He does it and when he gets home, his wife says she meant to call him to get these things from the store – and here they are! That kind of thing goes on all the time. That is the beginning of merging – just the beginning.

All of marriage is to learn to be more God-like in every way. Not just One with your spouse and your children, but One with Earth and One with the universe.

In order to *be* the Light of the world, you have to have the whole world in you. That means everyone and everything. So start merging! Merge your Divine consciousness with that of everyone else!

That does not mean you have to hug, kiss, mate, or anything like that. The merging is not with personality. When you merge with the Light in everyone, personality falls away. You cannot be hurt by anyone then. You cannot hurt God. There is no way that can happen.

Everyone should be inside of you – total Oneness, total Love, total Light. If we put anyone outside, we have failed. We were made in the image and likeness of the Divine, which means we *must* love. We must love everyone – the drunk, the mentally incapacitated, the hurt, the sick, *and* the well.

The objective is to start. Try it!

<u>A New Type of Family</u>

We are not taught anywhere how to exist as a God-family. The whole objective in having a family is oneness. Having a family is a quick way of achieving Oneness because there is a closeness in the family arising from the fact that the vibrations among the family members are nearly the same.

Imagine what kind of family there would be if each family member knew that he was Divine and did not ask for love from anyone or anything. What a family! It would be so powerful, so vibrant, so alive! As children are brought up this way, imagine what they are going to be like. Fantastic!

Let us imagine what a new type of family would look like. Let's use as an example a person who has just graduated from college and follow him through his life and the creation of a family the way it ought to be.

Let's assume he's a spiritual person. After two years of working, he finds a woman who appeals to his soul. Through meditation and prayer, they conclude that they would create a good family. They agree they should have children and they agree on how those children should be raised. They get married.

If a child is conceived as a result of sexual gratification, with no desire for having children, and if the couple run here and there thinking about getting an abortion, this kind of vibration affects the child. There is a feeling of not being wanted. There are so many children, so many people, who feel they are not loved or wanted.

So, prior to conceiving their first child, a couple should pray together a great deal. At a minimum, they would pray fifteen minutes face-to-face and fifteen minutes back-to-back. The fastest way of balancing the male-female through prayer is with the spinal columns pressed together. It also brings each person into a higher state of consciousness.

When they are ready to conceive a child, they would send out a call for a being to be born into their family. This would take about two to three weeks. Through prayer, the parents and the being awaiting birth can image a perfect child – a perfect body, perfect teeth, perfect everything.

The child associated with a fetus hangs around the mother, almost encapsulating her. So, the higher the mother's prayer vibrations, the better it is.

If, during the nine months of pregnancy, the mother and the child-to-be are surrounded by beauty – beautiful music and paintings – and if disturbances such as loud noises are prevented, this is a tremendous help in bringing forth a fantastic child. Every sound, every thought-wave is recorded in the fetus during the nine months of pregnancy. If there is a disturbance, it is recorded and there can be physical or psychological problems in the baby.

The soul and the astral body enter the physical body at first breath. Without the entrance of the astral body, the fetus is dead.

At birth, if we are talking about the way it *should* be done, there should be three people present: a psychic, a spiritual counselor, and a doctor. The psychic is there to present what the possibilities are in the astral dimension. The spiritual counselor should be able to see previous incarnations and the karma from those incarnations. The spiritual counselor also would indicate what the main purpose is for this particular lifetime and what the potential Divine missions are for this child. The astrological chart also should be given. The planets, whether we like it or not, have an influence.

The psychic reading, the information from the spiritual counselor, and the astrological reading should be recorded and it should be made available to the parents so they can help the child attain his spiritual mission and so that things will go smoothly for the child.

Somewhere about the age of two, the child can be told of the spiritual readings and of his Divine mission. Of course, the final determination of what course to follow must come from the soul itself. All of these readings are just to assist the child.

For the first five years of its life, the child should be provided with as much beauty and exposure to nature as is possible. During these first five years, there also is a need for prayer and love and beautiful sounds that are similar to those of the human heartbeat.

In addition to the intellectual growth of a child, there is a great need for spiritual growth. This is an area where there is very little presented to children. The spiritual growth that can occur by going to church for one hour a week is very small. Parents should be teaching their children the spiritual way of life along with regular education. Children who practice the Effective Prayer and who are taught the spiritual way of life are able to accomplish quickly what would take most people a long time.

In the future, teachers will teach telepathy and children will go on to learning adventures far beyond what most of us have had. With this training, there can't be any lies. I don't know if the world is ready for this openness.

We know that the ultimate goal of each person is Oneness with the Father. Jesus said, "I and my Father are one, yet the Father doeth the works." He also said, "The things I do you can do and greater." This gives us a goal – being one with the Father and doing the greater works. That is a Divine mission in itself.

We should be helped and trained – before conception, during birth, and as we are growing up – towards accomplishing that goal. Both the parents and the siblings should help. Everyone should help that child attain his Divine mission, his Divine goal.

Deep within every person on the planet, there is a knowing that the spiritual is more important than other people, is more important than anything. In finding the Divine within and in working with the Divine, a family automatically grows into a more spiritual, more advanced unit. And it brings joy, great joy, to all of the family members.

The children who are raised in this atmosphere turn to the Divine more quickly than their parents. They have no blocks – they do it immediately. And they are acceptable to others, because they love. All peer groups, of whatever age or type, want love more than anything. A child who grows up knowing the Divine Love is within and knowing that he is totally accepted by the Divine within is able to give love. He is acceptable to others because he has learned to love and give love.

This new type of person advances all of mankind. This type of person comes to planet Earth - not for personal development – but to help mankind. To help people is what we are here for.

What do we do for children and adults who haven't had this kind of ideal birthing and upbringing? Prayer vibrations – I don't care what age the individual is – can change the genes. Prayer can bring into this physical body the things it needs.

Love from the Mother

If you have ever observed the woman at birth, the love that flows forth is unbelievable. It's super-fantastic. That love is probably the highest on the planet. But it is still the wrong type. It's mother love for a child: "I have given life." Probably the most powerful love there is. The most powerful feeling. "I have given life." That is God in action. It's the Creator in action. The male aspect can't do that.

But the consciousness should be, from prior to conception, not that, "I am giving life," or anything like that. The mother does not give life. The mother is the vehicle for giving life. We need to get into the consciousness that this is a human being, that this is a citizen of the world, that it is full of Light and Love. That it is following the directions of the Creator within.

Every being that is born on planet Earth realizes the dependency on the female – rather than dependency on the Creator.

The feminine aspect is one of nurturing and controlling through love. That is dying, too. No longer is it available to us. We are being shorn of all of the tools of animal man and we are moving into a new type being.

Jesus ran away from his parents at 12 to illustrate to you and me that we must stand up and be true. Not controlled and directed. We must follow the Creator within.

The first words he uttered after becoming Christed were, "Woman, what do I have to do with you?" – talking to his mother. He eliminated the word "mother." What he was saying was, "I am free. Let me be free. Let me follow the Creator within. I know who I am now. I am One." She had directed him to make wine. From that time on, she stopped. Thirty years it took to break that bond, to break that control mechanism. When she said, "Jesus, make wine," she was speaking for all women. And the answer was fantastic. Mothers are not up here. Fathers are not up here. They are people.

He was really saying, "Women, see yourselves as you really are." See yourselves as women, but of a different type: ones tuned into the Creator. Accept the wonders of yourself as a woman. But don't make it a control state. Let that womanhood manifest the Creator. And you are free. You are. You are standing up. You don't have to ask men for the Equal Rights Amendment. Don't make us a god. Jesus was saying, "Woman, stand up on your own. Be you." You don't have to direct anyone. You don't have to control anyone.

Nesting

The woman has made the nest, has made having a family, a god. That nesting instinct is an animal instinct. True man is able to stand up and say, "Wherever I am, God is."

The nesting instinct must be changed to: wherever you are is holy ground. Wherever you stand is holy ground. Not a home. You can't make a home a god. You can't make a nest a god.

I am very grateful that Diana and I, in the first 10 years of our family life, moved 21 times. Talk about destruction of nesting! That was wonderful. It forced us to become world conscious. It forced us to realize that a nest doesn't mean diddly-squat.

Knowing that wherever you are is holy ground is the beginning of Man, of rising up out of the animal nature. We've been in the animal kingdom since Day One. It is time for us to raise ourselves up to our Divine nature and to declare that wherever we are and whomever we are with is Divine.

Discipline

"Well," you say, "what about disciplining the child?" If we were all into Divinity, the need for discipline would be almost zero. There would be so much Light and Love that the child – the young person – would respond and give forth Light and Love. It is natural for people to give love. What is unnatural is that their parents, siblings, and peer group knock that love out of them within one year of being born. It is driven down, hidden, forced out of existence.

Most children who cry so much have their cries misunderstood as hunger for food. Parents plop something in their mouths instantly. But, the crying is actually a hunger for Love – but not mother love or father love – that does not satisfy. When you give Divine Love and awaken Divine Love within, *that* Love satisfies and there is no hunger.

The TV and all these things distract attention away from the consciousness of Being. In all of our children, it is programmed that it be a seeing world for them. We place into their minds that TV is the best baby sitter ever invented. And we allow this TV to be the baby sitter. "Now, sit here and watch this. It's good for you." We need to start saying, "Sit here and be in Light."

If we trained children from the time of birth until they went to school, children would become solidified in Light and they would apply to their world and throughout their lives.

Starting Later than Childhood

I am painting an ideal state. But, we have not had an ideal state.

Let us suppose you now have a child who is under twelve. What can you do? The mores of his peer group, the mores of television, the mores of man have definitely affected him. They have altered him so much he doesn't even know that he has a Divine mission.

Steps can still be taken at this stage. Have the best psychic give a reading for the child. Find an excellent astrologer and get a reading for the child. And find a spiritual being – one who can see the soul – and have a soul reading done.

The adults should take this information and simplify it. Make it appropriate for the child's age. Make it one, two, three and then give it to the child and say, "These are the findings of the experts. Now you have a goal. Here is a Divine mission for you. Here is what has happened to you. Here is where you should go. Here is a goal in life, and we, your parents, will help you in every way possible to attain this goal – because your attaining this goal will help all of man. It will help Earth."

Now, let us suppose you are a child of fifty-six, and you never had this help. Do the same thing. Get it all laid out for you. But, do not make any of these messages or messengers a god. The final determination of your direction must come from the Divine within you. Do not run to a psychic or astrologer every week, because then you would be making these a god. You take the information you receive from these individuals and you pray to determine your direction. Then, once you have received that direction, you do it with all your might and main. Accomplish it. Do not hold back.

Jesus had help. He had help from Moses and Elijah [at the transfiguration on the mount]. It was a first-class conference. They gave him alternatives as they saw it, from three different levels, and it was up to Jesus to make his selection. That conference helped him solidify his knowledge of his Divine mission – and he was already thirty-three. It is never too late to get yourself involved in accomplishing a goal.

The Single Person Family

Many of you say, "I'm alone. I'm not a family." But, every person is the father, the mother, and the son. Every person is a family unit. It is up to every person to express love and to help his fellow man. The prayers of a family praying together are powerful because there are two or three gathered together in the name of the Divine. Your prayers can be just as powerful. You are a family unit unto yourself: you are two or three gathered together. The father image in you creates ideas. The mother image in you loves the idea and surrounds it with Divine Love so that it quickly manifests as the son, the Christ in operation.

As an example of this, look at the Father-Mother-Son illustrated by Jesus. He said, "The Father in me doeth the works." The Love in him made it possible to accomplish the works. That Love was from the mother image – the Divine Mother.

Jesus said, "Who is my father? Who is my mother? Who is my brother? Who is my sister?" Who indeed is our father, mother, brother, or sister? It is all within you. Therefore, everyone is your mother. Everyone is your father. Everyone is your brother and sister.

The answer is that the Christ within you, the great master within you, that which knows the Father-Mother, is providing all your needs. Never ask for Love, Light, Truth, or understanding from anyone or from any book. Only the Divine that is within you can provide these things. If you look to another person for love, you have lost everything, because God said, "I will have no other gods before me." And that's the way it is.

The Divine Family

There are no grandmothers. There are no grandfathers. There are no mothers and no fathers. There are no children – no sons, no daughters.

These words of relationships should be eliminated from our vocabulary. Jesus put his finger on this when he said, "Who is my mother? Who is my brother?" There is none. There is only God. Jesus tried to give us this understanding about the family so all of us could awaken, because our concept of the family is a major block to our development.

The question is, what was he trying to tell us? Jesus said, "Our Father which art in heaven" and "The kingdom of heaven is within." Meaning: the Father is within. And if the Divine Father is within, then the Divine Mother and Divine Son are within. This is the Divine family. There is no outside father or outside mother or outside sons or daughters or outside brothers or sisters. All are people, and all people have the Divine Father, Mother, and Son within.

A better word than Son is "Christ." The Christ is universal, male and female. The Christ principle is the doing principle. The Father and the Mother bring the ideation and the love so that the Christ which you are can accomplish its mission. That is the only family which exists.

We give birth to a person. That person has the Father-Mother and the Christ within. We need to teach that *instantly* to every person who is born and help keep it in their consciousness as they grow up so the person will look to his Divine Father-Mother, because anything other than the Divine Father-Mother will be false.

We should teach people to find the Truth from the first breath, when the soul enters into the fetus. At that moment, it is a whole person. It has the Father-Mother principle within. It has the Christ within. And if we hold to that teaching, it will be manifested by this person.

Unfortunately, we do not do that. We, the parents, want to be dictators or kings and queens: "Do it my way or else!"

We are forced to look to the earthly fathers and mothers for the answer because of the mores and traditions that exist all over this planet. But, these earthly fathers and mothers do not have the answers. Not one parent can give you Truth. They can only give you what they have been taught.

We have a commandment to love God with all our being. That means one hundred percent of the time. Nothing less. So, we begin by loving that which is Divine, the Divine family within ourselves. Love all aspects of your body, your mind, your soul, your psyche – every part of you – realizing that each part is Divine Love.

When we learn that every person is Divine, and we emphasize that, we will have a new planet, a new type of family on Earth, a newness that is unbelievable, that is fantastic, that is good.

This viewpoint begins to change your concept of who *you* are. This approach needs to be practiced by every person, now, so that this problem of the family, which is so heavy on the planet, can be corrected.

You do not *need* to be married, but, with eight children, I am the first to say, "Do it!" It is fantastic!

If you do decide to get married and have a physical family, the manifestation of it must be from recognizing the Divine in each person. We are all here to help the people of the planet. We were given this mission when Jesus said, "You are the Light of the world." It is our responsibility.

Each individual is the one family, the true family. There is no other family than this Divine family.

We *must* become the Divine family. Then there will be no more hurts, no more physical problems, no more mental problems. Every problem comes from not knowing Divine Love. And that's the way it is.

If every person can say, "I am a member of the Divine family," then the problem is over. We don't belong to a specific physical family. We belong to the Father-Mother.

The Ultimate Purpose

The ultimate goal of each person is oneness with the Father. Jesus said, "The things I do you can do and greater." He also said, "I and my father are one, yet the Father doeth the works." This gives us a goal, a Divine mission in itself.

We should be helped and trained from before conception, during birth and early childhood, to accomplish that mission. Not only should the parents help, but if there are siblings, they should also help. Everyone should help that child know and achieve his Divine mission.

<u>Begin Now</u>

We must begin now to create this new type of family. If you are in a family where the husband or the children do not want to pray, then pray with them while they are asleep. That way, you can be two or three gathered together.

Suppose you have family members who are four hundred miles away. What do you do? You can pray with them while they are asleep. You can do the Seven Steps of Effective Prayer for them and in that way join them in prayer.

A man and a woman came to see me who were in their late forties. I explained the Seven Steps of Effective Prayer to them and said that with prayer they could have any miracle they wanted. The man said the greatest miracle that could happen on planet Earth would be for his mother to say something nice. In all his lifetime, his mother had never said anything nice. His wife agreed totally, that having her mother-in-law say something nice would be the greatest miracle. The mother lived three hundred miles away, and I guaranteed them that within two weeks, she would be totally changed. They said, "How are we to know, because we're not going to call her." I said, "You do not have to worry. You will know." So, they did the Seven Steps for her and they prayed with her when they knew she was asleep. In three days, she called them and said for the first time in his forty-eight years, "I love you." Well, he almost passed out. And then she told his wife and children that she loved them also. Seven days later, she said it again. Weeks later she gave them a piano, which they had needed and wanted. Things changed. Love began to flow.

Prayer obviously is the answer. Jesus said, "Pray without ceasing."

Pray one hundred percent of the time. You can program the Creator in you to pray while you sleep. You can pray for the planet and for the peoples of the planet to help them with the problem of the family. Consider all of the billions of people on Earth as one family. Recognize that the Father-Mother God is the father-mother that is within each one of them. If that one couple could alter the mother in three days, then together, as a prayer family unit, we can alter this whole planet, because it *is* one family.

CREATING PEACE

Most people in the world today recognize the great need for peace. Murder is repugnant to everyone. But when nations go to war, we don't consider killing to be murder. Then, killing becomes a Cause – a Cause worth fighting for and supposedly blessed by God. We have a Christian commandment to love our neighbors. And yet, Christians have fought Christians – Argentina vs. England and England vs. Ireland. It doesn't make sense.

There are no laws against war, so it has the blessings of our consciences. The mass thought of war seems to have impinged on our genes and altered them. With this genetic altering, war seems to be an acceptable act. Since Peace is one of the innermost aspects of our Divine selves, what is it that allows us to suddenly reverse this inner Peace and begin killing in a massive way?

What does killing or a mass invasion of a country say? It says, "I'm afraid." And it says, "I want to be loved. If I'm loved, I won't invade, because there is nothing to fear if I'm loved."

We each can be pressured to the point of feeling like killing. Many experiments have been conducted in which people have claimed they would not kill under any circumstances. However, when the situation changes, these same people become ready to kill. For example, a conscientious objector – a Quaker – was in Vietnam with the hospital corps. He had seen many of his friends killed by the enemy, and he reached the point of becoming a killer himself. He won a

Congressional Medal of Honor for killing people.

The war consciousness pervades the planet. We, man, have implanted this war consciousness in all of the kingdoms. It has been implanted by people who have not been educated about their responsibilities or about the fact that they are creators. These people must be taken into consideration also because the whole peace process must begin with the individual.

This war consciousness keeps man in a retarded condition. It is a tremendous pollution that pervades the very structure of Earth. It reaches within the planet to a depth of 3,000 to 4,000 miles. It's in every cell and atom. It's in the air and the atmosphere and in one another. Let's say that a billion people have been killed in wars since planet Earth began. In all of these, fear has emanated at the time of death; and this fear of war is everywhere. The fear of dying and of being killed in war is all around us and around the Earth. When we die with these emotions, the mass thought becomes powerful and other people get caught in those fear vibrations.

However, we can change all of this. We can change that fear consciousness that pervades the whole planet to Light. We can replace war consciousness with Peace, Light, and Love. We can create Peace within our genes and within our innermost selves. One way to do it is to say, "The Creator in me creates Light, Love, and Peace throughout my being. The Creator in me replaces the war consciousness throughout my being with Peace. The Creator in me replaces the war consciousness around planet Earth and in all peoples of the Earth with Peace. The Creator in me creates Peace in every atom, every cell, every gene, and every kingdom that exists on planet Earth."

The Bible on Peace

The Bible mentions "peace" quite a few times. In Isaiah (26:3) we find, "Thou wilt keep him in perfect peace whose mind is stayed on Thee." If your mind is "stayed" on God, peace comes. And since God is within, in order to know peace, you must know the Divinity within yourself.

Jesus said, "I came not to send peace, but a sword" (Matthew 10:34), meaning that the Christ consciousness cuts through the darkness and brings Light. This separation of darkness from Light brings discord until one connects with the Light. Then there is peace.

Jesus' idea of peace went far beyond its being the opposite of war. "Peace I leave with you, my peace I give unto you; not as the world giveth, give I unto you" (John 14:27).

The only way to bring about peace is through prayer, and by prayer I mean being in constant touch with the Divinity within.

If Jesus could stop the wind from blowing and the waves from creating havoc just by saying, "Peace. Be still," then you who speak from the Christ within can still the unsettled planet and bring about peace to its very heart and soul. The main reason the planet is unsettled, the main reason we do not have peace in the world, is fear. "Peace. Be still," can calm that fear.

Perhaps the best description of peace is the blessed assurance that you have the Divinity within you and that you are at one with this Divinity. If you are aware of the innermost part of you, this assuredness comes from doing the works – healing and creating from the Divinity within. This is true peace. It is the peace that passeth understanding, because at that level you are far beyond understanding. You are at the level of knowing – knowing from the Divinity within you.

You can be extremely creative, yet not peaceful. If you are not creating from Divinity, you are not creating peace. Mankind creates problems by holding onto negatives. That is why step one of the Seven Steps to Effective Prayer is so important. Until we release those negatives – our fears and our past and all the rest – we will create from them. Until the Christ within separates darkness from Light, actually changing all to Light, we will create from that darkness.

In this state of consciousness, we are walled in by the darkness of negatives. The Bible tells us of the walls of Jericho – the walls that separate us from peace. When you are caught within the walls of the physical world, your eyes cannot see reality. What is truly real in you is that which is unseen. To bring about peace within yourself, you need to make that unseen world a reality. How do you do that? You continually declare from within, "I see the Christ in you. I see Peace in you. I see the Divinity within you...and in everything." That is true seeing, that is seeing through the walls of negatives, and from that consciousness you begin to live in Peace.

See Peace. Hear Peace. Think Peace. Speak Peace. Constantly think Peace. Whenever you enter a home or a building, think to yourself, "Peace be unto you and everyone and everything within." It's an old Jewish tradition, but we should all adopt it.

These words are just a way to become one with the Divinity within. In oneness with the Divine, you can merge with the earth and say, "Peace. Be Still." Merge with the leaders you see on television and recognize the Peace in them. And remember to be at peace in everything *you* do and say. As you remain peaceful through your daily life, so others around you will be affected. You have the power to declare Peace to their souls, to help the Christ within each one manifest Peace in the world.

The key to being a peaceful person is to be still and know who you really are. You are the Christ, and the birth of the Christ within you brings glad tidings of great Joy and Peace.

There are two aspects, then, of peace: the peace that comes from knowing the Divinity of yourself and the Peace that you hold for the planet and the people of the planet.

The peacemakers are not those who run around the world negotiating treaties. They are those that speak the word of Peace from deep within. We as peacemakers need to think of the world as being without walls or boundaries because walls create fear and block peace.

There is a need for one world, one law, one justice...one consciousness of the Divine working through everything. Your efforts can accomplish this. You can consciously merge with the planet and declare Peace from the Divinity within.

"Blessed are the peacemakers, for they are the children of God" (Matthew 5:9). You are the peacemaker. You are the child of God. You are the Christ.

The World Situation

World War I was supposed to end all wars, as was World War II. But, since World War II, we've had 138 wars. Although mankind as a whole has long supported the idea of world peace, we're still fighting and killing.

People are tired of all the killing and maiming and frightening situations resulting from the wars taking place around the world. Ever since the Vietnam War, when television brought it live into our homes, there has been an increasing desire for peace.

There are tremendous negative forms of war everywhere. Everywhere. It's in the consciousness of everyone. Just as each one of us has an astral body, so planet Earth has an astral body. In the astral consciousness of Earth is this war consciousness. It is prevalent in the unseen world. I see the killing desire in everything I look at.

Almost every person who has a negative emotion is asking for love. If we can create Divine Love in that person so that Divine Love radiates throughout their being, obviously they have to change.

Question from the audience: If the Divine created such a wonderful planet, why does He allow us to go into such destruction?

Answer from Jim: My answer is: "Why do you do it? You are the Creator and you create negatives. Therefore, you, I, all of mankind causes this." There is no Divine up there that says, "O.K., you've been bad long enough. Now, I'm going to wipe you out." It just isn't that way.

You are made in the image and likeness of the Creator. We, man, have created this planet in the negative form it is in. And we, man, have a responsibility for changing it.

It Is Our Responsibility To Bring Peace

If you could see what is going on, you would see that it is a very, very touchy time where our responsibility is really great. *We* are responsible. *We* need to take up the gauntlet and do something, continuously. It is not a time for sitting back and looking for happiness.

Pray without ceasing. Prayer does not mean asking God to do something. Prayer is not asking. Prayer is creating more Light, more Good, more Peace on planet Earth.

Instead of looking to God somewhere to do it – when we've heard from Jesus that the kingdom of heaven is within – we need to shoulder the responsibility. Jesus told us, "You are the Light of the world." What that means is that we have responsibility for planet Earth. It's *our* responsibility – not that of someone "up there." *We* were given dominion. *We* were given responsibility. This is what we have done to planet Earth. This is what we can change.

Jesus said that what he did, we could do, and greater. Right now, there is a tremendous need all over the planet for these greater works. In the Middle East, the Third World countries, in our own country – everywhere – people are hurting and their hearts have need of love. The need is not for human love, but for Divine Love from the Christ within us.

We are our brother's keeper. We have a responsibility to love our neighbor. To truly love. To Divinely love. Our brother Iran. Our brother Russia. Our sister India.

Everything that Jesus did was to teach us that this Christ is in each of us, but that just to be aware is not enough. We need to create, to use the Creative Life Force within to reach all people and change them. Through individuals like you praying effectively, this has begun.

The Prevalence of the War Consciousness...and How It Can Be Changed

We can't forget that the concept of war includes those conflicts that occur in our homes, in our jobs, and within each one of us. If you analyze your own behavior, you find that you get angry and that you make statements that are war-like. Sometimes you find that your actions are war-like. You find that you do things that reflect a desire to get even. So, this war-like consciousness is a part of us.

However, it is easily changed. Jesus gave us the commandment to love God, to love our neighbor, and to love ourselves. In loving ourselves we eliminate the consciousness of the war within self; we eliminate the various negative aspects built up within ourselves.

Our responsibility is really great – to alter the killing aspect that is prevalent everywhere. It is important that we begin now. Right now. There is a tendency to feel we must be perfect before we heal the nations or become the Light of the world. But, if you wait until you are perfect, you will never get started. Don't wait. Begin now.

Make Your House a House of Prayer

Though all people say they want world peace – that we cannot survive without it – there seems to be no one who knows how to attain it. Jesus gave us an answer: "Make my house a house of prayer." One way to interpret that would be for all the churches on the planet to be open twenty-four hours a day for prayer – and only for prayer. Hindu, Buddhist, Moslem, Jewish, or Christian – it wouldn't matter; anyone could enter and pray. The minister or other leader would no longer give sermons or lead prayers, but would just be there as an example of how to pray silently.

Jesus compared the physical body to a house or a temple. And when he tells us to make our bodies houses of prayer, he doesn't mean just once in a while. He means to live in prayer continuously.

We can program the Creator within us to act even while we sleep: "The Creator in me keeps the world in peace while I sleep. The

Creator in me holds my family in peace throughout the night. The Creator in me fills my whole being with peace no matter what I am doing."

Prayer is the only thing you and I can do to affect the leaders of the world, to affect the mass consciousness, particularly for the Middle East. It is thought by many military leaders that the one country that could start World War III is Israel. It has the atomic weapon and it would use it.

In the Book of Revelation, Jesus said that, "The Tree of Life is for the healing of the nations." We should take on nations rather than taking our personal problems to the Divine.

When people pray, their minds are focused on God and, therefore, the focus is on peace as well. When there is prayer in the same place day in and day out, an energy builds up. It becomes so strong it affects anyone who enters, healing their hearts and minds and souls.

We have tried to set up the Light Center as a house of prayer. The energy here, created by prayer, has healed people of all kinds of problems.

Wouldn't it be wonderful if this were the way of all churches. What if they all just took down their signs – Methodist, Catholic, Buddhist, whatever – and put up new ones: "This is a House of Prayer. Everyone welcome."

Another way to look at "Make my house a house of prayer" is to apply the idea to our own homes. Many of us pray as individuals, but there are few homes in which the family prays together. Before the Light Center was built, we as a family had four periods a day when everyone in the house came together for about a half hour of prayer.

The best type of family prayer is for everyone to join hands while each person says a little prayer out loud. Then the rest of the time can be spent in silent prayer. Much of this prayer would be for peace – peace in the world, peace in the family, and peace within each individual.
If each of us did this, wars would cease. There would be total peace in

one year. The world has experimented with diplomacy, handing out money, supplying food and using military force to bring about peace. Nothing has worked. Nothing has stopped the killing. We don't want to just stop wars; we must stop all killing.

Ways of Bringing Peace

So, here are five ways to bring about peace: 1) Make every church, temple, and mosque a house of prayer; 2) Make your home a house of prayer; 3) Make yourself a house of prayer; 4) Pray without ceasing; and 5) Love.

If each of us loves God in every other person and in our self as well, that will bring peace. To worship God means to honor God or the Creator in everyone equally. So, if we begin to truly love God, we will automatically love one another. And we will love ourselves, because we know God is there. As we learn to worship God, we will let go of the word "my."

All is God, and if we are loving God, we are loving all people equally, all things equally. This is the essence of peace.

Just keeping the world in a bubble of Light will bring about peace. We know that Light changes people. We know that as Light increases, more and more people will become Light and increase it further. We must not throw up our hands and say, "It's too much. There is no way to make every church, every home, every person a house of prayer." That isn't necessary. It takes only a certain number of people to be dedicated, to make themselves and their homes houses of prayer. If only you who are hearing my words worship God every moment, the whole world will respond.

How can you not? God is in every moment. Not to worship God in every moment, not to recognize God moment-by-moment is blindness, is deafness, is chaos – is death. Take this challenge yourself, right this minute. Become a house of prayer and pray without ceasing. Program the Creator within to continuously increase Light and Love and Peace throughout the planet, even as you sleep and do other things. Declare with all your being, "Planet Earth is a house of prayer." And it will be so. It will be paradise.

Be the Light of the World

Let us accept our responsibilities of being the Light of the World. Let us accept the responsibility of changing the mass consciousness of war to Light, Love, Peace, and Joy. When there is Joy, we cannot kill – we can only give Love. We can do the Seven Steps for planet Earth, saying, "The Earth releases all of its past to the Light. The Earth releases its consciousness of killing to Light. The Earth releases its consciousness of war to Light. The Earth changes the vibrations of war to Light."

The higher vibrations will begin a massive healing of man as soon as we take on the responsibility of changing war to Peace. It will heal us, too, because we've all been killed in war.

There is no law from God saying there must be a cataclysm, or that we must suffer or die, to attain the new heaven and new earth. You have the power to bring about the new heaven and new earth, without war, but you have to dedicate yourself.

TECHNIQUES AND PRAYERS FOR BRINGING PEACE

Prayer reaches the hearts and souls of everyone. Each of you should choose a leader of a country and through prayer change him or her to bring peace to this planet. Everywhere there is a need for us to totally dedicate ourselves so that the Creative Life Force we have begins creating more Good than has ever been before, to change the hearts, minds, and souls of all people so that each and every one is dedicated to doing the works of the Christ within. That is what the power of prayer can do.

Let us declare, "The Creator in me changes the consciousness of war, fear, dying, killing, and being killed to Light, Love, Peace, and Joy." This will heal us as well as everyone else on the planet. All of man will be changed automatically. We must continue working with this because the mass thought of man is continuing with the war consciousness – the killing consciousness and the fear of dying. As we do this for the entire planet, we will be healed. We will be the first to be healed of our inner physical and mental problems.

The Cosmic Christ is in everyone and everything. We need to change our consciousness to see everything as sacred, not just certain times, or certain people, or places, or events. Every moment is a time of sacredness, a time of joy.

There is a great need on Earth for successful examples of communities that function peacefully and lovingly, communities of people that exist in the consciousness of peace.

Another reason the Light Center was established is to help take care of a great need – the need to change all thoughts to thoughts of peace. To bring this about, we not only need continual prayer at the Light Center, but we need it in every home, as well. The power of prayer is fantastic. We need to pray for world peace, but more important, we need to pray for individual peace. "The Creator in the people of Earth fills them with love, heals them, and directs their lives to Light." The one thing people absolutely require is to be loved. If they have love, they are going to cease killing.

Become the people of the future NOW. Start this new world NOW. The greatest power there is, is prayer. In your prayers you will discover new ideas about peace that need to be implemented.

Give your ideas to the world. Don't seek recognition or a "well done" or a blessing. That's not important. God knows the work you have done. What *is* important is peace on Earth.

There is a great need to pray in a totally different way than we have been. It must be with authority. Speak with the authority of the Creator. *The war consciousness of Earth is changed to Light.* If you'll repeat that a million times, there must be a change.

Additional prayers:

- The Creator in me changes the war consciousness of Earth to Light and Love and Peace

- The Creator in me changes the war consciousness in the astral Earth to Light and Love and Peace
- The consciousness of the Middle East is changed to Light
- Do the Seven Steps for planet Earth and put Earth in a bubble of Light
- Do the Seven Steps for the astral consciousness of Earth
- The Creator in me creates Peace, Love, and Light in [name a country]
- The Creator in [name a world leader] creates Love and Peace. The Creator that is in the leaders of [name a country] creates Peace
- Thank you, God, for starting this new world, a world of peace, a world of good will among people, a world of trust, a world of loving one another, a world of serving and helping one another. Thank you, God, that all people on Earth are filled with love, are healed, are directed to Light. Thank you, God, for each one of us. Amen.

TERRORISM

Acts of terrorism are acts of seeking love. Most of our problems as individuals come from a lack of love – love from someone outside of self. We are always seeking love from someone outside of ourselves.

We start in early childhood when we learn to cry and we get picked up. Parents should pick up their children when they're *not* crying. Studies show that when a child is picked up when it is not crying, it tends not to cry as much.

But, throughout the world, we receive praise and love when we're bad. It's a problem throughout the planet – people reaching out for love from someone. We are always disappointed in that love we reach out for. People are not giving the type of love we really want. We want not only one hundred percent of their love – we want one hundred fifty percent of their love.

Attention is the one thing we really want. We have many ways of getting attention: winning athletic competitions, getting intellectual honors, being an entertainer – or getting sick.

When it comes to the terrorists, they think we do not treat them as we should. We, the Americans, do not treat the Arab countries as we should. We do not treat them with the respect, honor, or equality that we do Israel. Obviously, that is true. They have this feeling of not only wanting to be recognized but of wanting respect for themselves.

This is one of the ways of doing that: by tweaking the nose of America, they feel like they are accomplishing their mission. It isn't the way of gentlemen or the way of people who have couth. It seems to be the way of the un-couth, of the barbaric.

There are over 800 terrorist acts a year. Most come from the Arab nations, the Muslim world. And over a third are against America.

The reason they do it – if you analyze the family – the way children get attention today is by crying or showing their hurts. Then big father or big mother comes and hugs them. Similarly, in the world, America is the big father and big mother. The only place you can get attention is from America.

They're at the stage of total rejection. And when you get to the stage of total rejection is when you get into killing.

In our own country, most murderers are seeking love. The reason is that the present modes of love are unsatisfactory. They do not fulfill. The only love that fulfills the needs of people is Divine Love.

Maybe one of the solutions to this particular problem of the terrorist act in Lebanon [where, in 1983, barracks in Beirut were bombed, killing 220 U.S. Marines] is to come up with a method, once it's particularly resolved, of getting love to these people - rather than being rejected by the world. Being rejected is very difficult, and they're at the point of total rejection. Is there a possibility we could give them a solution to their particular needs? Obviously, if all 235 million Americans were to pray that they – all of the Muslim world – be filled with Divine Love, there would be a change. All of you have seen the effects of effective prayer.

So, if we, instead of getting uptight and angry and getting into a consciousness of "against" rather than "for"….Jesus, when he walked the planet, said, "Pray for those who despitefully use you." This is exactly what is going on. We are being despitefully used. It requires – not only in America but around the world – praying without any judgments. It requires praying effectively for these terrorists, for the Muslim world, for the Arabs – for them to feel they are accepted, that they are not rejected, that they are part of the world.

One of the good things that has happened is for an Arab to go up in the space shuttle and help launch a satellite not just for Saudi Arabia but for all of the Arab world. That was a wonderful happening. We need to get more involved in that type of thing. We need to be involved in, "What can we do to help these people?" These people are our well-beloved brothers. They believe in God. They are created in the image and likeness of God. Everyone is created that way. For people to reject another people is catastrophic. We must learn to love our fellow man. We must not only love them, but find ways to help them. It is time for us to get into the consciousness of helping our fellow man. Helping them out of their darkness. Helping them out of their despair. Helping them out of their feeling of rejection.

We've been praying for this area of the world and its people. One of the things that came to people was to implement something like a Marshall Plan for Lebanon, to help them rebuild their country, so that the people will not feel rejected anymore.

There is internal fighting in Lebanon – Arabs killing Arabs. The Shiites are killing the other Arabs there. This situation has been going on for quite some time.

The primary solution is for us to pray effectively for the Shiites, the Sunnis, the other Arabs, and the whole Middle East. The amount of negative thoughts over the Middle East now is unbelievable. The negatives that have been implanted there continue to grow. With so many people thinking negative thoughts, it adds to the burden over there. It causes them to want to kill.

We need to change that negative thought to love. When you eat, sleep, and drink Divine Love, you are not into the consciousness of killing. You are not into the consciousness of feeling rejected. You are not into the consciousness of wanting to get even. At that moment that you have Divine Love, you are willing to give. You are willing to help your fellow man. The idea of killing stops.

It may be that the negative thoughts of man are adding too much to their burden and causing this terrorism.

The Middle East is not the only place terrorism occurs. In our country, in America, when we beat our children, this is terrorism of another type. Why does that go on? It's the same reason: if parents had Divine Love, they would not do this.

There is a need all over the planet for people to learn to Divinely love each other. So that our abuse and killing of each other come to an end.

There is a great need to pray that these terrorists be filled with Divine Love, that Lebanon and Syria be filled with Divine Love. And when you think of Iran and the Ayatollah Khomeini and all of those involved there – total rejection. They have nothing. It is time for them to have Divine Love. It is time for change to take place. And of course Iraq, since there is a war between Iraq and Iran.

It is *our* requirement that we do something – not only in the physical in the way that we relate internationally with them, that we should be able to relate freely with them, and give freely to them without so much going on in our Congress and the special interest groups controlling so that we can't act like a true Christian nation ought to act, giving love and giving help where it's needed without restraint. The ones that are into killing are in the greatest need of help. It requires that we do something. It requires that we no longer reject. It requires that we go in with open arms. "We'll be glad to help. We'll be glad to give you anything that will help you be a nation of the world, accepted and acceptable. We have so many limitations we place upon our government – when we should be an example of helping. If we are a true Christian, we will do that.

Our government should request that the people of this country go into an all-day prayer for the countries of the Middle East. There will be a change when there is that much prayer for a people.

There are things we need to do individually. We as Christians should dedicate our lives to helping our fellow man, those that are in need, those that are despitefully using us, those that are the killers in our country, those that are the killers on our highways. We have the responsibility to help our fellow man.

We have the capability of doing this because this is the most enlightened country. We stood out magnificently when we did the Marshall Plan after World War II. Probably one of the greatest acts of help that has ever been done on planet Earth. Prior to that Marshall Plan, every nation that defeated another raped the country of everything – and raped the people. This was the standard way of doing things. The Marshall Plan instituted a new way that changed the world.

This is a way – to show that our goodwill is not limited to just a handful that are our neighbors. Every person, every country is our neighbor. It is time that we change our concepts that we give only to the good and we kill the bad. It is a time for all kinds of good to be done, especially Divine Love. This is the ultimate that we can do for anyone. That's the way it is.

THE MILITARY

*W*hy would a man who dedicated the last seventeen years of his life to prayer for peace have spent three decades associated with the military?

Jim never rejected the military. Quite the opposite: he saw it as being necessary, at least for a time. Nor did he reject weapons, even nuclear weapons. His fundamental belief was: it's not the weapons, it's the desire to kill that is the problem. He saw that the most effective way of transforming that desire to kill was through prayer. But, Jim believed that in the interim, until the prayer and the Light and the Love brought about a new world, the military plays an important role.

A basic premise of Jim's was that you do not want to be weak. As a boy growing up in Pueblo, Colorado, he had a reputation as being one of the better boxers: if you got in a scuffle, you had to defend yourself, and Jimmie Goure, known for his heart, was not going to be bullied or defeated. Later in life, after leaving the government, he said, The killing is not the answer. But, you can't be weak. All over the planet, there are examples of what happens to the weak. The gazelle is soon killed in the animal world – and most of man is still animal. And the weak is that person who is much preyed upon.

Another premise of Jim's was that force, in extreme cases, may be necessary. All over the planet, there are people who are power-mad and there are beings who are into the negative aspect. Sometimes, the only way we can get their attention is whip them. If we get their attention, then they might listen.

Jim also had high regard for the spirituality of military people. Military people, who have seen killing, who know killing, are the most spiritual people I have run across on the planet. They really pray. They *really* pray. Any time you've seen someone you love – and in the military they love one another, because their lives depend on one another – when you see that one you love die from war, you want to pray. There is no question. You *will* pray.

My being in the Pentagon, the most spiritual people I ran across were in the military. It was fantastic. And the best lecture on spirituality I'd ever heard was given by a four-star general. It was absolutely fantastic.

In the Pentagon itself, about five hundred people gather every day to pray. Show me a city that does the same. That's fantastic.

If we do our job with effective prayer, it will change the course of events. That is why most of the admirals and generals are very, very spiritual people, very much into prayer, all of them, because they know there has to be a better way. Nevertheless, they know there can be no weakness.

For all of his observations and premises, Jim drew parallels from the Bible. He noted that Jesus, when he whipped the moneylenders in the temple, used force: He whipped man. He used a force. To alter one of the greatest problems on the planet. To alter our concept of money. Greed. It took *that* to get our attention, to get their attention, to make them realize what they were doing not only to the building structure, the temple, but what they were doing to this temple, the body. It was a fantastic event.

In defense of having weapons, he said that Jesus had allowed his disciples to carry arms. He cited the story of Peter cutting off the ear of a man who threatened Jesus. The Bible states that at the time Jesus was betrayed by Judas, Peter, "having a sword, drew it and smote the high priest's servant, and cut off his right ear." Jesus said, "Suffer ye thus far," and touched the man's ear and healed him. Most people focus on the miracle of the healed ear, which Jim also took note of. But Jim also inferred from the story that Jesus had given Peter permission to carry a sword as a way to defend himself.

Jim's basic belief about weapons was that, If all of the countries of the world laid down their arms, then obviously within a few months there would still be a power struggle. So, we need to look into this concept of war and peace and things of this nature in a different way.

Anyone who has ever seen a nuclear weapon go off would obviously never use it. This is true of Russia and China and it is true of our country. We would not use it now because we know the devastation that would exist and *they* know no one can win in those conditions.

There is a proposal to the United Nations by our country that every five years we put on a demonstration of nuclear weapons – actually exploding them and showing what they do, so, at the end, all of the leaders will say, "We can never do this." As leaders who are aware of what nuclear weapons can do die off, the new leaders don't know. No matter what they say, they really don't know. If there were a demonstration of the destructive power of nuclear weapons every five years, eventually then, nuclear weapons would be done away with.

And to support his statement that military people can be highly spiritual, he mentioned the story of the military person who came to Jesus asking him to heal a servant "sick of the palsy and grievously tormented." Jesus told the centurion that he would come and heal the servant, but the centurion said, "Lord, I am not worthy that thou shouldest come under my roof. Speak the word only, and my servant shall be healed." Jesus "marveled, and said to them that followed, 'Verily, I have not found so great faith, no, not in Israel.'" Jim's take on that story was that, Jesus healed a person in another town, without going, a person who was near death or dead, just by speaking the word, deep within, and it was so. The amazing part of that story is he gave the highest credit to the man who asked him to do this, without going to his home. And the man was a military man. And he said in *all* of the whole of the world he had never seen anyone with that much faith, and that included his disciples. None of them had the faith that this one man, the military man. So, you might change your concepts about military people.

Jim was well aware that there is much work to be done before Earth can be a peaceful planet. How many souls of military people who have died still want war? How many military people who have been trained to kill – and their only objective is to kill – when they die, in the astral dimension, what about them?

During World War II, I ran into one of my schoolmates from grade school. All he could talk about was killing. All he wanted to do was kill. But, he was killed. And yet all he still wants to do is kill. It was ingrained in his soul. To have that energy in somebody's home or attached to some military person, is pretty heavy.

There is a great need for us to work on this. We need to free Earth from dead thoughts and dead emotions. Earth has been a killing planet. The people of Earth have been killers. It is a great project for us to take on: to free Earth of these thoughts and emotions.

We need to free Earth and have Peace so a new world can be established in the minds and hearts of the people of Earth. We need to work towards this goal with our whole being.

Total trust of each other is what we are evolving towards. With no fear of dying or of being killed or of being hurt. Everyone is alert now, just like you are alert now about your home: you keep it locked to keep out the negative aspects. Someday we won't need a lock. Someday we will be able to relate one to another. Someday we don't have to whip people to get their attention. Someday in loving one another we will get through it.

How are you individually going to live? Why not start now? Why wait until that moment? Start existing now the way you would like to exist when there is total peace and trust and love between people.

Jim had a unique perspective on nuclear fallout: There has been much said about radiations from fallout. Fallout was really a good thing back in 1947 to 1948 before real testing. The group of Man was about five thousand years behind in normal development. Radiation from fallout has speeded up the time span so Man could reach a higher state of consciousness. But testing is not longer "where it's at." Even underground testing creates problems, but at the same time it is good. Radioactivity is Light. It has forced us to be Light-conscious. At the same time, radioactivity can be poison."

Other

Q: It is hard for me to imagine a four-star general really aware of Divine Love in all people and to then take part in planning or actually ordering the extinguishing of a carrer of that Divine Love or actually extinguish part of the Light of the world. Could you give me insight into what goes on in that person's psyche?

A: Yes….He whipped man. He used a force. To alter one of the greatest problems on the planet. To alter our concept of money. Greed. It took *that* to get our attention, to get their attention, to make them realize what they were doing to the building structure, the temple, but what they were doing to this temple [the body]. It was a fantastic event.

The concept of people on the planet…obviously we do not trust one another. We have locks on our doors. We have locks on our cars. Obviously, we do not believe in God.
The reason for the locks is that we are afraid – of getting killed, raped, robbed, whatever.

All over the planet, there are countries that have this same problem. There are people who are power-mad. There are beings who are into the negative aspect. Sometimes, the only way we can get to them is to whip them to get their attention. The two-by-four story is a good example of that. We get their attention, then they might listen.

In my concept today, I believe it is possible, if all of the countries of the world laid down their arms, then obviously within a few months there would still be a power struggle. There would be control mechanism.
Then we need to look into this concept of war and peace and things of this nature in a different way.

When one of the great gurus of the planet spent a great amount of time in our country fighting against the nuclear weapon, as though it was the end of the world, when he was presented with the idea of the nuclear weapon...

Anyone who has ever seen a nuclear weapon go off would obviously never use it. This is true of Russia and China and it is true of our country. We would not use it now because we know the devastation that would exist and *they* know no one can win in those conditions.

There is a proposal to the United Nations by our country that every five years we put on a demonstration of nuclear weapons – actually exploding them and show what they do, so, at the end, all of the leaders will say, "We can never do this." Because all of the leaders of the world are aware of what nuclear weapons can do, as they die off, they don't know. No matter what they say, they really don't know. Eventually then, it will be done away.

But in the interim, the fear of control overrides. It's a lot like Jimmy Carter saying, when the Russians invaded Afghanistan, "I was so wrong in what I was doing to the military."

Everyone is alert now, just like you are alert now about your home: you keep it locked to keep out the negative aspects. Someday we won't need a lock. Someday we will be able to relate one to one another. Someday we don't have to whip another to get their attention. Someday in loving one another we will get through it.

There is no question that the military, who have seen killing, who know killing. In my relation with so many of them, they are the most spiritual people I have run across on the planet. They really pray. They *really* pray. Any time you've seen someone you love – and in the military they love one another, because their life depends upon one another – when you see that one you love die from war, you want to pray. There is no question. You will pray. You become spiritual because you know there is no force that can do....
The killing is not the answer. All of them know that. They all know that. But you can't be weak. It is examples of what happens to the weak all over the planet. The gazelle is soon killed in the animal

world – and most of man is still animal. And the weak is that person who is much preyed upon.

If we do our job with effective prayer, it will change the course of events. That is why most of the admirals and generals are very, very spiritual people, very much into prayer, all of them, because they know there has to be a better way. Nevertheless, they know there can be no weakness.

In the Pentagon itself, about five hundred people gather every day to pray. Show me a city that does the same. That's fantastic.

If I can truly recognize that Divine Love in you, if I hold to that, obviously you have to be healed. If I can see only Love throughout your whole being, then obviously you will be healed.

It doesn't make any difference how far away. Distance has no bearing. When Jesus healed a person in another town, without going, a person who was near death or dead, just by speaking the word, deep within, and it was so.

The amazing part of that story is he gave the highest credit to the man who asked him to do this, without going to his home. And the man was a military man. And he said in *all* of the whole of the world he had never seen anyone with that much faith, and that included his disciples. None of them had the faith that this one man, the military man. So, maybe you might change your concepts.

My being in the Pentagon, this is an aside, the most spiritual people I ran across were in the military. In the government. It was fantastic. And the best, if you will, lecture on spirituality I'd ever heard was given by a four-star general. It was absolutely fantastic.

I *know* the Love is inside of you. I know you need not seek outside of self. I know that if you hold to this in your loved ones – "The Divine Love is in you" – they will change. Whether they stay or go does not make a difference. You have done your mission: "I know you have Divine Love in you. I'll hold to it whether you stay or go."

Just as all of Jesus' disciples left him. Yet he loved them. He divinely loved them. Even one of them lied about him.

How many souls of military people who have died still want war? How many military people who have been trained to kill – and their only objective is to kill – when they die, in the astral dimension, what about them?

During World War II, I ran into one of my schoolmates from grade school. All he could talk about was killing. All he wanted to do was kill. But, he was killed. But all he still wants to do is kill. It was ingrained in his soul. To have that energy in somebody's home or attached to some military person, is pretty heavy.

There is a great need for us to work on this. We need to free Earth from dead thoughts and dead emotions.

Because Earth has been a killing planet. The people of Earth have been killers.

It is a great project for us to take on: to free Earth of these thoughts and emotions.

We need to free Earth and have Peace so a new world can be established in the minds and hearts of the people of Earth. We need to work towards this goal with our whole being.

Total trust of each other is what we are evolving towards. With no fear of dying or of being killed or of being hurt.

How are you individually going to live? Why not start now? Why wait until that moment? Start existing now the way you would like to exist when there is total peace and trust and love between people.

WORLDS TO PRAY FOR

*J*im worked hard to understand what was holding people back from recognizing and living their Divine nature. His experience was that there are forces – often hidden from view – that compel people to behave in ways that inwardly they know are not in their best interest. He spoke extensively about those forces and continually admonished people to pray for their transformation. What follows are his descriptions of some of these forces and the prayer antidotes that he recommended.

The Power and Control Worlds

The control world manifests itself in a boss-slave consciousness. It shows up in the way parents try to exert control over their children. Or it may manifest in a boss trying to control employees through the god of money. The time for this boss-slave consciousness – which has existed throughout the history of mankind – is over.

The power world is into ego and self-aggrandizement. It is the dog-eat-dog world people experience in businesses. It shows itself when businesses try to put others out of business. The power world also manifests itself in killing and in wars.

TECHNIQUES FOR CHANGING THE POWER AND CONTROL WORLDS

Say silently, over and over, "The Creator changes the power and control worlds to Light."

We all tend to think of our particular heads of government as being the boss. We get tired of this boss situation. But if we as a nation got into the concept that our head of government is working from the Creator within himself, for the good of everyone, and if we held to that in him, it would, it must, become a reality.

If you are a parent or a business executive, you can remove the idea of being the boss or the dictator. Get into the consciousness of, "I am working with the Creator for the good of everyone around me. I am working with the Creator to accomplish the mission of the Creator." When we work for the Creator, the money is the Creator's. It's not mine. The house is the Creator's. It's not mine.

What if we recognized the Creator in our husbands, our wives, our children? We would be giving them the maximum we can give to anyone. It would cause a tremendous happening – because the ultimate that can be done for any person is the recognition that the Creator in them is creating Light and Love. We can say silently about others, "The Creator in you is creating Light and Love throughout your whole being, filling you so full of Love that you have Peace."

The Astral Dimension

The astral world needs cleaning up. There are around one hundred forty million people who die each year and many of them stay around Earth and try to influence people still in the physical. Seventy to ninety-five percent of all people are controlled by one or more beings on the astral dimension.

The majority of the people of Earth stay within a ten mile radius of their home. In third world countries, the people don't have enough money to go *anywhere*. And where do they go when they die? They stay within the same ten mile radius they lived in when they were in the physical. They hang around their loved ones. They hang around homes. These are the so-called spirits or ghosts. If they have been alcoholics, they hang around bars. That type of presence is heavy upon the people in bars and taverns and lounges. Almost all of the 140 million who die each year – whether alcoholics or not - are negative.

With 140 million people dying each year, over a ten year period there potentially would be 1.4 billion spirits hanging around the astral, interfering with people. No one on Earth is free to be themselves. Everyone is open in their astral nature because we have not been taught about our astral bodies and how to protect them. There are many cases of people being possessed. This has been brought out in books such as *The Three Lives of Eve*.

None of us is completely free from being influenced by the astral dimension. But all of us want to be free. Earth needs to be free. The people of Earth need to be free from any control outside of self.

There is a need to conduct prayers that will free souls that have passed on and are hanging around the astral dimension. There is a need for prayer so that they are allowed to move on to the Light – rather than staying around their homes and interfering with people. There is a need to bring to their consciousness that there is Light.

What would heaven on Earth be like? The veil between the physical dimension and the astral dimension would be rent. We would be able to see people on all dimensions. We would see the people who have passed on. We would see the truth. People could no longer be dishonest without it being seen. You would instantly be aware of anything of a negative nature. There would be Divine Love flowing from the Creator within. You would be able to see the colors and the wonders of the mineral and the plant kingdoms.

TECHNIQUES FOR CHANGING THE ASTRAL DIMENSION

Say silently, over and over, "The Creator changes the astral dimension to Light."

Or, "The Earth and its astral body release all of its past. The Earth and its astral body are unified as one."

Or say, "The Creator in all people throughout all time who have passed on to the other dimension fills them with love, heals them, directs them to Light, and educates them on spiritual growth."

The Drug and Alcohol Worlds

There are beings on other dimensions – beings who were alcoholics or drug addicts when they were alive - who try to influence people into taking drugs and drinking alcohol. One drop of alcohol or even a whiff of marijuana connects you with these alcohol and drug worlds. You do not want to be controlled by these beings and you do not want your fellow humans controlled by these beings.

TECHNIQUE FOR CHANGING THE DRUG AND ALCOHOL WORLDS

Say silently, over and over, "The Creator changes the drug and alcohol worlds to Light."

The Sex World

Throughout the Bible, the finger is pointed at sex as the big problem. The male aspect of our beings is into sex, the animal nature of sex. The female aspect also is interested in sex. Ninety-five percent of people's thoughts are interconnected with sex. Everything we do regarding money is oriented to sex. Even in our homes, where we think we're safe, there are beings into sex who try to control us, causing us to have sex in our minds or in all kinds of forms that we don't want. You know in your inner self that this is not the right way.

The sex world is a separate, thick world around planet Earth. There are millions of beings on another dimension who are totally, one hundred percent, into sex. This sex world is a control mechanism. It affects us so dramatically that we are not able to direct our own lives. We can't even function as human beings. We're functioning as animals. So many thoughts and emotions have been put into the sex world that it has gone berserk.

Man – for thousands and thousands of years – has been practicing animal sex. He has seen animal sex and that is all that he has seen. He has not been taught any other way. So, man is caught at the level of animal sex. When done the way we do it, animal nature sex is death. Absolute, guaranteed death.

The animal form of mating is done primarily for gratification of animal desires. The animal nature of sex that we are involved with does not free us or bring us happiness. If it did, this would be the happiest planet in the universe.

There somehow is a direct connection in people's minds that sex is love. S-e-x does not spell l-o-v-e, does not correspond in any way, shape, or form to love. The whole idea that sex is love has to be eliminated.

I'm not saying that sex is wrong. But, we need to change our concept of sex. It is a matter of altering and elevating our concepts. This requires effort. A lot of effort. Because sex is the dominating thing on planet Earth.

TECHNIQUE FOR CHANGING THE SEX WORLD

This sex world needs our prayers. It is time that we change sex to Light. By saying, "The sex world is changed to Light. Sex *is* Light," you will begin the process of elevating sex and changing it into something that is life-enhancing.

BE DIVINE

Be Divine. Maybe this is the ultimate of the code of life. Maybe this is the *only* code of life, being Divine.

Jesus said, "Ye are Gods." The Old Testament has the same, exact words. But, we've been programmed by all of the religions to think otherwise. So, we don't pay attention to these words, "Ye are gods."

What would it be like if we had been taught for two thousand years that ye are gods? That each of you has that essence of God. That you indeed are God. Suppose that we were taught how to behave as gods. How to think. What to do. How to accomplish. Rather than the way it was. What would the world be like two thousand years after that? What would the relationships be, one to another? What would be the laws of the world? How would we live? What would be the conduct of man?

Let us look into what kind of state of consciousness we would be if we lived the statement, "Ye are gods."

Accepting Divinity

Some of us feel that to be a god we would have to dress and look differently. We would have to be perfect. Our bodies would have to be perfect. And our bodies are telling us we are not perfect. We feel that, "'Ye are gods' does not apply to me because my body is not perfect. It applies to...well, no one on Earth is perfect. But, maybe someone will come." That's the kind of consciousness we have. And there's been much ado about a second coming.

Most people are afraid to be a god because the rest of the world is not in that state of consciousness. We are afraid that we will be different and unacceptable if we had the consciousness of a god and acted like a god.

You are God. Accept it. "I accept Divinity in me." That's easy to say. If you say, "I am God," you're going to the loony house. But, if you say, "I accept the Divinity in me," everyone can accept that.

You *are* Divine. That's the way it is.

"I [God] exist right now." The oneness of that is fantastic. We then have let go of all of the troubles of man. We have let go of all of that which holds us back, which keeps us from functioning as Divine beings. We have no concern for the future because God is now.

We were made in the image and likeness of the God, according to the Bible, and that image and likeness of God includes the ability to be Divine. Being Divine means you have total oneness with Life, Love, Spirit, and Truth. You are one with all of the attributes of the Divine.

Stay locked into Light. The easiest way to stay in the flow and stay in this Light is to say, "Thank you, God, for me." Things begin to happen in every cell when you say that. They become alive. *You* become alive. Everything becomes alive.

How do we be Divine? It is oneness with this innermost part of ourselves and it is a matter of practice.

<u>Recognizing the Divine in Each Other</u>

The first part of being a god is the recognition of God in each individual. As soon as we recognize the Divine in each individual, it changes the way we see one another. Immediately we know that we can only worship the Divine and we know that Divine is in everyone. We feel the beauty and wonder of each individual as a God-being and we know this is something that commands our complete awe and respect.

If we would recognize the Divine in each other, that would automatically eliminate wars. War becomes impossible. Killing becomes impossible. Crime becomes impossible.

Recognizing who each person is, we would all work together.

If we say, "I love you. I love that Divine that is in you," if everyone on the planet is saying that, how much better is each individual going to be? What would be our own way of living then, if everyone else is seeing us as Divine – and we in turn are seeing everyone as Divine? There immediately would be a flow of Divine Love. Not human love. Not man love. But Divine Love. The highest type of love. If we could see Divine Love flowing between each of us and increase that in each other, then each of the gods would accomplish their Divine mission.

A change is occurring. We are beginning to know that everyone is Divine. When we see other people, we are beginning to think, "I know that you are special. I know that you have the Light in you. I know that the Light in you is fantastic."

Let this Light and let this Divine within you become strong and true. Let it be the primary feature of your life. Every time you see the Light or see the Divine in others, you increase the Divinity in them. Everyone is trying to be free - to be the Divinity they know is within themselves. And the time is now for us to get into this consciousness of Divinity. As we see the Divine in all things, all things change.

Every time we see the Light, every time we see the Divine in each other, we are increasing the Divinity in ourselves and in others. As we see the Divine in all things, all things change to greater Divinity. And the time is now for us to get into this consciousness of Divinity.

Doing Your Divine Mission

We must take responsibility for our own Divine mission. Each one of us has a distinct Divine mission. It may be a small thing and it may be a big thing.

So, we need to change our consciousness of God, our consciousness of heaven, our consciousness of existence, and live a new way of life. We need to see the Divine in each other, respect the Divine in each other, and help each other accomplish our individual Divine missions.

How much would be done if each one of you received total love? You would immediately heal anyone you saw. You would do it automatically without thinking about it, because you love.

Once we begin being that type of consciousness, there is a tremendous change that takes place in each one of us. As soon as we recognize the Divinity in everyone and in everything, there is an increase of the Divinity within us. It is an automatic thing.

How do we find out what our Divine mission is? The Divine reveals all. Every day, you can say, "The Divine in me reveals my mission."

Letting Go of the Mass Consciousness

This is a world that is into separation, into judging, into seeing things as plus-minus. In this plus-minus world we think, "I have to work. I have to make money. I have to get married." Let go of all of this.

Letting Go of the Past

There is no past. There is no future. There is only God. Right now.

Let go of the past. Let go of all past relationships. Let go of all things. The past is over. Let go of it. God is *now*! God exists right now!

Letting Go of the Future

Have no concern for the future. God is now.

There is no greater thing than God now. Rather than working toward a future event, go for God now. If you're saying to yourself, "I'll go for God consciousness when my body is perfect," that will be two million years down the pike. Go for God right now and let go of any desire to be perfect. Let go of your consciousness of perfection. No one here has any idea of what perfection is. The reality is: that which is Divine in you *is* perfect. The more you begin to express that Divine within yourself, the Divine spreads through your beingness. You begin to change.

Letting Go of Separation

The idea of separateness is the biggest problem on the whole planet. When you look at the planet, it is this "I" or "my" that is holding man back.

The Bible says that God is Light; God is Love; God is Spirit; and God is Truth. It also says that there is no place that God is not. That means God is everywhere present – in me, in you, in everyone and everything – inseparable. The scientific world has arrived at the same conclusion: we are not separate from anything or anyone.

All of us think we are separate and distinct from everyone else. All of think we are different.

But the scientific world has said it, the Bible has said it, and all the great gurus of the world likewise have said it – exactly the same thing – that we indeed are not separate.

We are programmed to separate everything and everyone. We separate ourselves: there is a part of me that is perfect. Most of me isn't. That type of thing.

In reality there is no separation. That is the biggest problem within ourselves. We are constantly separating. We go to church on Sunday, take our halo out of the closet, dust it off, put it on, go to church, that type of thing. Church is always, every moment of existence, of holiness, of this that is Divine.

It is time the walls came down – the walls we have built around ourselves, including the wall we create when we say to ourselves, "Nobody knows how great I am".

Let go of separation. Let go of being separate from each other. Let go of separation from anything. The Divine is everywhere. There is no place the Divine is not. That being the case, we are all One. We are merging into One. The consciousness of separation must go. Our consciousness must be, "I see the oneness of the Divine."

It is time we declared a unified world, unified in the Creator, evermore. Separation must cease.

Being the Light of the World

Jesus said, "Ye are the Light of the world." That statement says, "I must *be* the Light of the world." It says each person must be the Light of the world. It says *you* must be the Light of the world.

What does it mean to be the Light of world? It means being able to recognize and hold to and declare *Light* – in every person and in every thing and in the earth and throughout Earth. Declaring Light so powerfully that man will change his need to kill.

The Allness

Even saying the word "I" is a separation. Even saying the word "I" limits the Divine. The Creator can say "I" – but the Divine cannot. The Divine is. That Isness is everywhere in everyone.

So, take on not only your own Divine mission but the Divine mission of the Allness. Not only merge with the Creator but bring the Creator inside of you. Be big about it. Bring the Creator inside of you and love Him. Love that Creator. The Creator is likewise moving on into the consciousness of Divinity. He's a step ahead of us, in a sense. Moving into that Isness includes loving the Creator and the creation as one.

It goes beyond the statement, "The Creator and I are one." Being Divine, you cannot say, "The Creator and I are one." It's impossible.

You Are. And that's the way it is. You Are all – and beyond all. Life – that's You. That's You.

Merging

Being the Light of the world means becoming one with the world in every way. That doesn't mean I am one with the world out here. That means I am one with the world in here, inside. If it's out here, we're not one with the world. Bring it within you and love it when you have it within.

It's like being pregnant. When you have it within you, you give it life. You increase life. You want that which is in you to be perfect. You try with all your might and main to fill it with love and life. You feed it – give it what it needs. And so it is with the world: you give to the whole world everything it needs. That means you give every person, every cockroach, every tree, every stone, the center of the world, everything about it – you give Light and Love so it is fed, so that it has Life. "You are the Light of the world" means you have that responsibility.

You can put planet Earth in a bubble of Light and bring it inside yourself. Experiment! Everyone who has tried it becomes God-conscious just like that! [snaps his fingers]

When a woman is pregnant with a child, she is saying, if she's doing it right, "You are filled with Light and Love." So, when we become pregnant with planet Earth, "Earth, you are filled with Light and Love." Because everything in the Earth and on the Earth and around the Earth wants what you have to give: Light and Love.

What happens when you begin to live that is that you become an entirely different person. All of the rules immediately have been changed. You are a different type of person. You are Christ. And all rules are off for the Christ. There is no law except for one hundred percent love. There is no law of karma. There is no law of reincarnation. You are a totally a different person, and therefore, you are not controlled by anyone or anything.

As soon as you have that Earth within you, that moment is when you realize, "I cannot stop there." Because God is in Mars. God is in our Sun. Wherever God is, I must be. I cannot exist separate from that.

Not out there. We as humans place everything out there, wall it out. But as the Divine, we take it in and merge it inside of us – our sun, our stars, our galaxy, our universe, every being in it – so you can love them, so you can give them life, so you can increase that life – with your total being, because existence other than that is not living. Not having the universe inside of you is death! Ye are gods. You *are* Divine. And that's the way it is.

Thank you, God, for merging us all as One.

Thank you, God, for this Divinity, this of Thee in each of us, in everything, in all that is, in all dimensions. Amen.

CODE OF LIFE

*I*n 1948, Jim and Diana Goure wrote their personal bible. That bible can be found in Part I in the chapter entitled "Family." What Jim did in a lecture entitled "Code of Life" was to expound portions of that bible, without stating explicitly what the code's source was.

In order to be Citizens of Light, we need a code of life to live by. We need a set of guidelines to show us how to be aware of God at all times, how to worship God, and how to make God the number one priority in our lives. Here are ten guidelines that you may find helpful for living as a Citizen of Light.

1. <u>LISTEN TO GOD</u>, within self and within everyone and everything

Each day, set aside time to really listen to God. Do this every day at the same time – not just when you think you need to. When you do this every day, at the same time, perhaps for an hour, you make it a holy time. As you do so, you are programming the brain, and it becomes easier and easier to truly be still and listen to God.

Listening requires being still – stilling the body and the mind. When we allow the mind and body to continually speak to us, as they often do, we hardly have time to listen to God. The mind is so busy, saying, "I have to go to the grocery store at 10. I must go to the bank at 11. And I must do this and I must do that." Such thoughts continually run through this computer we call a brain. Even when we are trying to be still or to meditate, the brain keeps on running.

The brain, in a sense, is trying to keep you from becoming spiritual. It wants to be your master. The body, too, wants to be your master. So, when you attain a deep, quiet moment, the body starts signaling. There's a little itch down there and another one up here and maybe a few aches and pains in various places. All kinds of things go on in the body that are saying, "Pay attention to me. Don't become one with God. If you do, then I won't be boss. You won't feed me when I need it, and you won't give me water when you're supposed to." Our minds and bodies are so busy that they don't give the Divine an opportunity to speak to us.

There are techniques for stilling the mind and the body. In order to still all the thoughts being produced by the mind, declare, "The Creator in me stills my brain so I can hear the Divine within." Another method for getting through the confusion within us is to practice saying, "I see Light," as we look at each other. And, "I see Light in the trees, in animals, in plants." Yet another method is to declare with authority, "I am still. God speaks to me in the stillness." You can also say to your body, as David did, "*Be still! And know that I Am God!*"

2. PRAY REGULARLY

Consider prayer as tithing and give one tenth of each day to God – 2.4 hours of prayer, or, to make it easy, two-and-a-half hours of prayer a day. Make a schedule for yourself so that you'll pray regularly. It will change your life! Just try it, and after a month, see how you feel. See what has happened in you and in the world around you. See the difference!

Take every opportunity there is to pray. Some of you may wake up in the night at two or three o'clock. This is an opportunity for you, in the stillness of the night, to reach out around the world. When you wake in the middle of the night, get up and pray. Because so many people's thoughts and emotions are still at this time, your prayers can affect the whole world. These moments of prayer will alter you, too. They will become moments of gold, moments of Life.

3. THINK LOVE, THINK LIGHT

We are past masters at thinking about grocery stores, menus, cleaning, going places, and doing things. We spend very little time in thinking Light and Love. There is so much time we waste! We think when we are scrubbing the floor that we must do just this job and that's it. But we have the capability to think Love and think Light from our whole beings whenever we are doing anything, even when we're talking or answering the phone. Everyone and everything is affected by thought processes. With our whole beings, we should be thinking Love and Light so that vibrations of Love and Light radiate out from us in all directions. Continue the practice throughout your day. Silently say to yourself, "I see the Divine. I see Light" as you go through the rest of the day.

4. LET LOVE AND LIGHT DO IT

We tend to think we must do all things: *we* must work to make money; *we* must love our mates in a certain way; *we* must heal. We have all these things we think we *must* do.

Instead, let Love and Light do it. Program every moment of your existence to be one where Love and Light accomplish whatever needs doing. You can command, "Let everything this day be accomplished by Love and Light. Let Love and Light hear, see, speak, and breathe for me." Declare this with the authority of the Divine.

5. LET GOD DIRECT YOUR LIFE AND YOUR RELATIONSHIPS

We automatically reject criminals and alcoholics and other people whose behavior we object to. We keep on rejecting until we end up with a handful of people who think like we do and with whom we get along. In all of this, we are actually rejecting God. Everyone is Divine, so we need to declare, "Let Love and Light make all my relationships smooth, beautiful, and wonderful." God in you loves everyone and everything, so change the way you relate. Let God direct your life and your relationships.

6. LET LOVE PUT PEACE AND GOODWILL IN ALL HEARTS

When it comes to people in government and people in power, rather than focusing on the evil we see, and thereby increasing that evil, we must declare for every person, "You are filled with Peace and Goodwill." The Bible says that "the government shall rest upon the shoulders of the Christ." *All* people are the Christ in action. So, declare Peace and Goodwill in the hearts and minds of your fellowmen, of those in government, and of those in power. Every person on planet Earth must awaken to the fact that God is present throughout Earth and in every individual.

7. LET LOVE AWAKEN ALL TO GOD AND HIS GOODNESS

God declared that everything is GOOD. But, we haven't yet experienced that fantastic Goodness. Man has declared that we must experience evil, negatives, depressions, and all kinds of hard times. We must change that way of thinking, that way of existence. We must awaken man to God and God's Goodness. When Goodness becomes a way of life for every person on Earth, all problems will be solved. So, declare with Divine authority, "Let Love and Light awaken the hearts and minds and souls of all people to God and His Goodness." Because that command will be from your God-self, it will change things, for the Good.

8. BE PEACEFUL AND CALM

So many of us feel stress, and we tend to get totally caught up in going over and over our problems and the problems of our immediate world and the problems of the planet. So, declare with authority, "I am peaceful and calm throughout this day and throughout the night."

9. GIVE THANKS TO GOD

Everything is God in action – but we tend not give thanks to God for all that is. The simplest things are fantastic. Breath – the breath of

God – is one of the greatest events of our existence. The way we breath can change us, can bring to our awareness things that we were not conscious of. Breath is holy. Breath is full of Life! When we are aware that the air we breath is holy and Divine, even pollution becomes holy. Give thanks for breath as God in action: "I am breathing in God; I am exhaling God."

Be thankful for every event that occurs. Be thankful for a flat tire. It may have saved your life: it may have prevented you from being in a dangerous place at the wrong time. Don't ever – *ever* – criticize a situation or relationship.

We're not thankful for the things we don't like. Do we say things such as, "Thank you, God, for being fat"? No. Because we judge mankind and its ways and feel we can't be thankful for man.

But we need to be thankful for man. We need to be thankful for everything. So, program thankfulness with prayer: "Thank you, God, for Life, for being here now, for my body, for being on this planet. Thank you, God, for man and his ways and his evolving into You."

10. BE PATIENT, BE KIND, BE HELPFUL, AND BE LOVE

In America, we expect everything to happen instantaneously. And in instant America, those on the spiritual path want instant God, too. We become impatient when we pray for five minutes and we don't see a change. We then either stop praying, because we think something is wrong with God or wrong with us. Be patient with God in action. Remember: we do not see with the total eye of God.

Being unkind is often an unconscious act. It comes from thinking of ourselves first and wanting the best for ourselves. Because we are spiritual and have healed someone, perhaps we think we deserve recognition of our special-ness. But, we need to be careful of our actions and of the ways in which we can hurt others, even with body language. With just a look or a certain subtle movement of the body, we can be showing others that we reject them. We need to be aware of this so we can prevent it before it happens.

When we *know* that God is in everyone, we know that being hurtful means that we are rejecting God. We also know that helping others is helping God. Being aware that God is in everything and everyone makes us want to be helpful in every way possible.

To BE LOVE does not mean being a goody-goody type person. It means being still and radiating Divine Love to everyone and everything. Our problem is that our reference point is human love and we use that as a guide to living and receiving love. But human love can hurt, while God's Love is far beyond anything human. God's Love gives one hundred percent to everyone and everything. The Creator within us is unlimited and gives unlimited Love. So, Being Love is just that: giving only Divine Love, all of the time.

Experiment with these ten steps in the Code of Life. Use them to become the spiritual person you have always wanted to be. Live by this Code – and discover a whole new way of life!

THE CREATOR IN DAILY LIFE

Putting the Divine into daily life requires just a little switch of consciousness to this: All that is is Divine. With this consciousness, you can say, "I know that money is Divine. Money is a Divine flow to me, from me, to all. There is an abundance of money." And you can say, "I know the Divine is in action in everyone. I know the Divine brings this person to me for more understanding of the Divine. For growth. For love. For giving. For giving Light. For giving Love. Whoever comes into my presence, 'I hold to the fact that it is the Divine doing it. Not me.'"

Instead of saying, "I have to...go home, take a shower, go to work, etc.," put the Divine into it first: "The Divine is at work. The Divine is in the car, the shower, etc. The Divine is in operation." This frees you from the tensions of having to do anything.

Prepare things ahead. Jesus sent John the Baptist. In other words, he sent the Light. You can do the same. Know that the Light goes before you, preparing your way. Hold to that. Put that to which you are traveling in a bubble of Light. Light the way ahead of you.

In doing this, you will find you have plenty of time. You will wonder what to do about your time. You will say, "But I should be busy." But the time is being made available to you so you can be the Divinity in action and increase the Good for the whole planet.

If you really analyze your day, you have tremendous amounts of time – time to create Good. When walking down the street, you can create Good. You don't have to close your eyes. The Divine has never closed its eyes. How could you miss a second of seeing the creation in action while you're creating it? You have the pleasure of watching the Good in action – and increasing that Good.

Take every opportunity to be the Good in action. When you're watching TV, create Good through the actors. The program itself has been created to gratify the male-female or animal nature. You're not really interested in this. But you can still watch TV with your peer group – just watch it differently. Become involved with the actors, creating Light for all who watch. It's a joy. Think of it: when there's a program being watched by millions, you're in the homes of millions of people, bringing them a greater awareness of the Good.

Jesus said, "I bring you abundant life." Create from that consciousness of infinite, Divine abundance.

Create Life in yourself: "I create Life in every one of my cells. I create Life throughout my heart. I create Life throughout my mind. Every part of me is Life. Abundant Life. Christ Life."

Create Life at all times. As you travel in your car, say, "I create Good. I create Life in this automobile. I create Life in this cemetery I'm driving past. I create Life in this building. I create Life in everyone I see."

Go beyond this. Hold to governments resting upon the shoulders of the Christ. When the government rests upon the shoulders of the Christ, everyone works together – instead of working in different directions. Create Life in government, in our leaders. State that, "The government rests on the shoulders of the Christ."

You are the Light of the world. Bring that world within you. You are not separate from the world. Is God separate from anything? Is there anywhere that God is not? No. So, wherever you are is holy ground.

Hold to that. Say, "I create Life throughout my being and throughout this world that is within me." And since the entire world is within you, you have a responsibility for planet Earth, for the kingdoms of Earth – the plant, animal, mineral, man, and angelic kingdoms.

You cannot limit the giving of this tremendous Life and Light that you have. Don't hold back. "I create Light, Life, Love in everyone and everything. In all the stars and the planets. In all dimensions. In everyone and everything. The seen and the unseen are all a part of me. All are inside of me. I create Life throughout me. Throughout everything."

Being the Good-in-action requires that you pray more. In praying more, you will find that things are being accomplished more quickly. As that occurs, you have even more time available for the Divine, available for the greater works, for increasing the Good, for being the Light of the world.

Keep things going even though you may not feel like you're accomplishing anything, even though you may feel like you're saying the words by rote. Even if they are by rote, something is happening because every word you say is filled with power. Every word spoken silently within is a vibration that is accomplishing something. It is Divinity in action.

So, take your opportunities. Every day.

CITIZENS OF LIGHT

I am requesting that we become the people of the future. Now. Make the future now. Start this new world now. Become a Citizen of Light.

In your own life, anything less than being a God-person, anything less than being a Citizen of Light, is unacceptable to you.

To bring this into existence requires the greatest power there is, which is prayer, both individual and collective prayer. Be the leaders of Light in the sense of giving Divine prayer, so people all over the planet can adjust to the tremendous Light coming to Earth.

The ability to change anyone and every thing, without having to speak, is in you. But, do not seek credit. What is important is peace on Earth, goodwill towards people. God knows the work that you have done already. What greater praise can you get than that?

The declaration from Godman, from a Citizen of Light, is Love, is Light. Declare it with authority. From the God that you are.

Be the Light of the world by radiating the Divine Light from your Light center and radiating the Divine Love from your Love center to everyone and everything. Train your eyes to see this Love and Light in one everyone.

The Love is so overpowering that you want everyone to have it. It is so fantastic that you cannot contain it. The only reason for existence is that Love. It is so overpowering that it is beyond the comprehension of man.

You know that you must give it with your total being. Not just from your heart. Not just from your mind. But from your total being. You know that you must give it constantly. And the more you give, the more it fills.

You are free, as Godperson, to be anywhere on the planet. Your consciousness is free to be anywhere on the planet where there is a need for what you have to give. And every place your consciousness goes will enhance you.

As Godman, you will be able to see the Total Man of the universe, on his hands and knees, calling out to you, calling out to this one planet, because we are becoming Godman. This Earth is that which brings Life.

So, from this moment onward, dedicate your life to being a Godperson. You will dedicate yourself to this – not for personal aggrandizement – but for the universe. Because there is this tremendous need throughout the universe for you to be a Godperson - totally loving, one hundred percent giving, not asking from anyone, not needing the things of man, not needing anyone or anything.

A PRAYER FOR CITIZENS OF LIGHT

Deep within, and silently, let's repeat, "I create Good. I create Good throughout my being. I create Good in everyone here. I create Good in this country. I create Good in and around and through planet Earth, so that everyone and everything opens to the Divine. I create Good in our solar system. I create Good throughout the universe. The universe in turn, radiates Good back to planet Earth and to everyone, so that everyone and everything becomes universal and aware of the universal Christ. And thank you, God, for making it so. And now, as we go forth into the world, let this Light and Love that Thou art, be in us, around us, and through us, so we are in the right place at the right time, doing Thy Good. Amen."

THE COSMIC DILEMMA AND THE COSMIC ANSWER

I looked out into the universe and I saw the Total Man of the universe. The total man was on his hands and knees, and that was me. And that is you.

When you see the total man of the universe, he's dark and he's on his hands and knees. *Jim was almost crying as he said this.* To find that the total man somehow missed the mark, to see that nowhere in the universe was there True Man, was devastating. To think, man, made in the image and likeness of God, on his hands and knees throughout the universe. It is catastrophic.

The total man of the universe needs to stand up and say, "I AM. I AM THAT."

So, the prayer for the universe began. And it was revealed that the mission of Earth is to become a Light, so brilliant, so fantastic. And this brilliance of Light will go throughout the universe – to various galaxies and solar systems - and light them up. And in doing that, the universe will become Light and man will stand up and the mission of this finite universe will become a reality.

This cosmic plan will manifest, rather than the universe decaying into nothingness, again.

The manifestation of this plan is going on right now. We the people of Earth are going to do it. Because you are here. You are changing this Earth – every atom, every cell in it is being changed. Everything is being changed. So this Earth can instantaneously go anywhere.

What Universal Man needs and what he wants is what *you*, the ones who are awakened to the Creator within, have to give: Divine Love. *You* can do this, because the Creator in you is not limited.

A NEW WORLD

A new world is beginning. A world of peace. A world with no fear of dying, no fear of being killed or hurt. A world of total trust of each other. A world of goodwill towards all people.

We, the people of Earth, need to be active participants in the creation of this new world. It is time for us, the people, to cause a change. Our creation must be from the Divine. It must be from the Light. Not from our personalities. Not from our human minds. We need to call upon Divine Mind to guide us, to guide the leaders of nations, to guide all the people of Earth.

We need to work with our whole being to establish a new world of peace in the hearts and minds of the people of Earth. There is an urge in everyone to have the peace of the new world. It doesn't matter who they are or where they are. They want it.

We are creating a world of magnificence, a world of beauty, a world of people who are Creators-in-action. As a result of great numbers of people going into Effective Prayer and as a result of people changing their consciousness, we will start building a totally different planet. We'll make the planet a Christed being. And a Christed being can do anything.

In creating Light, in a few more years, there won't be such things as accidents. Wars will cease. There will no murders. There will be no rape. There will be total respect for each other, because everyone will become aware that they are working for the Creator. They'll realize that every person is the Creator, and therefore every person requires our complete love. One hundred percent love. Every person. Because we are seeing God face to face. We'll have total respect and honor for each other.

And when that happens, all diseases must leave. All the accidents must stop. All our aches and pains will no longer exist. If man received total respect, would there be any kind of physical or mental sickness? Of course there wouldn't.

All of the things of the past will be changed. It will not necessarily be done instantaneously. We have spent several million years forming the ways of man. But, all of the old mores and traditions must go. Becoming Godman requires an entirely different type of body and consciousness.

Our whole purpose is to create more Light in Earth and make this a planet of Light. We dare to transform Earth into God beingness. We dare because we know there is no separation in God beingness. We do not see Earth as separate. We know it *is* us. Alive. Everything in Earth is alive with the life of Christ, with the life of God, with Light. It is not separate from any aspect of you.

And in that oneness we join together as one mind – God-mind to God-mind. We are merged together and therefore we think as one. We create as one. We will be mind-to-mind. Heart-to-heart. Soul-to-soul. There will be a great joy of togetherness. Everyone on planet Earth will become one Light being.

Future World

It is fantastic what this planet will be. It will be an example of true heaven for all to see.

We were given dominion over Earth. Our being made in the image and likeness of the Creator gives us the quality of the Creator.

We can make this planet a paradise. It will be greater than it was in the beginning, because it will be filled with people of Christ capabilities and a joyful beingness.

We as Creators are going to improve planet Earth. Right now, it is rather helter-skelter.

We will increase the Divinity in every person and every thing, and it is recorded that everyone on Earth will see the Light simultaneously. *All* will see this Light. All will know.

We are going to make Earth beautiful. The gardens in Japan add to nature and make it a thing of beauty. We will create a fantastic, beautiful garden – all over this planet.

Earth has great underground rivers. One of the reasons for rain and snow is to keep those underground rivers full of pure water so that when we have matured as Christed beings we will use this water to make this one of the most beautiful paradises in the universe.

Everything you see will be to elevate you. The flowers will be more magnificent because they will be Light and only Light. Radiant Light. A radiant Light that fills you.

Every drop of water, every breath of air, will be holy. Everything will enhance you. The whole planet will enhance you.

A creative energy will cause great happenings. The dance, the music, will touch everyone and increase everyone and cause a joy to pervade everything.

You will create crystal walls and crystal cities. Colors that go through these crystals will help all – from the center of the crystal. These crystals will be Life.

You will be crystal, "Christ-all," in all that you do. Giving out colors, giving out Life, you will help all that you see to accomplish their Divine mission. You will help not only individuals but the totality.

There will be no night. There will be only Light. It will be the Light of God from you. The have been numerous reports of people from around the world, alone at night, waking up and suddenly finding their room filled with Light and only Light. Similarly, there will always be a Light in and around and through Earth. The idea that the Sun and only the Sun can give you Light will dissolve into the magnificence of God. Because you are the Light of the world.

So, Earth will be Light. There will be no darkness. And everyone will see each other as God. Everyone will not only see it but will help increase that Divinity in each other. The great joy in giving this Love is fantastic.

Our makeup will change so that we will no longer be bound by the laws of nature. We will not be held by the laws of birth and death. We no longer will create people through a nine month gestation. We will create people full grown. As God-people. Because our mission is so great. So important. So fantastic. Your consciousness about having to eat will change. You will have the consciousness of energy and the use of energy and of increasing the energy for everyone. As one unified Divine Being, we will control the weather.

Going through the Universe

You are increasing Love. You are increasing Light. Not just for planet Earth. You are changing the solar system, the universe.

When you are able to see this whole universe, this whole creation, you will see this great need for you to increase Love, to increase Light, to increase Life, to increase Truth, to increase Joy.

All of the great gurus and masters heretofore have left us high and dry. They've gone to sit on the right hand side of God and have said, "You do it." But they didn't tell us how.

We're not going to leave Earth and sit on God's right hand side. *We* are going to do this Earth as God-man would.

We will take this planet as an example. And not only as an example: We will be *doing it* wherever we go. We will be increasing the Light in every solar system we go to, every galaxy we go to. All the spirals of man will become Light. All the spirals of galaxies will become Light. In doing so, we will increase the Light.

This going out to this universe will raise up Total Man. And then the universe will be able to accomplish its Divine mission.

There is a knowing that we must go through the universe. Each person. Each planet. Each star. So that all of these may attain what you are.

We will present the image for the hearts and minds and souls of all people, simultaneously, as God-person merged with God-person. We will present the image of what we were like and how we behaved with each other. We will beam that into their consciousness so they can see what it was like. All of the past of the story of man on Earth will be recorded and presented to all of the planets that we visit. And they will see us as the dark planet. They will see us as killers.

Everything will be for this one Divine mission of Earth going through and changing, increasing Light and Love. By being present with these other beings, they will see and feel. They will feel the Light. They will feel the Love. And by doing so they will be changed. Everywhere we go there will be a change. This is the beginning of Love.

Start Now

How are you as an individual going to live in this new world? Why not start now? Why wait until the new world is upon us? Start existing *now* the way you would like to exist when there is total peace and love among people. Be an example of this new world wherever you are *now*. We need this example. We need this effort to establish this new world. We can't wait until the leaders of nations do it. You are the leaders.

Become a person of the future. Now. Start this new world now. To bring this new world into existence requires the greatest power there is – prayer. The power of people who pray is fantastic. We need this prayer on a continuous basis.

PRAYERS FOR THE NEW WORLD

Thank you, God, for starting this new world. A world of peace. A world of goodwill between people. A world of trust. A world of loving one another. A world of serving and helping one another. Thank you, God, for bringing this new world into existence now. Thank you, God, for filling all of the people that are in the astral dimension around Earth with love, that they may be healed, that they may be directed to Light, that they may be educated in Thy way. Thank you, God, for each person in my life. Thank you, God for living, for being me. Amen.

Thank you, God, for the Light guiding us and filling our beings with Light. Thank you, God, for filling the world with Light. Thank you, God, for beginning a new life for the people of Earth. And so it is. Amen.

The Creator in each person on Earth fills them with love, heals them, and directs their life to Light.

Silently and deep within, repeat: The Creator within creates Light and Love throughout my being. The Creator within creates Light and Love in everyone here. The Creator within creates Light and Love throughout this area. The Creator within creates Light and Love throughout our country. The Creator within creates Light and Love throughout the world. The Creator within creates Light and Love throughout the government of the planet. The Creator within creates Light and Love throughout the nations of the planet. The Creator within creates Light and Love throughout the religions of the planet. The Creator within creates Light and Love throughout economy of the planet. The Creator within creates Light and Love throughout the energy of the planet. The Creator within creates Light and Love in the food, water, and shelter for man. The Creator within creates Light and Love throughout the solar system. The Creator within creates Light and Love throughout the universe. And now universal Light and Love from the Creator flow back to Earth, in and through and around everyone so that everyone becomes aware of universality and each one here is now one with all that is. Thank you, God, for making it so. And as we go forth into the world, this Love and Light in and around and through us is always in the right place at the right time, creating Light and Love. And that's the way it is. Amen.

PRAYERS

Thank you, God, for Thy Love, Thy Divine love, flowing forth from Thy center in me to everyone and everything. Thank you, God, for Thy Divine Love being present in everyone and everything. Thank you, God, for the flow of Thy Divine Love from everyone and everything to everyone and everything. Thank you, God, for making it so. Amen.

Thank you, God, for Thy Love in us. Thank you, God, for this Thy Love, flowing forth from us to each other. Thank you, God, for this Love and Light flowing forth into our whole area, filling everyone and everything with Thy Love and Light. Thank you, God, for this Light and Love flowing forth from Thee within us to our country, to every person and every thing so that the government rests upon the shoulders of Thee. Thank you, God, for Thy Light and Love filling our planet, so that everyone and everything is filled with Thy Light and Love. And Earth becomes a planet of radiance, a planet of Light and Love. And this radiance flows out to everyone and everything in the universe. And thus everyone and everything in the universe sends Divine Love back to Earth. And everyone and everything on Earth becomes universal and aware of loving. And thank you, God, for making it so. Amen.

Thank you, God, for this togetherness. For the unity and love, for the oneness, for being. Thank you, God, for more awareness of Thee. And thank you, God, for the love flowing between us and filling our beings. Amen.

Thank you, God, for this togetherness and for Thy Light and Love filling our beings, guiding us to Thee. Amen.

There is only the Divine, in, around, and through me and through all aspects of my beingness. There is no place the Divine is not. There is no place that I Am not. The Divine is Good. The Divine is Love. The Divine is Light. Therefore, I Am Good. I Am Love. I Am Light. I Am everywhere equally present. I Am everywhere equally knowing. And that's the way it is. Amen.

THE CREATOR PRAYER

Silently and deep within, let us say, "I create Divine Love throughout my being. The Creator in me creates Divine love in everyone, filling their beings with Divine Love. The Creator in me creates Divine Love throughout this area, so that everyone and everything is changed by Divine love. The Creator in me creates Divine Love throughout our country, so that everyone and everything is changed to follow Divine Love. The Creator in me creates Divine Love throughout the planet, so that everything and everyone is blessed by Divine Love. The Creator in me creates a radiance of Divine Love and Light, flowing out to everyone and everything, to all the other planets and our sun, so that the planets and the Sun are touched and blessed by this Divine Love. This radiance of Divine Love and Divine Light continues to flow out into the universe, touching all the other stars and all the other planets and all that is. This radiance of Divine Love and Divine Light from all the stars and all the planets flows back into planet Earth and into our world and into everyone's hearts and minds and souls so that everyone's hearts and minds and souls are touched by this Divine Love and Divine Light. We are universal. We are one with all that is. Thank you, God, for making it so.

"And now, in the stillness, we declare, 'Divine Love and Light is flowing throughout my whole being, changing me to Light.'

"And now, as we go forth into the world, this Love and Light is in us, around us, and through us, so we are always in the right place at the right time, doing and saying the right things at the right time for the good of all.

"And that's the way it is. Amen."

A LIGHT PRAYER

Deep within and silently, "I create Love and Light flowing forth throughout this area. I create Love and Light filling this area. I create Love and Light filling our country. I create Love and Light filling our planet. I create Love and Light filling the animal kingdom. I create Love and Light filling the plant kingdom. I create Love and Light filling the mineral kingdom. I create Love and Light filling the angelic kingdom. I create Love and Light filling the man kingdom. I create Love and Light filling the astral dimension. I create Love and Light filling the soul dimension. I create Love and Light filling the Christ dimension. I create Love and Light throughout the creation, unifying all that is. And this oneness of Light and Love flows into each one here, so that all know Thee. Thank you, God, for making it so. Amen."

SOURCES AND ACKNOWLEDGEMENTS

SOURCES AND ACKNOWLEDGEMENTS

One of the pleasures of conducting research for this book was finding so many people enthusiastic about sharing their experiences with Jim. For many, their times with him were the most extraordinary moments of their lives. Among the more than thirty people who were interviewed for this book were family members, Naval Academy classmates, and those who spent time with Jim during his Black Mountain years.

All were helpful and all made a significant contribution to my understanding of Jim and of how he affected the lives of others. The kindness of everyone I interviewed is greatly appreciated. Some of those interviewed requested anonymity, and rather than thank some by name but not others, I will simply give hearty thanks to all who helped.

There were two people without whose extremely generous help this book would have been a wispy shadow of itself. These two were Diana Goure and George Goure. Diana was highly supportive of this project from the beginning and has shared with me letters and photographs and other papers from her files. As remembrances of Jim came to mind, she was inspired to send me several letters with the details of those experiences. Diana did not review a draft of this book, and no inferences should be made that she approved any of the book's material.

George and his wife, Kathryn, were gracious hosts when I visited them in Pueblo, Colorado, where Jim grew up. George also was generous in sharing with me photographs and documents from Jim's youth. Virtually all photos in this book are courtesy of either Diana Goure or George Goure.

Other sources for this book have included tapes of Jim's lectures, books about some of the key people in Jim's life, and several web sites that provided background information about places and the times in which Jim lived.

Over 400 of Jim's lectures at the Light Center in North Carolina and in other parts of the country were recorded. I transcribed all or a part of close to 50 of these lectures, and excerpts from several of them, lightly edited to enhance readability, form the core of the third section of this book, the one that contains summaries of his teachings. For this section, I also made use of edited summaries of Jim's lectures that appeared in the United Research newsletter, *UR Light*. Those interested in hearing some of these lectures may obtain CDs of them by emailing United Research at dome@urlight.org, writing United Research at P. O. Box 1146, Black Mountain, NC 28711, or by calling the United Research Light Center at 828-669-6845.

United Research also has books that are transcriptions of Jim's lectures and you may inquire about those at the above addresses and phone number.

Special thanks go to Lorna Loveless and Sandy Fletcher. Lorna edited a draft of the book, for which I'm grateful. But much bigger thanks go to Lorna for living the love Jim taught us. Sandy Fletcher is also thanked for being a friend whose happy heart encouraged and uplifted me throughout the writing of this book.

Other than the interviews with those who knew Jim, the book's sources, organized by topic, include:

ATOMIC ENERGY COMMISSION

www.osti.gov

CHEROKEE INDIANS AND THE GREAT SMOKY MOUNTAINS

The Spiritual Reawakening of the Great Smoky Mountains, Page Bryant, 1994

THE COLORADO FUEL & IRON (CF&I)

Annotation, The Newsletter of the National Historical Publications and Records Commission, Vol. 31:1, March 2003. U.S. National Archives & Records Administration

The Bessemer Historical Society and the Colorado Fuel and Iron Archives by Jonathan Rees in the May 2003 issue of *New Resources for Labour History*, www.historycooperative.org

The Pueblo Chieftain, January 19, 2002, www.chieftain.com/metro

The Pueblo Guidebook 2005, A short history of Pueblo, www.puebloguidebook.com

GRACE FAUS

Grace and Truth: The Story of Grace Lightfoot Faus – Ordained Minister in the Nation's Capital, Lula Zevgolis, DeVorss & Company, Marina del Rey, California, 1985

Proof of Truth: The Spiritual Journey of Dr. Grace Lightfoot Faus, Minister of Divine Science, Dorothy Elder, Doriel Publishing Co., Denver, Colorado, 1994

BUCKMINSTER FULLER

http://blackmountaincollege.org/content/view/12/52/

http://en.wikipedia.org/wiki/Bauhaus

http://en.wikipedia.org/wiki/Buckminster_Fuller

http://en.wikipedia.org/wiki/Geodesic_dome

http://en.wikipedia.org/wiki/Josef_Albers

www.bfi.org/domes

www.ibiblio.org/blackmountaincollege/weblinks/webdef.htm

www.pbs.org/wnet/americanmasters/database/black_mountain_college

REFERENCES TO THE LIGHT IN OTHER RELIGIONS

www.integralyogany.org

UNITED STATES NAVY

The Bluejacket's Manual, Thomas J. Cutler, Naval Institute Press, Annapolis, Maryland, 2002

THE 1960s

After Heaven: Spirituality in America Since the 1950s, Robert Wuthnow, University of California Press, Berkeley and Los Angeles, California, 1998

The Sixties: Cultural Revolution in Britain, France, Italy, and the United States, c. 1958-c.1974, Arthur Marwick, Oxford University Press, Oxford and New York, 1998

What They Didn't Teach You about the 60s, Mike Wright, Presidio Press, Novato, California, 2001

WALTER AND LAO RUSSELL

"Artist To Turn Virginia Mansion into Museum of Own Creations," *New York Times*, October 30, 1948

Remembered for Love: Lao Russell of Swannanoa, J. B. Yount III, Howell Press, Charlottesville, Virginia, 2004

"Sculptor's Estate To Become 'Shrine,'" *New York Times*, May 1, 1949

The Man Who Tapped the Secrets of the Universe, Glenn Clark, The University of Science and Philosophy, Waynesboro, Virginia, 1946, 2000

"Walter Russell Is Dead at 92; Self-Taught Artist and Educator," *New York Times*, May 20, 1963

University of Science and Philosophy web site, www.philosophy.org

SANDIA NATIONAL LABS

www.sandia.gov/about/history/highlights

THE TEMPLE OF UNDERSTANDING

www.templeofunderstanding.org

Printed in the United States
64848LVS00006B/25-30